Housing in Post-Growth Society

In a globalising world, many mature economies share post-growth characteristics such as low economic growth, low fertility, declining and ageing of the population and increasing social stratification. Japan stands at the forefront of such social change in the East Asian region as well as in the Global North. It is in this context of '*post-growth society*' that housing issues are examined, using the experiences of Japan at the leading edge of social transition in the region.

The post-war housing system was developed during the golden age of economy and welfare, when upward social trajectories such as increasing population, high-speed economic growth with rising real incomes, housing construction driven by high demands, increasing rates of home ownership supported by generous government subsidies generated new housing opportunities and accompanying issues. As we have entered the post-growth phase of socio-economic development, however, it requires a re-examination of such structure, policy and debates. This volume explores what roles housing plays in the reorganisation and reconstruction of economic processes, social policy development, ideology and identity, and intergenerational relations.

The volume offers a greater understanding of the characteristics of post-growth society – changing demography, economy and society – in relation to housing. It considers how a definitive shift to the post-growth period has produced new housing issues including risks as well as opportunities. Through analysis of the impact on five different areas: post-crisis economy, urban and regional variations, young adults and housing pathways, fertility and housing, and ageing and housing wealth, the authors use policy and institutions as overarching analytical tools to examine the contemporary housing issues in a post-growth context. It also considers any relevance from the Japanese experiences in the wider regional and global context.

This original book will be of great interest to academics and students as well as policy makers and practitioners internationally in the fields of housing studies, urban studies, social policy, sociology, political economy, comparative analysis, and East Asian Studies.

Yosuke Hirayama is Professor of Housing and Urban Studies, School of Human Development and Environment, Kobe University, Japan.

Misa Izuhara is Reader on Comparative Policy Research at the School for Policy Studies, University of Bristol, United Kingdom.

Explorations in Housing Studies
Series editors: Ray Forrest, *Lingnan University, Hong Kong*
Janet Smith, *University of Illinois, Chicago*
Keith Jacobs, *University of Tasmania, Tasmania*

Explorations in Housing Studies is a series of high quality, research monographs which aims to extend and deepen both theoretical debate and empirical research in the housing studies field. The series is being introduced at a time when housing, in its various dimensions, is particularly closely intertwined with the impact of demographic change, economic instability, the shaping of life chances and wealth distributions and with the uncertain impacts of environmental and technological change. This series aims to engage with these and related issues from a variety of perspectives and methodologies.

Housing in Post-Growth Society
Japan On the Edge of Transition
Yosuke Hirayama and Misa Izuhara

Housing in Post-Growth Society

Japan on the Edge of Social Transition

Yosuke Hirayama and Misa Izuhara

Routledge
Taylor & Francis Group
LONDON AND NEW YORK

First published 2018 by Routledge

2 Park Square, Milton Park, Abingdon, Oxfordshire OX14 4RN
52 Vanderbilt Avenue, New York, NY 10017

Routledge is an imprint of the Taylor & Francis Group, an informa business

First issued in paperback 2019

British Library Cataloguing-in-Publication Data
A catalogue record for this book is available from the British Library

Library of Congress Cataloging-in-Publication Data
Names: Hirayama, Yosuke, author. | Izuhara, Misa, author.
Title: Housing in post-growth society : Japan on the edge of transition / Yosuke Hirayama and Misa Izuhara.
Description: 1 Edition. | New York : Routledge, 2018. | Series: Explorations in housing studies | Includes index.
Identifiers: LCCN 2017038461 | ISBN 9781138085008 (hardback) | ISBN 9781315111575 (ebook)
Subjects: LCSH: Housing—Japan.
Classification: LCC HD7367.A3 H57 2018 | DDC 307.3/360952—dc23
LC record available at https://lccn.loc.gov/2017038461

ISBN: 978-1-138-08500-8 (hbk)
ISBN: 978-0-367-33192-4 (pbk)

Typeset in Sabon
by Apex CoVantage, LLC

MIX
Paper from responsible sources
FSC www.fsc.org FSC™ C013985

Printed in the United Kingdom
by Henry Ling Limited

Contents

Figures

Tables

Foreword

Explorations in Housing Studies is being introduced at a time when housing, in its various dimensions, is particularly closely intertwined with the impact of demographic change, economic instability, the shaping of life chances and wealth distributions and with the uncertain impacts of environmental and technological change. It is intended that books in the series engage with these and related issues from a variety of perspectives and methodologies, and drawing on a wide range of social and cultural contexts. As editors we are looking for research and scholarship at the cutting edge of housing studies, for texts which stimulate theoretical and policy discussion and which situate housing studies firmly within wider debates in the social sciences. They may be historical, comparative or focused on current housing issues within a specific society.

This first book in the series, appropriately, ticks a number of these boxes. Through an exploration and analysis of the key housing challenges facing contemporary Japanese society, it offers a fresh understanding of the interconnections between Japanese demographic change, its housing market and the still struggling, post bubble Japanese economy. In doing so, it also connects with very similar issues emerging across a wide range of societies. Japan has been at the forefront of demographic aging and has been the earliest modern economy to face the consequences of the accelerating transformation from societies of young families to societies of elderly couples and singles, and, indeed, an associated shift to growing numbers of young single people. Japan's fertility rate has also been considerably below replacement rate for some time and shows little sign of any significant shift upwards. The reasons for this are bound up with neoliberal policy impacts with regard to employment and housing policy. Young people face less secure employment futures and more difficult access to housing. As the title of the book indicates, on a number of measures, Japan can be described as a post growth society—economically and demographically. It is also a society in which there would appear to be striking contrasts between the older and young generations. Here again, Japan has led the way in growing references to generational fractures and the view that the post-war growth in home ownership which characterised the capitalist core societies was fuelled by a set of social and economic conditions which are no longer operating—at least not in societies such as Japan, the USA, Australasia and the UK. Younger people, it seems, face a much less certain future in Japan and have a more pessimistic attitude towards their housing and economic prospects. And at an international level, more young people are staying longer in the parental home and those living independently are increasingly found in the private rented sector. At the same time, there is an accumulation of housing wealth among older generations the 'golden age' home owners. And this phenomenon is strikingly evident in Japan. What happens to this wealth and the extent to which it benefits particular sections of younger generations, is of considerable social, political and economic interest.

The extent to which the issues raised in this book are understood and constructed as problems, challenges or opportunities depends partly on one's perspective. There is certainly no argument that Japan has faced an economically damaging set of events over a period of more than two decades-a local economic crisis, a regional economic crisis, a global economic crisis and natural disasters. These events have had international ramifications and have impacted negatively on many Japanese households. But there may be different views about whether children should leave home earlier (is that good or bad for family life?), what 'post-growth' growth should look like, and whether the finance of housing should continue to play such a prominent role in our lives? Perhaps we need different models and different priorities.

At the same time, current trends in Japan are in sharp contrast to the social and economic changes experienced by younger generations in other Asian societies—most notably China. There, the proportion of young urban home owners is now among the highest in the world and despite regular, gloomy predictions, there is little evidence yet of a post-growth society emerging. But in both China and Japan, and more generally, there is a common experience of more polarised, two-speed societies—of the more privileged pulling further away. In housing terms, this is most clearly expressed in more differentiated house price trends—which may have urban-rural, inter-city, intra-city or intra-neighbourhood dimensions. These are the 'hot' and 'cold' spots referred to in this book. In Japan and elsewhere, housing markets offer more visible markers of inclusion and exclusion, of connection and disconnection. This book is also, however, a reminder of how global influences such as cross-national housing investment flows and financial crises interact with intensely local factors with regard to policy and demographic change to produce very specific housing consequences and responses.

Ray Forrest
Lingnan University
Series co-editor

Introduction

In a globalising world, many mature economies are following not necessarily common but converging paths of socio-economic, demographic and institutional transformations. Such shifts have been taking place in increasingly precarious economic climate for the last few decades. The rise and fall of property bubbles brought about economic crises such as Japan's post-bubble economic downfall in the early 1990s, the Asian Financial Crisis (AFC) in 1997/98 and the Global Financial Crisis (GFC) in 2007/08. Post-crisis economies across countries still remain in a low-growth trap. This indicates in many advanced economies that consumption and investment will remain sluggish while low labour productivity continues to mean weak wage growth (OECD, 2016). Post-growth characteristics are also evident elsewhere as the low-growth trap has a tendency to accompany high financial risks. Many central banks including the Bank of Japan, the Federal Reserve, the European Central Bank and the Bank of England have kept interest rates extremely low or even negative, leading to instability in financial markets. Embedded in such economic stagnation, mature societies also share other distinctive post-growth trends such as changing demography. In many advanced societies, fertility has declined to below replacement levels, while societal ageing has been, and will continue to be, progressing. These societies are now experiencing much slower growth or even decline in the population. The number of marriages has decreased and unmarried individuals, divorcees, single-parents and co-habiting couples are increasing in number. The average ages of first marriage and first childbirth have also risen. The decline in conventional marriage is transforming patterns of family formation, household structures and the contours of people's life-course.

One of the key elements that reflects and shapes the processes of transitions to post-growth society is housing. Across countries, housing systems are embedded in the broader context of socio-economic, political and institutional changes (Forrest and Lee, 2003; Kemeny, 1992). Post-war housing systems were developed on the back of economic and demographic growth. Population growth and an associated increase in the number of new households combined with rapid urbanisation generated rising demand for housing. In many societies, a dramatic expansion of the home ownership sector signified a clear departure from pre-war housing systems dominated by private tenancy. The promotion of home ownership led to the spread of middle-class lifestyles to the wider segments of society and thus functioned as a means to widening social inclusion. There was a robust cycle that the mass production of owner-occupied dwellings fuelled economic growth, which in turn further encouraged households to access home ownership. With entering the post-growth age, however, housing systems have begun to face more volatile and uncertain economic conditions. An increasing number of tenants on more insecure employment have progressively found themselves excluded from entry to the home ownership sector, while many owner-occupiers have experienced vicissitudes in property markets and a consequent decline in the security of residential properties as assets. In addition, demographic changes have encroached upon the conventional household model on which post-war housing systems were based. The shrinking of the middle class, associated with an increase in the number of one-person, single-parent and elderly-only households, has meant a decrease in those who follow conventional housing paths. It is in this framework of post-growth society that this volume will explore the role of housing in the reorganisation of wider socio-economic and institutional processes.

The post-growth context

Examining the context of transitions to a post-growth society in relation to the development of wider social theories will provide a basis for analyses in the subsequent chapters concerning more specific themes. The concept of post-industrial or post-Fordist economy is highly relevant to the analysis of the post-growth social context for this volume. Although the post-growth narratives are not confined to the analysis of industrial restructuring or the modes of production and consumption since wider social and institutional transformations including demographic change and policy development and reforms equally matter, the core and associated socio-economic phenomena constitute overlapping causes and consequences of social change. In terms of production and consumption, shifts from the high-growth period to the new period of post-growth have corresponded with transformations to a post-industrial or post-Fordist society. In post-industrial societies, manufacturing sectors that had played a key role in economic development during high-growth have been replaced by service sectors as the dominant industry. This has coincided with the increasing valuation of knowledge and the advancement of information and communication technologies (Bell, 1974; Touraine, 1971). Post-Fordist societies have arisen from shifts in production and consumption from mass marketing to flexible specialisation. The Fordist system of a large-scale mechanised production line on which workers repeated standardised tasks was pioneered in Henry Ford's automobile factories in the early twentieth-century US. In contrast, the post-Fordist system has aimed for more diverse products targeted at differentiated small groups (e.g., Aglietta, 1979; Amin, 1994; Jessop, 1994). The theories of post-industrial or post-Fordist society not only ascertain and scrutinise the changing nature of production and consumption but also extend to exploring the accompanying social changes with a greater level of risks and uncertainty and increasing stratification. The marked significance of knowledge in post-industrial societies has meant a general increase in expertise, leading to a new way in which society is stratified with an increasing number of urban professionals such as financial specialists, information-technology experts, researchers and scientists, and creative industry managers. The amplified flexibility of labour markets in post-Fordist societies has generally increased risks and uncertainty with respect to employment and income and has resulted in polarisation between high-income professionals with specialised skills and those on low income in more insecure employment.

In line with the shift to a post-industrial or post-Fordist society, pervasive neoliberal imperatives have led many governments to reform social policies emphasising market solutions. Neoliberalism is an economic and political ideology asserting that economic progress is best advanced by liberating individual entrepreneurial freedoms within an institutional framework of private property rights and competitive markets (e.g., Davies, 2016; Harvey, 2005; Springer et al., 2016). Post-growth economic and demographic stagnation has underlain such neoliberal policy reforms: an accelerated rise in the proportion of older people combined with a decline in growth rates has imposed growing pressure on cutting back on social spending and public subsidies, and rationalising the retrenchment of state welfare provision. Immediately after the Second World War, many European countries constructed welfare states by developing more comprehensive public welfare systems. However, since the early 1970s, when capitalist economies fell in crises due to the 1971 Nixon Shock, the 1973 Oil Crisis and the 1973 collapse of the Bretton Woods system for exchange rate management established in 1944, economic slow-down stimulated policy reforms. In the early 1980s, the US and the UK introduced a neoliberal model in formulating and implementing policy, which were followed by many other countries. In the East Asian region, the state played a leading role in coordinating and facilitating high-speed economic development within the framework of the developmental state model, where economic expansion was regarded as a primary means of providing welfare to the nations (see, for example, Park et al., 2012; Wade, 1998; Weiss, 2003). However, neoliberal prescriptions have penetrated not only Western but also East Asian countries in terms of policy reforms. There are diverse welfare approaches: for example, European and Anglophone welfare states build on variegated models with regard to how state-market-family relations are formed (Esping-Andersen, 1999), while developmental states in East Asia are distinctive in terms of the state's initiative in orchestrating economic development. Nevertheless, under the influence of prevalent and even normative neoliberalism, many countries have progressively converged around similar directions of policy reforms, accentuating the role of the market in providing welfare.

The widening of social inequalities is a marked feature of the shift to a post-growth society. What economic growth and decline could bring to society is a key question of debates on distributive justice (Muraca, 2012). A decline in growth rates has combined with post-industrial and post-Fordist socio-economic changes as well as neoliberal policy reforms to expand disparities in economic conditions between older and younger generations, between higher and lower income groups, between conventional and unconventional households, and between prime cities and provincial regions. The post-war baby-boomer generations in many developed economies experienced stable employment and steady income increases during the growth period, whereas the younger generations in the post-growth age has been confronted with more unstable labour markets. Many neoliberal governments have promoted deregulations of employment practices, resulting in a rise in short-term contracts without social protection. An increasing number of single-person and single-parent households are more prone to new social risks related to the working poor and long-term unemployment compared to conventional households (Bonoli, 2005; Taylor-Gooby, 2004). In addition, the high pace innovation of digital technology leads to a widening skill gap among workers (Castells, 1996). Tax systems have become much less redistributive, exacerbating income disparities even more. National economies are increasingly integrated into the global economy while at the same time being decentralised. This creates spatial economic cleavages between principal cities having the 'global city' status and provincial cities (Harvey, 1985). Although post-growth might conjure the image of paths to a mature, idyllic and more relaxed society with less competition and a higher quality of life (Hiroi, 2001), this positive connotation strongly contradicts the relentless reality of widening social inequalities, increasing insecurity and spatial disparities across and within generations.

Meanwhile, it is also important to note that 'post-growth' is not a synonym of 'decline' in society. Thus, we avoid labelling or characterising every aspect of post-growth society as simple decline and seek to provide more explanatory and structural analyses of the processes and outcomes of post-growth social transitions. In many advanced countries, there are undebatable falling trends in various indicators such as GDP per capita, interest rates, fertility, and household size, to name but a few. In some societies in East Asia and Europe, current ultra-low fertility will lead to population decline. However, popular discourses on 'decline' can sometimes be misleading. For example, arguments about the 'demographic time bomb' problematize the future shortage of the labour and the expected overload of welfare costs relating to pensions and health care, using the changing balance of the 'dependency ratio' between the 'working' population (usually defined as those aged 15–64) and the 'dependent' population. Within this context, in the mid-1990s EU, an ageing population was considered responsible for labour decline, lower competitiveness and slower growth (see Hantrais, 1999). It is well argued, however, that the dependency ratio does not necessarily paint an accurate picture of demographic impacts on labour markets. Ageing and old age are indeed social constructs, as not all of the 'working population' are engaged in paid work while an increasing number in the 'dependent' age group are healthy, wealthy and productive (Phillipson, 1998). Labour productivity can also be enhanced by new technologies. It is true that post-growth economic and demographic stagnation pose new challenges to the foundations of societies. However, this volume avoids simply describing the transition to a post-growth society as a pure 'decline' in favour of analysing and explaining the structure of social transformations and exploring possible avenues to a new social paradigm.

The housing context

Housing studies were developed during the 'golden age' of economic and demographic growth when increasing populations, rapid economic development, rising real incomes, high volume housing construction fuelled by expanding demands, and widening access to home ownership were composing 'linear upwards social changes'. As we have entered the 'global age' of more insecure economic processes and demographic changes, however, the post-growth social context now requires a re-examination of housing debates. The condition of housing systems in many mature economies has fundamentally shifted from 'expansion' to 'fluctuation' in terms of housing market developments. During the growth period, housing markets expanded rapidly: many people followed upward housing paths towards home ownership with generous state subsidies. However, housing markets in the post-growth era are more unstable, with an increasing number of households confronted with sluggish economies and reduced state subsidies when trying to secure housing and access property ownership. A focus of housing studies has been the affordability of housing, with housing costs analysed in relation to inflationary economies in the growth period. With entering the post-growth phase, however, it is now becoming necessary to examine affordability issues within the context of increasingly fluctuating housing and labour markets. Changes in the labour market in response to the rise of the post-Fordist mode have led to a notable rise in precariousness in employment. This has combined with the rolling back of the state in the housing-related field to result in the increasing number of households who face difficulties in accessing affordable housing.

The growth of housing markets has been increasingly driven by the expansion of mortgage markets. Widened access to the debt financing of housing purchases has encouraged more households to enter the home ownership sector. Such financialisation is a key feature of neoliberal housing systems (Aalbers, 2016; Forrest and Hirayama, 2015). Governments in many mature economies have progressively liberalised financial markets and situated the expansion of residential loan markets within the framework of growth strategy. Within the post-growth context, however, various restrictions are now being imposed on the expansion of mortgaged-housing markets (Aalbers, 2012; Forrest and Hirayama, 2015). Excessive financing for housing purchases by households on lower incomes culminated in the rise and fall of property bubbles and the excessive collateralisation of real estate provoked the subsequent financial and economic turmoil (Forrest and Yip, 2011; Schwartz and Seabrooke, 2009). More structurally, the growth of housing loan markets was underpinned by a particular set of conditions that included an increase in new households who wish to acquire owner-occupied homes; the long-term stability of employment as a basis for mortgage repayments; and inflationary economies and associated aspirations to property ownership. In the emerging post-growth era, however, population ageing, a decline in conventional family households, more flexible and insecure labour markets, and increasingly volatile housing markets have effectively combined to discourage the expansion of mortgage markets. This raises theoretical and socio-political questions concerning the extent to which debt-led housing systems are sustainable.

With entry into the post-growth phase, housing systems, which have played a significant role in enhancing social integration, are now becoming a key driver of social stratification. Older generation households moved up the housing ladder towards property ownership in the growth period and the expansion of property ownership underpinned social cohesiveness. As upward residential mobility has become more stagnant in the post-growth era, however, younger people delay in leaving parental homes, securing their own housing and accessing home ownership, resulting in generational fractures in housing opportunities (Forrest and Yip, 2013). Post-industrial labour markets lead to an increase in those on more insecure employment who find it increasingly difficult to access adequate housing, while changes in patterns of family formation mean that an increasing number of one-person, single-parent and elderly-only households tend to be excluded from housing markets unless they secure considerable incomes. Compared to the post-war period of social housing provision, housing policies in some European societies now employ market-based solutions. The provision of state subsidies aimed at supporting social housing sectors have thus been substantially reduced. Such housing policy reforms disadvantage lower income household in terms of housing access.

Housing markets in the post-growth age fluctuate over time and bring out spatial divisions. Such 'time-space fragmentation' of housing markets encourages the stratification of families in terms of property asset accumulation. Despite increasingly volatile economic circumstances, property-rich families have strategically navigated the processes of ups and downs in housing markets to further augment their assets. For such families, houses are more of an investment vehicle than a consumption objective. Housing markets are indeed unstable, yet propertied families perceive investment in housing to be safer in light of long-term wealth accumulation – especially in comparison with investment in stock and other financial products, which are excessively unstable. On the other hand, the instability of housing markets has resulted in an increasing number of 'losers' in regard to asset accumulation in some societies (Hamnett, 1999). Moreover, spatial divisions in housing markets between and within cities encourage the stratification of property ownership. In many advanced countries, despite instability in economic processes, housing markets in major global cities such as New York, London, Singapore, and Hong Kong have been largely buoyant with upsurges in house prices where rich people have invested in upmarket properties. Many large cities have also experienced gentrification of some neighbourhoods. This provides young urban professionals with opportunities for investment in real estate. In contrast, provincial cities, smaller towns and 'shrinking cities' (e.g., Hino and Tsutsumi, 2015; Pallagst et al., 2014) have undergone declines in housing markets due to disinvestment and outflows of population, where a number of households have experienced a devaluation of properties that they acquired in the past. Even within large cities, central areas have been associated with rises in property prices, whereas housing markets in peripheral areas have persistently been stagnant.

In post-growth economies that have a large housing stock, the distribution of existing housing wealth over generations within families acts as a mechanism in social stratifications. For the analysis of inequality, labour market position has been considered the most important factor in determining people's class position in light of understanding the structure of stratification. However, as growth rates decline, the role of existing property assets in expanding and reorganising inequalities comes into focus (see Piketty, 2014). Within the context of societal ageing and rollbacks of state welfare, the concept of housing-asset-based welfare has drawn extensive academic attentions (e.g., Dewilde and Ronald, 2017; Doling and Elsinga, 2012; Doling and Ronald, 2010; Izuhara, 2016; Groves et al., 2007; Malpass, 2008; Toussaint and Elsinga, 2009). Outright homeowners maintain property assets while simultaneously benefiting from minimal housing costs after completing mortgage repayments. It has therefore been presumed that the expansion of home ownership can be a deterrent to a high level of social spending, substituting for a decline in state welfare provision. However, property ownership systems are increasingly functioning as a driver for widening inequalities (Forrest and Hirayama, 2017; Hirayama, 2010; Kurtz and Blossfeld, 2004). Moreover, a high rate of home ownership among the older generation in some societies combined with low fertility means more opportunities for the future generations to inherit their family wealth. Inequalities pertaining to housing assets within the older generation are thus likely to perpetuate over generations. Social policy in many countries has become less redistributive and thus the distribution of housing wealth within families plays a more deterministic role in stratifying societies.

Japan on the edge of transition

This volume uses Japan as an important exemplar in looking at changes in housing systems within the post-growth context. Japan is the most 'mature' society in East Asia in terms of socio-economic and demographic developments and political institutions. Immediately after its defeat in the Second World War, Japan began to address fundamental reforms centring on demilitarisation and democratisation to construct a new, modern society. In line with the post-war reconstruction, the housing system, which was directed at driving mass construction of owner-occupied housing, played a significant role in not only providing shelters but also facilitating social and economic development. The Economic White Paper in 1956 declared that the era of post-war confusion had come to an end and the economy and the industry began to develop at a tremendous pace. The construction, housing and real estate sectors occupied the core of post-war industry in driving high-speed economic growth. By the late 1960s, Japan became the only Asian country comparable to the West in terms of economic prosperity and took the position as the world's second largest economy after the US. Expanding home ownership among middle-income households was instrumental in the promotion of social inclusion, underpinning the creation and maintenance of a property-owning democracy. Nevertheless, since Japan entered a post-growth phase in the 1990s, there have been inevitable and fundamental changes in socio-economic and demographic circumstances surrounding the housing system. With its sharp shift from growth to post-growth phase, Japan provides a prominent case study regarding transformations in housing conditions in contemporary society.

Post-growth Japan is above all characterised by remarkable demographic changes. The 2012 projection by the National Institute of Population and Social Security Research showed that the nation's population, which was 128 million in 2010, will decrease significantly by 32 per cent to 87 million by 2060. This is mainly due to its ultra-low total fertility rate, which is far below the replacement level of 2.1 – for example, 1.46 in 2015. Moreover, immigration policy is another factor for the demographic decline: the Japanese government has strictly controlled the inflow of migration. The government is now beginning to examine the possibility of opening up the nation to immigration to compensate for the decline in the population and the labour force. However, whether and to what extent the immigrant policy will change the nation's demographic trend remains to be seen. Societal ageing in Japan is phenomenal, deriving from the combination of low fertility and increased longevity. Post-war baby-boomers who were born in the latter half of the 1940s have now reached their retirement age *en masse*, accelerating the ageing of the population. The rate of those aged 65 and over, which was a little more than a quarter (26.7 per cent) of Japan's total population in 2015, is projected to reach one-third (33.4 per cent) by 2035. The figure is and will continue to be higher than that of any other countries. Demographic change is a shared phenomenon in post-growth East Asia. Many societies in the region will follow in Japan's footsteps regarding ageing and shrinking of populations due to low fertility. It is predicted that by 2040 the rates of societal ageing will reach over 30 per cent in Hong Kong (32 per cent), South Korea (31 per cent), Taiwan (31 per cent) and Singapore (30 per cent), while the total population is expected to start declining in Taiwan in 2020s and in China and South Korea a decade later in the 2030s (Department of Economic and Social Affairs, United Nations, 2015). In addition, the patterns of family formation have notably transformed with a shift in the dominant household type from a conventional nuclear household to a single-person household. During the growth period, the housing system was focused on facilitating mass construction of housing with emphasis on encouraging nuclear households to purchase their own home. Therefore, the shrinking and ageing of the population and the decreasing number of conventional households pose a considerable challenge to the home-ownership centred housing system that was developed in the growth period. It will certainly become more difficult for the state and corporations to maintain the high level of investment in housing.

Japan's post-growth characteristics are prominent in terms of economic change. The rise and fall of housing bubbles has been seen across many mature economies and in this respect, Japan provides an advancing and acute case. The bubble economy grew with an extreme rise in real estate prices in the last half of the 1980s and burst in the early 1990s. The nation subsequently fell into a financial and economic crisis and entered an extraordinarily prolonged period of recession. Shifts to a post-Fordist labour market combined with the post-bubble recession to undermine the stability and security of employment, while an economic shift to deflation or minimal inflation resulted in reduced real incomes. The 1997/98 AFC and the 2007/08 GFC followed Japan's economic crisis. In Japan, as in many other developed countries, the housing system in the growth period was implicated in the inflationary economy, encouraging upward residential mobility towards the owner-occupied housing sector. Owning a house produced considerable capital gains and thus provided an efficient means of asset accumulation. Since the bubble burst, however, an increasing number of those on less secure employment have undergone difficulties in entering home ownership, while owner-occupied housing has generated capital losses due to house price deflation, leading to an increase in homeowners captured by a negative housing equity. The post-bubble economy has thus eroded the foundations of the post-war housing system oriented towards mass home ownership.

Furthermore, the case of Japan is worth examining in terms of institutional and policy shifts in the post-growth era. The state of post-war Japan has been characterised as a developmental state with distinctive features such as the state's autonomy with less intervention from civil society; production enhancing, growth-oriented priorities; and the state-managed market economy with institutionalised formal and informal government-business cooperation (Institute of Social Science, the University of Tokyo, 1998; Johnson, 1982; Weiss, 2003). In line with this, the state-guided housing system in post-war Japan was focused on driving mass construction of owner-occupied housing as a key engine for economic growth. Such government-led economic development and related mass production of housing provided a model for other East Asian nations in forming their own growth strategies. In terms of welfare approach, family-reliance with corporate-based welfare has been a distinctive feature in Japan. Property ownership combined with family and corporate welfare provided a material basis for sustaining well-being of the households. In East Asia, Japan developed the most comprehensive system of social insurance schemes for pensions, health care, employment and workers' injuries with a new addition of the long-term care insurance reflecting the accelerated ageing of the population. When introduced, such public welfare system did not replace the existing functions of family and corporate welfare but has incorporated them under the state umbrella (Tamai, 2003). With the entry into the post-growth phase, the government has accentuated the role of the market in formulating and implementing policy. This is most notable in the fields of employment and housing. Labour market liberalisation occupies the core of neoliberal policy in Japan as in many other countries. The market has dominated the production and consumption in the field of housing. Therefore, the adoption of a more neoliberal direction has resulted in a prompt retrenchment of government housing policy. It would be a misunderstanding to consider that neoliberal policy has replaced developmental state policy entirely due to the path-dependent nature of public policy. However, the post-bubble economic downturn and the associated decline in political stability have fuelled the reorientation of labour and housing policies towards market solutions.

Finally, Japan can be seen as an important exemplar with regard to acute shifts to social stratification. Until the 1980s, the country was arguably "successful" in light of constructing a more egalitarian and less meritocratic society along with growing prosperity. The perceptions of the 'middle-classness', which grew during the period of high growth, coined the popular phrase *'ichioku sou churyu'* meaning 'all 100 million of Japan's population regarded themselves as a member of the middle-class'. Opinion polls on living standards that have been conducted by the government since 1958 revealed that the percentage of those who considered the level of their living standards as 'middle' increased from 72 per cent in 1958 to 87 per cent in 1965, then exceeded 90 per cent in 1973 and remained at around 90 per cent until the end of the 1970s. Some scholars and commentators argued that a large and homogeneous 'new middle mass' in Japan had emerged with the rise of the 'affluent society' (see, for example, Murakami, 1984). The expansion of home ownership was effective in extending such perceptions of middle-classness in society, underpinning and enhancing social cohesion (Hirayama, 2007). Since 1990s, however, the arrival of post-growth society contracted the size of the 'middle class', while inequalities in terms of income distribution and employment security have been widening. A growing body of literature has provided substantial evidence of widening disparities, drawing social and academic attention to the rise of *'kakusa shakai'* (gap society) (e.g., Chiavacci and Hommerich, 2016; Ishida and Slater, 2011; Sato, 2000; Shirahase, 2014; Tachibanaki, 1998). Changes in housing conditions are reflected in a decline in the number of households who follow upward housing paths to home ownership, resulting in widened housing inequalities in access and assets. Thus, it has become more important to examine questions as to whether and how the housing system can provide housing and home ownership opportunities within the context of the shift to post-growth society.

The structure of the volume

This volume aims to fill a gap in the existing literature by placing housing at the heart of debates on post-growth society. The majority of arguments concerning post-growth social transitions have been focused on demographic processes, economic shifts and related changes in labour markets, environment and sustainability. However, housing is a foundation of social change. In particular, housing systems play a key role in shaping people's life opportunities at both individual and household levels, while simultaneously intertwining with broader socio-economic, political and institutional changes at large. What type of housing people can secure is crucially definitive in determining how they lead their lives in terms of physical security, access to services, employment and transportation, rent and mortgage payments, the accumulation of property assets, and membership in mainstream society. Moreover, a house is not only a material basis for people's lives but could also provide a sense of ease and comfort and ontological security (Dupuis and Thorns, 1998). Meanwhile, housing systems are implicated in wider social processes. Housing thus occupies a pivotal position in mediating micro-macro interactions, linking people's lives directly to broader socio-economic, demographic and policy shifts. It is within this context that we focus on housing in exploring social transitions.

Following this introductory chapter, changes in housing conditions in post-growth Japan will be examined in Chapter 1, with particular emphasis on the shrinking of the housing market and the expansion of housing inequalities. The chapter begins by looking at the characteristics of Japan's post-war housing system that was developed in the growth period. In terms of implementing housing policy, the government has consistently driven mass construction of owner-occupied housing while residualising the direct provision of low-income public rented housing. This was embedded within the framework of developmental state policy that was orientated towards facilitating economic development. The chapter then identifies and explores three key ingredients that shape post-growth social transitions for our analyses of changes in housing circumstances, namely, shrinking and ageing population, continuing economic stagnation, and policy shifts to a more neoliberal model. This is followed by explorations of the shrinking of the housing market and the associated reorganisation of mechanisms that produce social inequalities. With entry into the post-growth era, the upward residential mobility – from tenancy to owner-occupation, from a condominium to a detached house, and from a small house to a more spacious house – becomes stagnated, corresponding to a decline in the housing market. This leads to the increased importance of the role played by the distribution of the existing housing wealth within families in stratifying societies, representing the changing structure of social inequalities. The chapter finally highlights the significance of the post-growth context in light of investigating contemporary housing and social processes, providing a basis for the subsequent chapters to examine more specific issues.

Housing systems in post-growth society are primarily underpinned by more volatile and uncertain economic conditions. The rise and fall of property bubbles has led to major economic crises such as the GFC of 2007/08. Housing issues in the post-growth age are thus situated within the post-crisis economic context. In Chapter 2, we focus on Japan's 'post-bubble housing' in light of exploring housing situations in the era of economic instability. The chapter begins with a discussion on the theoretical salience of economic bubbles in regard to changes in housing systems and subsequently explores the trajectory of Japan's post-bubble housing within the context of prolonged economic stagnation and neoliberal policy reforms. We then analyse post-bubble changes in housing affordability and housing assets in detail. During the growth period, the inflationary economy accelerated a rise in housing costs, which resulted in a decrease in the affordability of housing. After the bubble burst, the financial pressure of acquiring housing did not mitigate but rather increased due to the deflation of real incomes. There has thus been a shift from house price inflation to income deflation in terms of the main cause of the decline in housing affordability. In addition, residential properties have fallen in value, resulting in a marked decline in the safety of houses as assets. We also look at changes in the housing conditions of low-income groups in relation to the policy shift to a neoliberal course and finally conclude with an examination of the implication of post-crisis economies on housing systems in the post-growth era.

Chapter 3 highlights the spatial dimension of housing development regarding the processes and outcomes of regional and urban policies in post-growth Japan. In response to intensified international economic competition, and within the context of pervasive neoliberalism, the Japanese government has implemented urban generation, placing special emphasis on the redevelopment of Tokyo. The new competition-orientated policy has, however, produced economic and spatial disparities between Tokyo and the rest of the country, and within Tokyo itself. Together with various policy measures aimed at restructuring Tokyo as a global city, a vast amount of investment has been poured into numerous residential projects in the capital city, whereas other regions have continued to suffer from disinvestment. Within Tokyo, housing investment has been concentrated in the 'hot spots' in the city centre, while the property market in the 'cold spots' at the periphery of the city has continued to stagnate. The chapter first examines the concepts of developmentalism and neoliberalism in terms of changes in the redistributive aspects of regional and urban policies and then looks at the development of the competition-driven policy. Subsequently, we analyse changes in the housing market in Tokyo in detail, while exploring economic stagnation in provincial regions with regard to housing issues, with investigations into housing situations in the Tohoku region, which was hit by the 2011 Great East Japan Earthquake, as an extreme case of post-growth economic and demographic decline. The chapter concludes with consideration on the prospects of housing opportunities in regard to regional and urban transitions in the post-growth era.

The impact of the transition to the post-growth society has been uneven across generations and has been particularly significant on the younger generation. In Japan, as in many other developed economies during the period of high economic-growth, many households climbed up a housing ladder towards home ownership. With entry to the post-growth age, however, an increasing number of young adults on more precarious employment have found themselves excluded from the home-ownership society. In Chapter 4, we look at divergence in housing pathways of young people within the post-growth context. The chapter proposes to focus on the 'individualisation' and 'familisation' of people's life-course in terms of exploring the diversification of housing trajectories. The combination of individualisation and familisation has led to increases in the numbers of one-person households living in private rented dwellings, unmarried young adults who continue to live in the parental home indefinitely, couples who purchase properties with assistance from their parents, and those who inherit residential properties from their parents. This means that conventional nuclear households who own their own home become less dominant. This chapter also explores transitions in urban space in relation to diversified housing pathways of young people. One-person households are concentrated on urban central areas, while an increase in the number of parental home dwellers is observed in fringe areas. A decrease in the number of conventional households has been reflected in a notable increase in the rates of vacant properties in suburban communities. Finally, the chapter examines the implications of changes in housing conditions of young people for post-growth societies.

One of the critical issues associated with post-growth society is very low fertility. Chapter 5 uses housing as a lens to explore women's issues, especially issues emerging from their multiple roles in work, reproduction and care in post-growth Japan. Gender issues tend to be absent from the contemporary housing debates since it is often households not individuals which are used as a unit of measurement in housing statistics. In pro-family societies like Japan, therefore, marriage has been a strong determinant for women's access to housing. The chapter begins with locating women in the family and welfare systems in order to ascertain how the current housing situations of women have derived and what were conventional expectations for women to access housing in the growth context. It then moves on to examine the relationships between work, family and housing in women's life-course. We will investigate the link between fertility and housing, and how current housing policy attempts to address fertility issues. Echoing the previous chapter, the policy measures are also familial in this context encouraging young families to co-reside or live near-by to extensively draw upon family resources for care provision. Housing or family policy addressing the nation's fertility agenda in relation to reproduction and work are, however, not necessarily effective in the post-growth contest. Alternative approaches to address gender issues in housing will be considered in conclusions. Many of the discussion in this chapter are concerns of women in their reproductive age.

Low fertility further accelerates the population ageing in the post-growth context, and housing issues in super-aged Japanese society is the central theme in Chapter 6. There are two main aims in this chapter. As the post-war baby-boomers have already reached their retirement age, one of major housing questions in super-aged Japan is how social stratification in housing, which has existed earlier in people's life-course, is now translated and accentuated in their later life. This is an important question at both micro and macro social levels. Therefore, we first explore the divisions which exist in housing tenure, conditions and asset levels among older people and how post-growth characteristics such as asset volatility and deregulation contribute to widen such inequalities. Current older people are the 'housing rich' generation since they have accumulated their housing wealth in the economic growth period. Our second theme is thus the role of housing, especially housing wealth in later life, in the mechanisms of asset transfer and its implication in post-growth society. The feasibility and limitations of the housing asset-based welfare approach in the Japanese context will be examined in Chapter 6.

In the concluding chapter, we highlight significant issues facing housing policy and practice in post-growth society and explore new approaches in order to reorganise the conventional housing systems developed in the post-war economic growth period. First, policies need to be developed to shift (away from the construction orientated housing system); in Japan, how the second-hand housing market can be developed and how a rising number of deteriorated vacant properties can be addressed are pressing post-growth policy questions. Given widening housing inequalities, developing more effective redistributive mechanisms in society are also critical. The chapter considers the ways in which the current state reliance on family resources exacerbated social inequalities. Last but not least, the chapter argues prospects for promoting social cohesion in post-growth society. Post-war housing policy and practice in Japan were built on social homogeneity based on the standard life-course with particular employment and welfare systems. Increasing diversity in people's life-course, employment and household structures is a cause and a consequence of the shift to post-growth society.

Housing policy and practice are now required to reflect and respond to such diversity.

References

Aalbers, M. B. (ed.) (2012) *Subprime Cities: The Political Economy of Mortgage Markets*, Oxford: Wiley-Blackwell.

Aalbers, M. B. (2016) *The Financialization of Housing: A Political Economy Approach*, New York: Routledge.

Aglietta, M. (1979) *A Theory of Capitalist Regulation*, London: Verso.

Amin, A. (ed.) (1994) *Post-Fordism: A Reader*, Oxford: Blackwell.

Bell, D. (1974) *The Coming of Post-Industrial Society*, New York: Harper Colophon Books.

Bonoli, J. (2005) The politics of the new social policies: Providing coverage against new social risks in mature welfare states, *Policy & Politics*, 33(3), 431–449.

Castells, M. (1996) *The Rise of the Network Society*, Oxford: Blackwell.

Chiavacci, D. and Hommerich, C. (eds.) (2016) *Social Inequality in Post-Growth Japan: Transformation During Economic and Demographic Stagnation*, New York: Routledge.

Davies, W. (2016) *The Limits of Neoliberalism: Authority, Sovereignty and the Logic of Competition*, Thousand Oaks: Sage Publications.

Department of Economic and Social Affairs, United Nations (2015) *World Population Prospects: Volume 1: Comprehensive Tables*, New York: United Nations.

Dewilde, C. and Ronald, R. (eds.) (2017) *Housing Wealth and Welfare*, Cheltenham: Edward Elgar.

Doling, J. and Elsinga, M. (2012) *Demographic Change and Housing Wealth: Home-Owners, Pensions and Asset-Based Welfare in Europe*, Heidelberg: Springer.

Doling, J. and Ronald, R. (2010) Home ownership and asset-based welfare, *Housing and the Built Environment*, 25(2), 165–173.

Dupuis, A. and Thorns, D. C. (1998) Home, home ownership and the search for the ontological security, *Sociological Review*, 46(1), 24–47.

Esping-Andersen, G. (1999) *Social Foundations of Postindustrial Economies*, Oxford: Oxford University Press.

Forrest, R. and Hirayama, Y. (2015) The financialisation of the social project: Embedded liberalism, neoliberalism and home ownership, *Urban Studies*, 52(2), 233–244.

Forrest, R. and Hirayama, Y. (2017) *Late home ownership and social re-stratification*, paper for international conference on *Unreal Estate? Rethinking Housing, Class and Identity*, by Research Committee 43 on Housing and the Built Environment, International Sociological Association, June 18–21, City University of Hong Kong.

Forrest, R. and Lee, J. (eds.) (2003) *Housing and Social Change: East-West Perspectives*, London: Routledge.

Forrest, R. and Yip, N-M. (eds.) (2011) *Housing Markets and the Global Financial Crisis: The Uneven Impact on Households*, Cheltenham: Edward Elgar.

Forrest, R. and Yip, N-M. (eds.) (2013) *Young People and Housing: Transitions, Trajectories and Generational Fractures*, London: Routledge.

Groves, R., Murie, A. and Watson C. (eds.) (2007) *Housing and the New Welfare State: Perspectives From East Asia and Europe*, Aldershot: Ashgate.

Hamnett, C. (1999) *Winners and Losers: Home Ownership in Modern Britain*, London: UCL Press.

Hantrais, L. (1999) *Gendered Policies in Europe: Reconciling Employment and Family Life*, Basingstoke: Palgrave MacMillan.

Harvey, D. (1985) *The Urbanization of Capital: Studies in the History and Theory of Capitalist Urbanization*, Baltimore: Johns Hopkins University Press.

Harvey, D. (2005) *A Short History of Neoliberalism*, Oxford: Oxford University Press.

Hino, M. and Tsutsumi, J. (eds.) (2015) *Urban Geography of Post-Growth Society*, Sendai: Tohoku University Press.

Hirayama, Y. (2007) Reshaping the housing system: Home ownership as a catalyst for social transformation, in Y. Hirayama and R. Ronald (eds.) *Housing and Social Transition in Japan*, London: Routledge, 15–46.

Hirayama, Y. (2010) The role of home ownership in Japan's aged society, *Journal of Housing and the Built Environment*, 25(2), 175–191.

Hiroi, Y. (2001) *Teijo ka Shakai: Atarashii Yutakasa no Koso [Stationary Society: A Perspective on New Prosperity]*, Tokyo: Iwanami Shoten.

Institute of Social Science, the University of Tokyo (ed.) (1998) *Kaihatsu Shugi [Developmentalism]*, Tokyo: Tokyo University Press.

Ishida, H. and Slater, D. H. (2011) *Social Class in Contemporary Japan: Structures, Sorting and Strategies*, New York: Routledge.

Izuhara, M. (2016) Reconsidering the housing asset-based welfare approach: Reflection from East Asian experiences, *Social Policy and Society*, 15(2), 177–188.

Jessop, B. (1994) Post-Fordism and the state, in A. Amin (ed.) *Post-Fordism: A Reader*, Oxford: Blackwell.

Johnson, C. A. (1982) *MITI and the Japanese Miracle: The Growth of Industrial Policy, 1925–1975*, Tokyo: Charles E. Tuttle.

Kemeny, J. (1992) *Housing and Social Theory*, London: Routledge.

Kurtz, K. and Blossfeld, H-P. (eds.) (2004) *Home Ownership and Social Inequality in Comparative Perspective*, Stanford: Stanford University Press.

Malpass, P. (2008) Housing and the new welfare state: Wobbly pillar or cornerstone? *Housing Studies*, 23(1), 1–19.

Muraca, B. (2012) Towards a fair degrowth-society: Justice and the right to a 'good life' beyond growth, *Futures*, 44(6), 535–545.

Murakami, Y. (1984) *Shin Chukan Taishu no Jidai [The Era of the New Middle Mass]*, Tokyo: Chuo Koron Sha.

OECD (2016) *Global Economic Outlook*, November.

Pallagst, K., Wiechmann, T. and Martinez-Fernandez, C. (2014) *Shrinking Cities: International Perspectives and Policy Implications*, New York: Routledge.

Park, B-G., Hill, R. C. and Saito, A. (eds.) (2012) *Locating Neoliberalism in East Asia: Neoliberalizing Spaces in Developmental States*, Oxford: Wiley-Blackwell.

Phillipson, C. (1998) *Reconstructing Old Age: New Agendas in Social Theory and Practice*, London: Sage.

Piketty, T. (2014) *Capital in the Twenty-First Century*, Cambridge: The Belknap Press of Harvard University Press.

Sato, T. (2000) *Fubyodo Shakai Nihon [Inequality in Japanese Society]*, Tokyo: Chuo Koron Shinsha.

Schwartz, H. M. and Seabrooke, L. (eds.) (2009) *The Politics of Housing Booms and Busts*, Basingstoke: Palgrave Macmillan.

Shirahase, S. (2014) *Social Inequality in Japan*, New York: Routledge.

Springer, S., Birch, K. and MacLeavy, J. (eds.) (2016) *The Handbook of Neoliberalism*, London: Routledge.

Tachibanaki, T. (1998) *Nihon no Keizai Kakusa [Economic Inequality in Japan]*, Tokyo: Iwanami Shoten.

Tamai, K. (2003) Development of social policy in Japan, in M. Izuhara (ed.) *Comparing Social Policies: Exploring New Perspectives in Britain and Japan*, Bristol: Policy Press, 35–48.

Taylor-Gooby, P. (ed.) (2004) *New Risks, New Welfare: The Transformation of the European Welfare State*, Oxford: Oxford University Press.

Touraine, A. (1971) *The Post-Industrial Society: Tomorrow's Social History: Classes, Conflicts and Culture in the Programmed Society*, New York: Random House.

Toussaint, J. and Elsinga, M. (2009) Exploring 'housing and asset-based welfare': Can the UK be held up as an example for Europe? *Housing Studies*, 24(5), 669–692.

Wade, R. (1998) *Governing the Market: Economic Theory and the Role of Government in East Asia Industrialization*, Princeton: Princeton University Press.

Weiss, L. (2003) Guiding globalization in East Asia: New roles for old developmental states, in L. Weiss (ed.) *States in the Global Economy: Bringing Domestic Institutions Back in*, Cambridge: Cambridge University Press.

1 Housing and shifts to a post-growth society

Introduction

This chapter examines changes in Japan's housing conditions within the post-growth context, placing particular emphasis on the shrinking of the housing market and the widening of housing inequalities. Many mature economies have begun to experience post-growth social changes characterised by slower economic growth, ageing of the population, lower fertility, and increasing social stratification. Japan stands at the leading edge of such transitions into a post-growth society, providing a vivid case study with regard to housing developments after the era of high growth. The chapter begins by examining the nature and characteristics of Japan's post-war housing system that was developed in the growth period. This is followed by identifying key elements such as the demographic, economic and policy shifts that are shaping post-growth social changes. It then moves on to analysing the shrinking of the housing and mortgage markets and the role of housing in reorganising inter- and intra-generational social inequalities. Finally, the chapter highlights the importance of the post-growth context in light of exploring contemporary housing and social processes, providing a basis for the subsequent chapters to examine more specific issues.

Building the post-war housing system

It is necessary to investigate the development of the housing system during the high-speed economic growth period before analysing emerging housing conditions in the post-growth era. Japan's housing system during high growth was characterised by particular orientations towards facilitating mass housing construction and promoting home ownership among the emerging middle class (Hirayama, 2003, 2014). The post-war Japanese state was characterised as a 'developmental state' that prioritised and orchestrated economic development as a means to legitimise itself and to sustain social stability (Fukui, 1992; Institute of Social Science, the University of Tokyo, 1998; Murakami, 1992). Within this framework, the housing system was directed at the acceleration of the mass construction of owner-occupied houses, where an increasing number of households were encouraged to own their own homes.

The government established post-war housing policy based on the 'three pillars': the Government Housing Loan Corporation (GHLC) Act in 1950, the Public Housing Act in 1951 and the Japan Housing Corporation (JHC) Act in 1955. The GHLC provided middle-income households with long-term, low-interest loans for building or purchasing their own home. Public housing was allocated to low-income households at low rent, while the JHC together with local public corporations constructed multifamily apartment complexes for both rent and sale for middle-income households. Of the three pillars, the supply of the GHLC's loans was particularly emphasised as a means to facilitate middle-income home ownership. According to the Housing and Land Survey (see Table 1.1), since the 1960s, despite rapid urbanisation, with the provision of GHLC loans aimed at encouraging home ownership, the level of owner-occupation has been maintained at approximately 60 per cent, representing its position as the dominant housing tenure. The ratio of private rented housing has been the second highest, accounting for a little more than a quarter of all dwellings – for example, 28.0 per cent in 2013. However, the government has not supported the provision of private rented housing. There has been little assistance for the

Table 1.1 Housing tenure in Japan (1958–2013)

	Owned houses	*Public rented houses (owned by local government)*	*Public rented houses (owned by public corporation)*	*Private rented houses*	*Company houses*	*Total housing units (including tenure not reported)*
Year	*(%)*	*(%)*	*(%)*	*(%)*	*(%)*	N
1958	71.2	3.5		18.5	6.7	17,432,000
1963	64.3	4.6		24.1	7.0	20,374,000
1968	60.3	5.8		27.0	6.9	24,198,000
1973	59.2	4.9	2.1	27.5	6.4	28,731,000
1978	60.4	5.3	2.2	26.1	5.7	32,189,000
1983	62.4	5.4	2.2	24.5	5.2	34,705,000
1988	61.3	5.3	2.2	25.8	4.1	37,413,000
1993	59.8	5.0	2.1	26.4	5.0	40,773,300
1998	60.3	4.8	2.0	27.4	3.9	43,922,100
2003	61.2	4.7	2.0	26.8	3.2	46,862,900
2008	61.1	4.2	1.9	26.9	2.8	49,598,300
2013	61.7	3.8	1.6	28.0	2.2	52,102,200

Note: Unoccupied houses were not included.

Source: Author's calculations from the Housing Survey (1958); Housing Survey of Japan (1963–1993); and Housing and Land Survey of Japan (1998–2013).

construction of private rented units and almost no provision of cash-based rent subsidies. The direct provision of rental units by the public sector was positioned as a residual measure (Harada, 1985; Ohmoto, 1985). The ratios of means-tested public housing for low-income households and public corporation rented housing have been minimal – 3.8 per cent and 1.6 per cent in 2013, respectively. Japan's housing policy has thus been characteristically tenure biased (Hirayama, 2014).

Within the framework of the developmental state, post-war housing policy not only served to provide housing but was also operated as an engine for economic growth (Oizumi, 2007). As a result of post-war high-speed economic growth, Japan became the world's second largest economy by 1968. From the mid-1950s to the early 1970s, the average annual GDP growth was approximately 10 per cent. The construction, housing and real estate sectors played a leading role in driving economic development. The 'iron triangle' between the Liberal Democratic Party (LDP), government bureaucrats and the construction sector, which constituted the political core of the developmental state system, was devoted to encouraging mass housing construction (Honma, 1996). The LDP, a party of established conservatives, has held power almost exclusively since it was founded in 1955. The government led by the LDP provided many households with GHLC mortgages, which was instrumental in accelerating housing construction. This in turn led to the maintenance of political support for the LDP by the construction industry as well as the housing and real estate sectors. With the enactment of the 1966 Housing Construction Plan Act, the government began to draw up Five-Year Housing Construction Plans periodically as a foundation for housing policy. The majority of public funding for housing construction took the form of GHLC loans. The strategy of the conservative administration was focused on expanding the construction of housing, especially owner-occupied housing, by indicating a targeted amount of housing production.

With the oil crisis of 1973 as a turning point, housing policy became more of a measure to stimulate the economy. Although the economic climate recovered after a short recession caused by the crisis, the era of high growth ended and a period of low growth began. This shift led to further strengthening the 'iron triangle' – the politico-economic relationship between business, especially the construction industries, the bureaucracy and the ruling LDP. The government further geared housing policy towards the mass construction of owner-occupied housing in order to revitalise the economy, providing more incentives for households to purchase their own home with GHLC loans. As a consequence, since the early 1970s, among the three pillars of housing policy, only the construction of owner-occupied dwellings was promoted, while the public rented sector was further residualised.

The post-war housing system of encouraging an increasing number of middle-income households to acquire an owner-occupied house was expected to create and maintain a 'social mainstream' (Hirayama, 2003,

2014). Backed by the rapid economic development, the increased flow of households who ascended the 'housing ladder' towards entering the home-ownership sector led to the spread of middle-class lifestyles to wider segments of society. The government formulated tenure-biased housing policy, placing emphasis on expanding the home-ownership sector, where housing measures for low-income households were marginalised. Public funds for housing were therefore not largely redistributed but rather concentrated on middle- to high-income households that wished to purchase a house. This was rationalised and justified as a means of providing more households with opportunities to climb up the ladder towards property ownership as membership in the social mainstream.

Within the context of shaping the social mainstream, the government implemented family-oriented housing policy and advantaged conventional family households in securing housing while excluding unconventional households (Hirayama, 2003; Hirayama and Izuhara, 2008). For example, the GHLC did not provide one-person households with mortgages until 1981. Of single-person households, GHLC loans were only available to those aged 40 or older until 1988 and to those aged 35 or older before 1993, when the age restriction was eventually removed. In addition, the GHLC did not provide mortgages to those who wished to build or purchase small houses. This was aimed at encouraging the construction of spacious 'family homes' while at the same time implicitly excluding one-person households. The public housing schemes for low-income people also excluded one-person households. It was only in 1980 when the elderly single-person households had become eligible for public housing as a result of a court battle (Kawano et al., 1981). However, younger single households continued to be excluded from public schemes. The JHC provided rental housing mainly to family households with a small number of dwellings for single-person households. Thus, only people who established a family household centred on marriage counted as legitimate members in mainstream society and were regarded as worthy of government support.

In parallel to housing policy, the taxation and social security systems have favoured family households. The family system in Japan was traditionally based on the 'male breadwinner family' model (Yokoyama, 2002; also see Chapters 4 and 5 for more discussion). Within this framework, married women, or homemaker wives, who may be part-time workers on low wages, have been provided with an entitlement to a basic pension without having to make contributions while assisting their husbands in qualifying for income tax deductions. In the labour market in Japan, the status of women has been much lower than that of men in terms of stable employment, promotion opportunities and remuneration. This has combined with the tax and social security systems that have given institutional advantages to male breadwinner families to prompt many women to get married.

Moreover, the development of Japan's post-war housing system was linked to the formation of a 'company society' (Fujita and Shionoya, 1997).

Major companies adopted the systems of life-long employment and seniority-based promotion and salary while providing employees with a variety of occupational welfare, including housing assistance (Sato, 2007). The government supported the security of employment and facilitated the provision of occupational benefits by means of regulatory measures and tax incentives. Corporate-based housing measures were placed in the Japanese housing ladder. Low-rent employee dwellings and rent subsidies were supplied for young employees, while employees at higher rungs of the ladder had access to a company loan system for house purchase. The occupational welfare system of major companies was characteristically aligned with the male breadwinner family model. Employee dwellings as well as family allowances were only provided to male employees whose spouses were housewives or part-time workers, corresponding with the tax and social security systems.

In addition, the home ownership system was situated within the framework of the 'Japanese style welfare society' (Hirayama, 2014). From the late 1970s to the 1980s, it was well debated whether or not European welfare state models were applicable in Japan, considering the contrast between Japan's growing affluence and a continued low level of state welfare. With a decline in growth rates in the 1970s, however, LDP politicians and government bureaucrats began to stress the necessity of developing a Japanese-style welfare society (Shinkawa, 1993). The basic idea was to revitalise the traditional Japanese practice of reciprocal help and to define families and corporations combined with property ownership as the cornerstone of the welfare system. According to the conservatives, the European welfare models were not necessarily desirable due to high dependence on public resources, while Japanese values and practices were effective in maintaining the nation's vitality. The LDP government used the term 'welfare society' while avoiding use of the term 'welfare state', denoting its intention to rationalise the limited development of state welfare. Within this framework, property ownership combined with the family and company systems has thus constituted the foundation of Japan's welfare approach.

Entering a post-growth era

Demographic change

The condition of the housing system was fundamentally transformed following the end of high growth. In this section, we identify three key ingredients that constitute post-growth social transitions for our explorations of housing developments, namely, shrinking and ageing population, continuing economic stagnation, and policy changes towards a more neoliberal direction. First and foremost, demographic decline is one of the most important elements responsible for Japan's shift to a post-growth society. According to the 2012 projection by the National Institute of Population and Social Security Research, the population, which was 128 million in 2010, is predicted to decline significantly to 107 million by 2040 and then to 87 million by 2060 (see Figure 1.1). This is partly due to Japan's ultra-low fertility. The total fertility rate (TFR) in Japan, which was more than 2.0 until the mid-1970s, decreased to a record low of 1.26 in 2005 (see Figure 1.2). The rate has since increased slightly but has remained at a very low level – for example, 1.39 in 2010 and 1.46 in 2015. The population decline is being paralleled by a rapid increase in the proportion of older people in society. Japan became a 'super-aged society' in 2007, when the rate of those aged 65 or older in the total population exceeded 21 per cent. This figure is forecast to increase to as much as 36.1 per cent by 2040 and 39.9 per cent by 2060. The proportion of older people in Japan will remain the highest in the world.

Such demographic changes have major effects on transformations in the condition of the housing system. The government has traditionally encouraged the mass construction of dwellings to stimulate economic growth. Pressure from the demand for housing will be, however, significantly lessened in the future due to the shrinking and ageing population. It will thus become more difficult to maintain a high level of investment in housing production. If the number of households continues to increase with a decline in

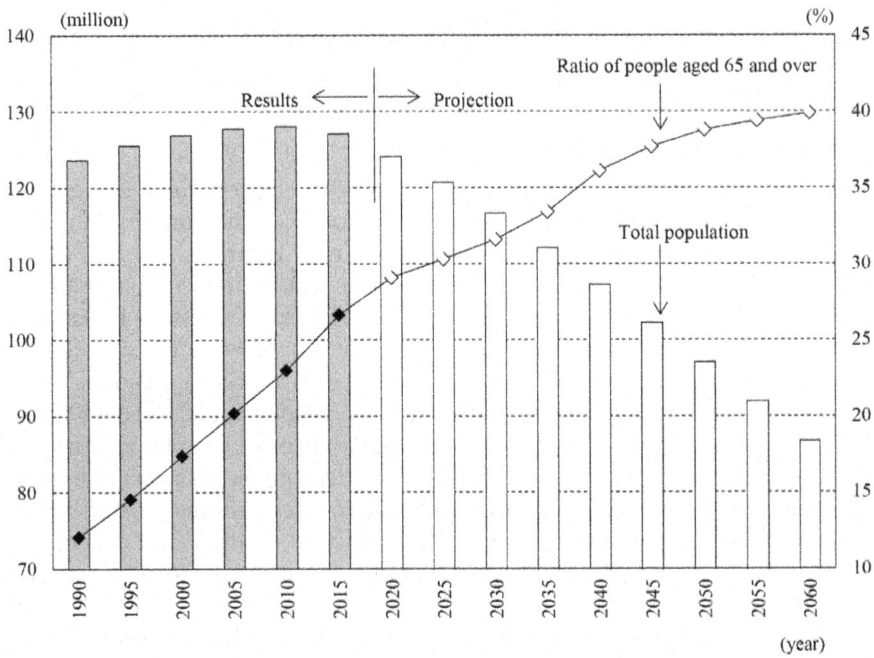

Figure 1.1 Population change in Japan (1990–2060)

Source: Statistics Bureau, Population Census of Japan; National Institute of Population and Social Security Research, Population Projection for Japan.

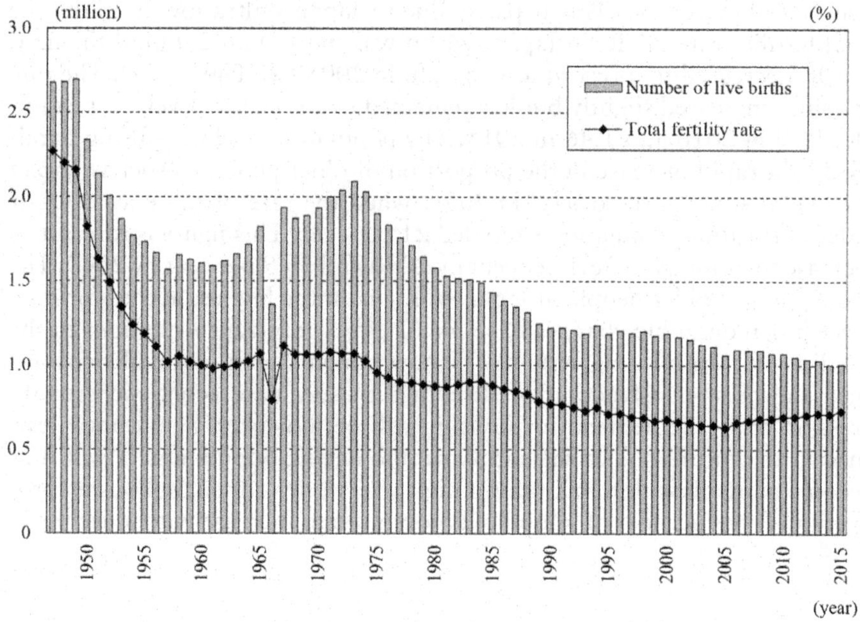

Figure 1.2 Live births and total fertility rates in Japan (1947–2015)
Source: Ministry of Health, Labour and Welfare, Vital Statistics of Japan.

household size, it might be possible to sustain the high volume of housing construction despite the population decline. However, the number of households is also expected to start declining in the near future.

In addition, the shift to post-growth society has been accompanied by a decline in the number of marriages and associated changes in household patterns. In post-war Japan, acquiring an owner-occupied house was closely linked with family formation (Hirayama and Izuhara, 2008). In some Western societies, not only married couples but also single people and cohabiting couples aspire to own a home, whereas in Japan most people do not purchase a dwelling until they get married. The government placed significance on encouraging marriage-based households to access home ownership in implementing housing policy, while the tax, social security and corporate-based welfare systems gave a range of financial advantages to conventional households. The combination of marriage and home ownership was indeed at the heart of Japan's post-war social development. In other words, the decline in marriage has in turn meant a fundamental challenge to the post-war housing system based on home ownership. Unconventional households often on low incomes have largely been excluded from policy measures and the housing market. Therefore, the increase in the number of unconventional households suggests an increase in those who are disadvantaged in securing adequate housing, not to mention accessing home ownership.

An increase in those who either delay marriage or never married has been evident. According to the Population Census, between 1980 and 2015, the percentage of unmarried people in the 30–34 age group rose from 21.5 per cent to 47.1 per cent for men and from 9.1 per cent to 34.6 per cent for women (Figure 1.3). Unmarried rates are much higher for males than for females. Moreover, the ratio of never-married individuals at 50, who are defined as 'lifelong never-married' in Japanese statistics, increased to 23.4 per cent for men and 14.1 per cent for women by 2015. This figure is, according to the 2013 projection by the National Institute of Population and Social Security Research, expected to increase to 29.0 per cent for men and 19.2 per cent for women by 2035. With a decline in marriage, household patterns have indeed changed. Between 1980 and 2015, the percentage of one-person households increased from 15.8 per cent to 34.6 per cent, while that of households comprised of married couples and children decreased from 44.2 per cent to 26.9 per cent (Figure 1.4).

Continuing economic stagnation

The economic bubble, which swelled in the latter half of the 1980s with an abnormal upsurge in real estate prices, collapsed at the beginning of the 1990s. This marked a turning point in which Japan entered a new era of

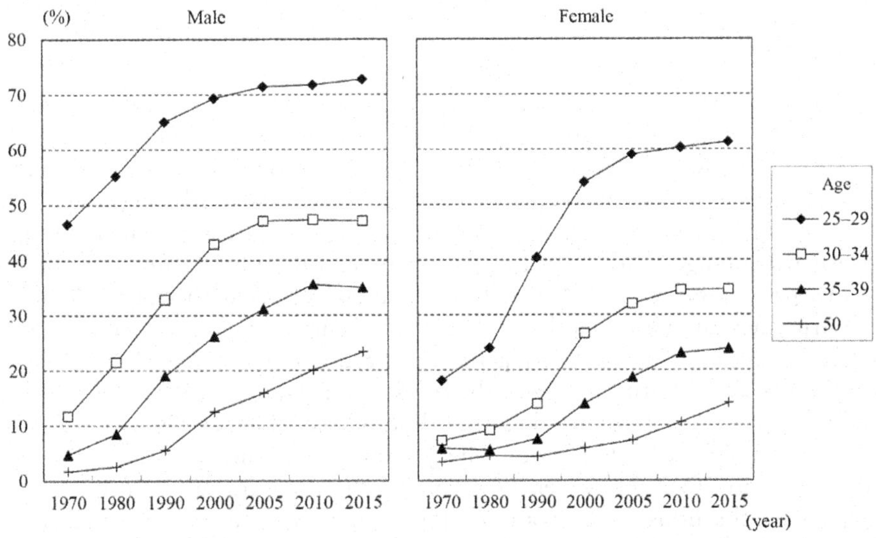

Figure 1.3 Unmarried rates by age and sex (1975–2015)

Source: Author's calculations from Population Census of Japan.

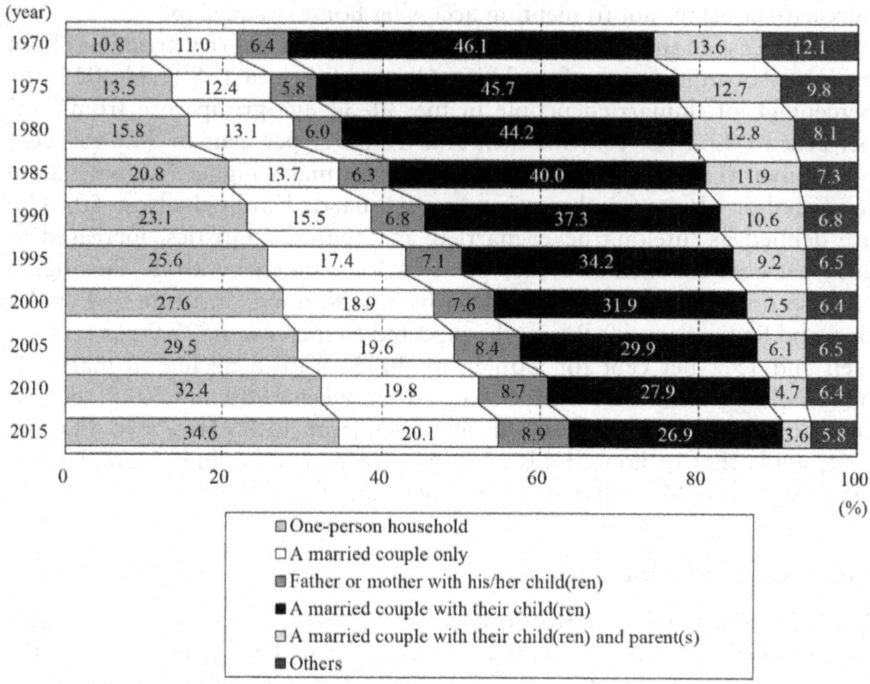

Figure 1.4 Change in household type (1970–2015)

Source: Author's calculations from Population Census of Japan.

post-growth stagnation. Annual real growth rates in GDP on average, which were more than 5 per cent in the 1970s, fell to less than 5 per cent in the 1980s, to below 2 per cent in the 1990s, and then to even below 1 per cent in the 2000s. Post-bubble recession was extremely prolonged and traumatic, with minimal or negative real growth in GDP (see Figure 1.5). The banking sector was plunged into crisis due to a significant number of unrecoverable loans, provoking the 1994 and 1997 financial crises with chain-reaction bankruptcies of major banks and security firms as well as corporations in other sectors. The AFC, triggered by the downfall of the Thai baht in 1997, was an additional blow to the recession in Japan. Real incomes were reduced and the labour market was destabilised. The 1990s came to be known as Japan's 'lost decade'. The Japanese economy eventually began to recover in 2002. However, the economic upturn did not translate into improving the household economy. Japan then entered another recession in 2008, having become entangled in the GFC triggered by defaults in US subprime mortgages. Subsequently, the European debt crisis began to affect many economies including Japan in 2009. Some scholars and commentators

Figure 1.5 Real growth rate in GDP (1980–2015)

Note: The benchmark year of 1990 is used for data for 1980, 2000 is for 1981 to 1993, and 2011 is for 1994 and after.

Source: Cabinet Office, National Accounts of Japan.

therefore asserted that Japan now had two 'lost decades' (e.g., Fukao, 2012; Fukuda, 2015). Thus, since the early 1990s, economic insecurity has come to be perceived as 'normal' rather than 'abnormal' and has increasingly been considered a phenomenon arising from some structural transformations in the economy rather than from pure economic cycles.

In addition, demographic changes have accelerated economic downturns. The population decrease combined with an increase in the proportion of older people means a substantial decline in those who are of 'productive' age. The percentage of those aged between 15 and 64, which was 63.8 per cent in 2010, is projected to decrease to 53.9 per cent in 2040 and to 50.9 per cent by 2060. As argued in the previous chapter, the 'productive age' population includes those not engaged in paid work and an increasing number of older people extending their working life. It is true, however, that the workforce is declining substantially, which will put a structural barrier against economic recovery.

Economic decline and neoliberal policy reforms aimed at deregulating the labour market have led to the 'casualisation' of employment (Genda, 2001). Japan's post-war development was associated with the formation of a 'company society'. However, within the context of the post-bubble economic downturn, and in response to intensified competition brought by the globalising business environment, an increasing number of corporations, struggling for their survival, carried out large-scale personnel restructuring and downsizing. This weakened the foundation of the company society model. The labour market has thus been reoriented around declining employment stability with an associated increase in non-regular, low-wage employees. According to the Employment Status Survey, the number of regular employees has declined from 38.1 million to 33.1 million between 1992 and 2012, while the number of non-regular employees including dispatched workers, short-term contract-based employees, part-time workers and temporary employees has more than doubled from 9.5 million to 19.2 million in the same period. The percentage of non-regular employees in the total number of employees rose to 36.8 per cent in 2012 (see Figure 1.6). It was not only economic downturn but also neoliberal policy that has accelerated the reorganisation of the labour market. The major amendments to the 1986 Dispatched Labour Act in 1999, 2004 and 2015 played a particularly important role in promoting the casualisation of employment practices. The Japan Federation of Employers' Associations (1995) published an influential report in 1995 that emphasised the necessity of deregulating employment practices to enhance competitiveness in business. The associations merged

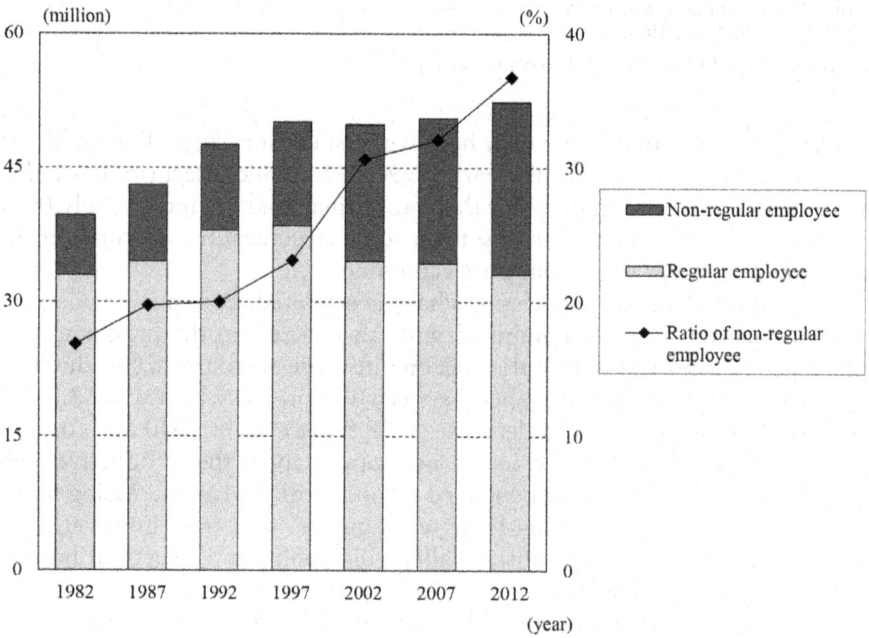

Figure 1.6 Number of regular and non-regular employees (1982–2012)

Source: Author's calculations from Employment Status Survey.

with the Japan Federation of Economic Organizations to form the Japan Business Federation in 2002. As the most powerful corporate organisation in the country in terms of political influence, the new federation has been prompting the government to further deregulate the employment market. A labour policy reorientation towards more flexible employment has thus been achieved in the context of political pressure applied by business circles.

During the post-war growth period, many households with rising real incomes acquired owner-occupied houses and accumulated valuable real estate assets. Since the bubble burst, however, prolonged stagnation and neoliberal policy reforms focused on deregulating the labour market have fundamentally affected the economic circumstances surrounding the housing system. A decline in real incomes has made it more difficult for many tenants to enter the home ownership market. At the same time, within the home ownership sector, residential properties have been substantially devaluated, resulting in a decline in the security of residential properties as assets.

Housing policy reforms

Entering the post-growth period, the Japanese government implemented various policy reforms emphasising market solutions in alignment with pervasive neoliberalism. Since the early 1970s when capitalist societies underwent economic crises such as the 1971 Nixon Shock and the 1973 Oil Crisis, declines in growth have stimulated the rise of neoliberal imperatives, which have been increasingly influential in re-orientating public policies. Compared to some Western nations, Anglo-Saxon societies in particular, progress on the implementation of neoliberal policy was slow in Japan (Forrest and Hirayama, 2009). Policy shifts started in the early 1980s in the UK and the US, while the Japanese approach to policy reforms only began to emerge in the mid-1990s. Political and economic factors were responsible for the delay in advancing neoliberalism in Japan. The LDP government had played a key role in the operation of post-war developmental state policies. Therefore, the adoption of radical neoliberal policy by the party meant an attack on itself, generating contradictions within its political base. Moreover, unlike developed Western economies which had experienced a prolonged recession since the Oil Crisis in the early 1970s, Japan's economy had maintained a relatively strong performance. This accounted for the delay in the restructuring of state policies. The post-bubble stagnation was, however, remarkably extended. The LDP lost the 1993 general elections for the first time. Although the party returned to power in the following year, it lost the election again in 2009 and it took until 2012 for the party to return again to govern the nation. Thus, enduring recession has combined with a decline in LDP-dominated political stability to erode the foundation of the developmental state, leading to the introduction of a neoliberal course.

Shifts in social policy towards liberalisation were particularly noticeable in the areas of employment and housing. The deregulation of the labour market has been at the core of neoliberal policy in Japan as well as in many other economies. Housing policy has been positioned at the periphery of social policy because compared with education, health care and social security, housing is much more likely to be provided in the market domain. For this reason, housing policy was promptly involved in the market-oriented policy shift. It would be misleading to consider neoliberal policy to have fully replaced developmental state policy (Park et al., 2012). Government policy cannot be separated from its past trajectories, assuming a path-dependent nature. The Japanese government has continued to give priority to and take the initiative in addressing economic issues, while many LDP politicians continued to support developmental state policy. Together with the economic and political crises, however, post-war social policy has lost ground in phases, and significant reforms have been carried out in the areas of employment and housing.

Post-war housing policy has been fundamentally reformed. The Housing Construction Plan Act, which had provided a foundation for post-war housing policy, was abolished in 2006. This was followed by the 2006 enactment of the Housing and Livelihood Basic Act, which developed a new market-based system. Along with increasing emphasis on the role of the market in financing, producing and consuming housing, the three pillars of post-war housing policy were disintegrated. New developments of low-income public housing have declined since the early 1970s and have almost completely halted since the mid-2000s. In addition, there has been an increase in cases where the reconstruction of public housing developments results in a reduction in the number of housing units, which has led to a decline in the volume of the existing stock. The Housing and Urban Development Corporation, the successor to the JHC, was reorganised into the Urban Development Corporation in 1999 and again into the Urban Renaissance Agency in 2004. The new agency reduced its commitment to housing schemes substantially so as not to compete with the private sector. The GHLC was a central mechanism in expanding home ownership. Nevertheless, the government began to reduce the provision of GHLC loans in the mid-1990s, and the corporation was ultimately abolished in 2007. The dissolution of the state agency, which had constituted the core of the housing system, was a particularly important watershed in the post-war history of Japan's housing policy. While the Housing Finance Agency was established to replace the GHLC, it mostly withdrew from the primary mortgage market and thereafter dealt mainly with the secondary market of mortgage securities.

The shrinking of the housing market

Reduced housing construction

The next issue is to explore how housing conditions have transformed within the post-growth context. Changes in the circumstances of the housing system have been seen at the micro level of individuals and households, which are simultaneously intertwined with broader social processes at the macro level. Therefore, housing situations at both micro and macro levels are examined in this section in order to explore transitions into a post-growth society. Since the end of high growth, the moves of individuals and households up the home ownership ladder have decreased, while the housing and mortgage markets have increasingly become shrunken. Such micro and macro stagnation in the housing sphere has begun to undermine the sustainability of the post-war social mainstream.

One of the most important features of changes in the housing situation at the macro level is a substantial reduction in the volume of housing construction. Mass production of housing has underpinned Japan's post-war economic development. Immediately after the Second World War, housing shortage was acute. A significant number of dwellings were lost in the war-devastated cities, while housing construction had almost completely stopped during the War. The government estimated the housing shortage at 4.2 million dwellings, which was more than one-fifth of the total number of existing dwellings at that time. In addition, the population increase combined with a trend towards smaller households to multiply the number of households in the process of rapid urbanisation. As a result of acute housing shortage, the demand for housing continued to augment, necessitating a high volume of housing production. This led to post-war industrial developments in the housing, construction and real estate sectors, which further stimulated economic expansion.

As mass housing production progressed and urbanisation subsided, however, the imbalance between housing demand and supply was rectified and a new period of housing surplus began in the 1980s (Miyake, 1996). The number of existing dwellings in Japan doubled from 31 million in 1973 to 61 million in 2013, while the vacancy rate increased from 5.5 per cent in 1973 to 9.8 per cent in 1993 and to 13.5 per cent in 2013 (see Figure 1.7). As the housing market has matured, housing construction has inevitably declined. Furthermore, upon entering the post-growth phase, demographic and economic stagnation has contributed to shrinking the housing market. The number of housing starts continued to increase rapidly during the growth period and peaked at 1,905,112 in 1973 (see Figure 1.8). Thereafter, a new pattern of housing construction emerged in which a cycle of ups and downs in housing starts was observed. In general, however, housing construction declined. The annual number of 'housing starts' (new construction) on average, which was 1,507,152 between 1990 and 1994, significantly decreased to 1,180,770 in 2000–2004 and to 880,465 in 2010–2014.

The second-hand housing market has remained underdeveloped in Japan. This is a distinctive feature of the Japanese housing system. A decline in new construction has therefore translated directly into a decline in the total amount of investment in housing, as investment in the existing housing stock is not expected to compensate for the decline in investment in housing

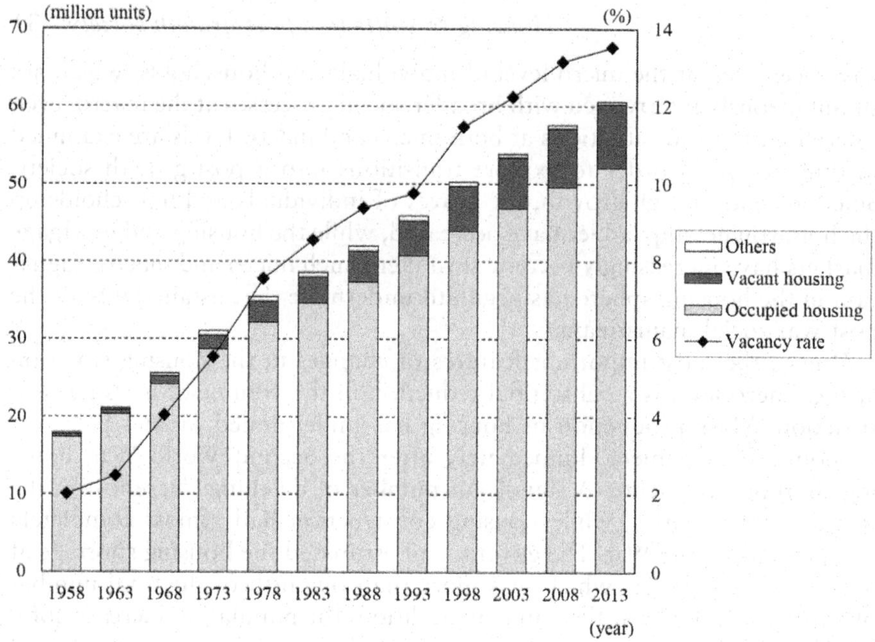

Figure 1.7 Housing stock (1958–2013)

Source: Author's calculations from Housing Survey (1958), Housing Survey of Japan (1963–1993); Housing and Land Survey of Japan (1998–2013).

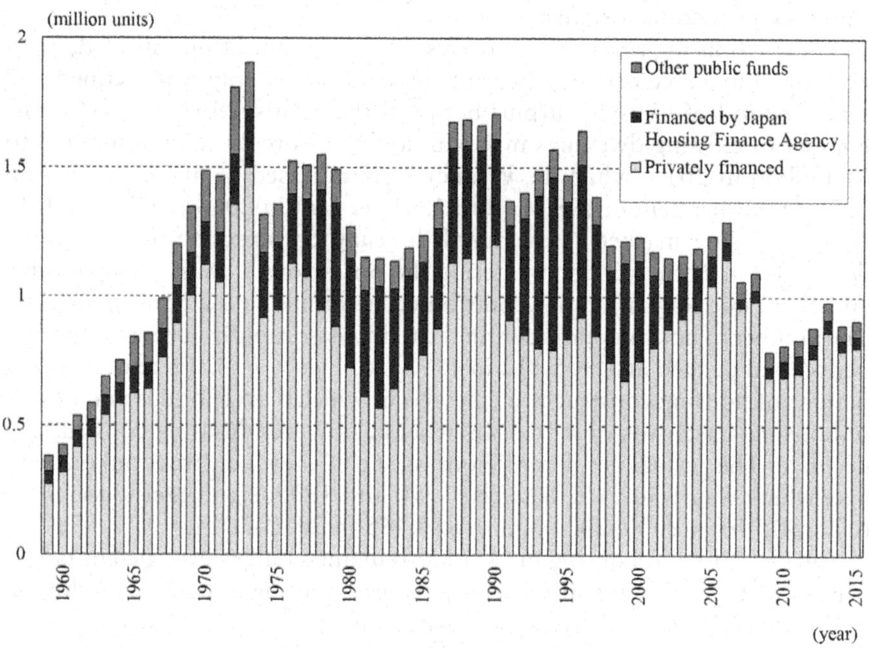

Figure 1.8 Housing new starts by type of fund (1959–2015)

Note: Japan Housing Finance Agency is formerly known as the Government Housing Loan Corporation.

Source: Ministry of Land, Infrastructure, Transport and Tourism, Housing Starts.

construction. Between 1990 and 2015, the annual investment in housing decreased significantly from 26.9 trillion to 15.8 trillion yen (from 215 billion to 126 billion euros [1 euro = 125 yen, May 2017]) and its percentage versus real GDP dropped sharply from 5.9 per cent to 3.1 per cent (see Figure 1.9). The government has placed importance on expanding the construction of new dwellings in formulating housing policy, aimed at stimulating the economy. Institutions involved in house purchases have characteristically offered incentives to households seeking to buy new houses in order to support housing construction. For example, the GHLC provided borrowers who were purchasing new housing with mortgages under more favourable conditions compared to those who were buying second-hand properties. In addition, the tax system gave advantages to those who bought new houses. Such institutional mechanisms indeed discouraged the development of the second-hand property market. Since the 2000s, the government has begun to place more weight on the expansion of second-hand housing transactions. This is due to changes in the conditions of the housing market including the onset of the population decline and the increasing number of vacant dwellings. However, the policy shift has, at least so far, only led to the very slow improvement of the marketability of the existing housing stock. This

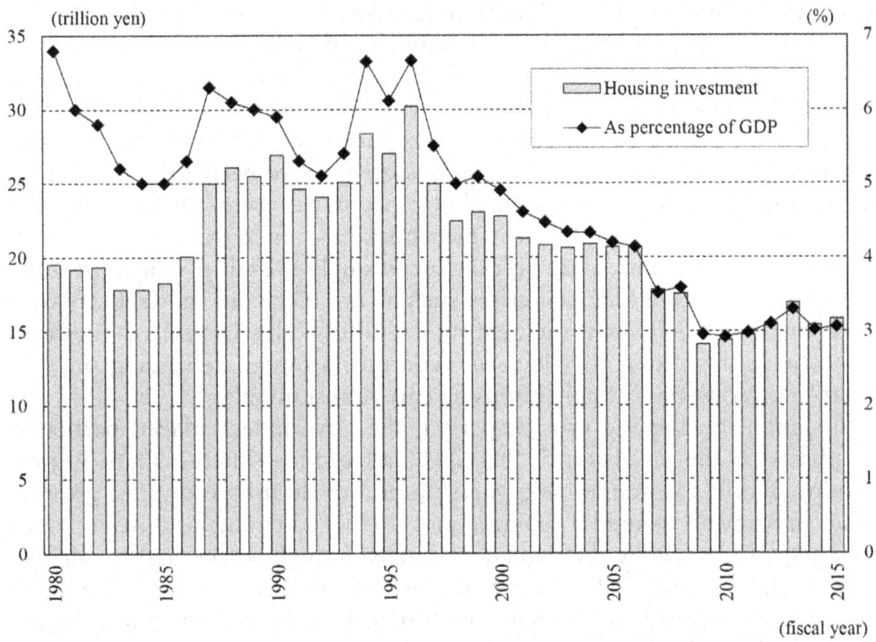

Figure 1.9 Housing investment and its percentage of GDP (1980–2015)

Note: Regarding GDP, the benchmark year of 2000 is used for data for 1993 and before, and 2011 is for 1994 and after.

Source: Cabinet Office, National Accounts of Japan.

suggests that considerable time is required to develop the second-hand housing market in terms of making a more fundamental shift away from the construction-oriented housing policy.

Limits on mortgage market expansion

In many developed countries including Japan, facilitating the supply of housing loans has been increasingly instrumental in expanding housing markets and stimulating economies. During the economic growth period, inflationary economic conditions urged many households to enter the home ownership market. In addition, governments in many countries provided a variety of assistance such as tax incentives and direct subsidies to those who wished to procure loans for home purchase. This effectively protected households with mortgages from fluctuations in the financial market. However, as growth rates began to decline in the early 1970s and neoliberal imperatives grew more prevalent, mortgage market institutions were transformed to further liberalisation. This encouraged the devising of more diverse mortgage products, leading to the expansion of housing loan markets. Such 'financialisation' of housing constituted a key feature of neoliberal housing systems (Aalbers, 2015; Forrest and Hirayama, 2015). Streeck (2014) argued that there had been a shift from inflation to public debt and to private debt in neoliberal policy to cope with economic crises. This was best reflected in an increase in mortgaged houses. Households, rather than governments, were encouraged to take on debt to stimulate their economies, which resulted in a rapid increase in indebted homeowners. This was embedded within the broader framework of a growth strategy that Crouch (2009) dubbed 'privatised Keynesianism'. Thus, mortgage systems have been expected to play a key role in buttressing economic buoyancy in the era of declining growth rates. Nevertheless, the way in which housing loan systems interact with economic circumstances has become increasingly unstable, which has been reflected in extreme financial crises such as the AFC and the GFC (Forrest and Yip, 2013; Schwartz and Seabrooke, 2009). This has raised questions concerning the extent to which an economic strategy depending on debt financing for owner-occupied housing can be sustainable.

In Japan, during the growth period, the government placed particular emphasis on the provision of the GHLC's fixed-low-interest loans in promoting middle-income home ownership and facilitating economic growth. The corporation formed a separate and privileged circuit of housing loans and helped to alleviate the influence of the volatile financial market on borrowers. In the early 1970s when the era of low growth began, the supply of GHLC mortgages became more important as an economic measure. By the mid-1970s, it had become difficult for tenants to purchase housing due to house price inflation. The policy of stimulating the economy, which directed a significant amount of investment into the housing market, further pushed up the prices of residential properties. In response to rising house prices, the GHLC increased the loan limit and lengthened the repayment period to improve lending conditions. In addition, a series of new programmes to encourage housing acquisition was developed by the GHLC. The Step Repayment System, in which the amount of repayments was set at a low level for the first five years, was introduced in 1979, while a loan relay system was established in 1980 allowing loans to be carried over two generations within families. A clear cycle was thus established, where the improvement of loan conditions expanded demand for owner-occupied housing and boosted housing prices, which then fed back to the further improvement of loan conditions. The government increased the supply of GHLC loans whenever the economy fell down into recession. The percentage of GHLC-financed dwellings against all newly constructed owner-occupied dwellings rose from 25.6 per cent in the 1970s to as high as 47.6 per cent in the 1980s and 49.3 per cent in the 1990s. This confirms that the state housing loan system played a key role in the expansion of home ownership in the post-war period.

In response to the post-bubble recession, the Japanese government began to re-orientate housing policy towards market solutions. This included the privatisation and marketization of housing finance. In 1994, the housing loan market was deregulated in terms of allowing private banks to set interest rates, and subsequently the GHLC was abolished in 2007. During the post-war growth period, banks concentrated on financing investments in industrial development, while the GHLC dominated the provision of residential mortgages. In the 1980s, however, the banking sector turned to financing for real estate as large companies moved to procure capital from equity finance. Banks thereafter came to position the sale of mortgage products as core business. Therefore, the significant void in the mortgage market created by the dissolution of the GHLC was immediately filled by the rapid increase in the supply of mortgage products by private banks. Furthermore, since the late 1990s, interest rates have declined to an extraordinarily low level in response to the post-bubble economic downturn, while the government has practiced various financial deregulations to an unprecedented extent. This has been expected to stimulate the financial and housing markets and economic recovery.

Nevertheless, within the post-growth context, it becomes more difficult to expand or even maintain a high volume of mortgage transactions. The housing market has been saturated within the context of demographic and economic stagnation. This has inevitably imposed limitations on the expansion of the mortgage-led economy. The total amount of outstanding housing loans for individuals increased dramatically from 45.1 trillion yen (361 billion euros) in 1980 to 183.4 trillion yen (1,467 billion euros) in 2000, and its percentage versus the GDP rose from 18.6 per cent to 36.2 per cent during the same period (see Figure 1.10). The amounts have, however, been largely stationary since the early 2000s. Meanwhile, new issues of mortgages have begun to decline (see Figure 1.11). The annual average amount of newly-issued housing loans for individuals decreased from 30.1 trillion yen (241 billion euros) in 1995–1999 to 20.0 trillion yen (160 billion euros) in 2010–2014. As for the composition of housing loans, the proportion of bank loans has rapidly risen with a decline in GHLC loans (see Figure 1.10 and 2.11). The government has launched itself on the privatisation and marketization of housing loans in order to withstand economic slow-down. Post-growth demographic and economic shifts to stagnations have, however, hindered the expansion of the mortgage market.

Stagnated upward residential mobility

In terms of changes in housing conditions at the household level, the upward residential mobility – from tenancy to owner-occupation, from a condominium to a detached house, and from a small house to a more spacious one – has become stagnated. This is a cause and a consequence of the shrinking of the housing and mortgage markets at the macro level. During

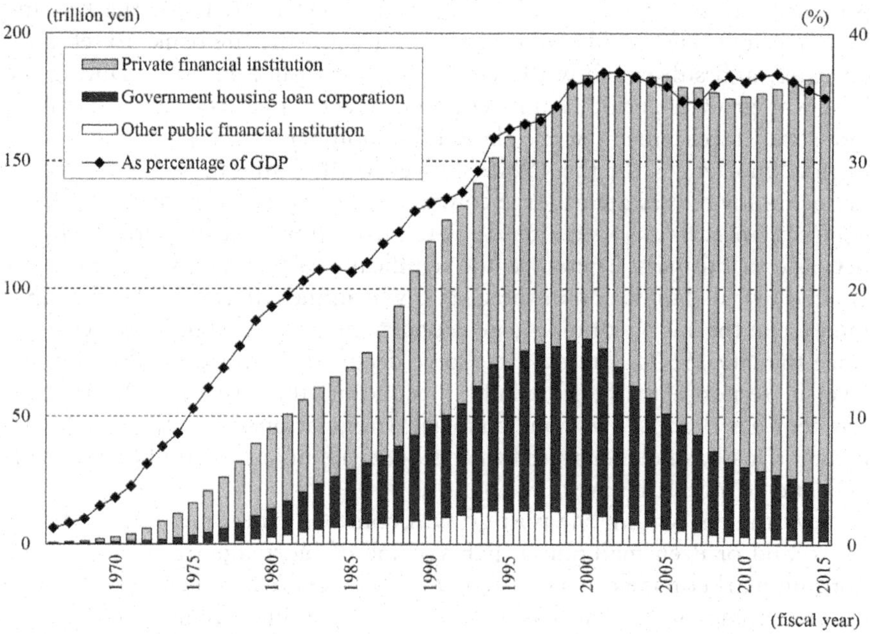

Figure 1.10 Outstanding housing loans for individuals as percentage of GDP (1966–2015)

Note: Government Housing Loan Corporation was reorganised into Japan Housing Finance Agency in 2007. Regarding GDP, the benchmark year of 1990 is used for data for 1979 and before, 2000 is for 1980 to 1993, and 2011 is for 1994 and after.

Source: Japan Housing Finance Agency, Cabinet Office, National Accounts of Japan.

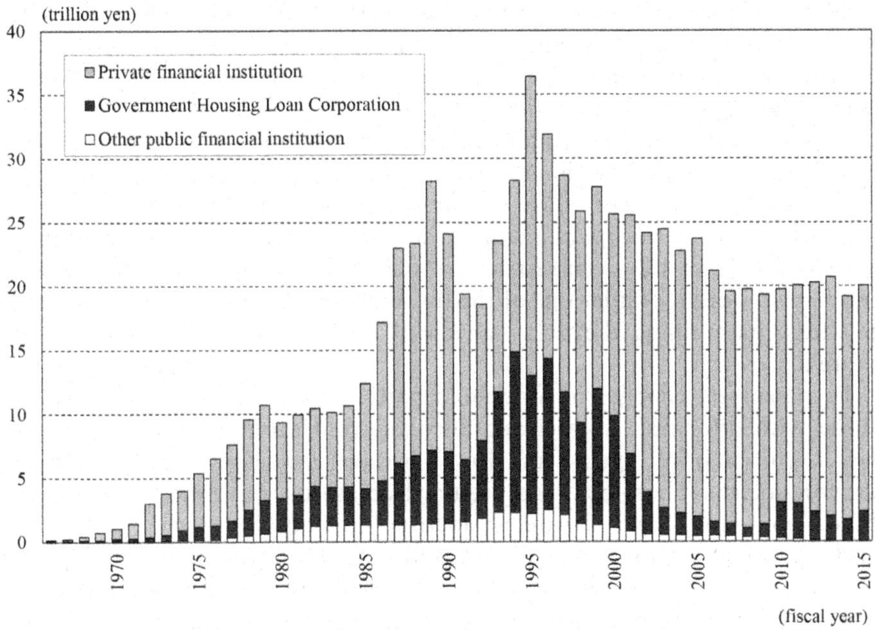

Figure 1.11 New issues of housing loans for individuals (1966–2015)

Note: Government Housing Loan Corporation was reorganised into Japan Housing Finance Agency in 2007.

Source: Japan Housing Finance Agency.

the growth period, house price inflation was the main reason for undermining the affordability of home ownership. The rate at which house prices went up was far beyond general price and income growth. The population growth and a rapid increase in the number of households combined with urbanisation widened supply-demand imbalances in the housing market, accelerating house price inflation. After the bubble burst, the overall economy became deflationary, and a sharp drop in housing prices was observed for the first time in the post-war period. Once the pressure from the population growth and urbanisation on the housing market was eased, housing supply-demand imbalances were reduced. Nevertheless, the affordability of home ownership did not improve largely due to reduced real incomes. In contrast to house price inflation in the growth period that urged households to purchase a house, post-bubble income deflation discouraged many households from buying a dwelling. In the post-growth era, therefore, an increasing number of households with declined incomes have remained in the rented housing sector with less prospects of climbing up the housing ladder towards home ownership (for a full discussion, see Chapter 2).

Within the owner-occupied housing sector, the burst of the economic bubble led to a devaluation of housing assets, undermining the system of leading homeowners to higher rungs on the property ladder. During the growth era, home ownership generated capital gains and facilitated asset accumulation. Many households moved to a better house of higher value by using capital gains as a springboard. Since the bubble collapsed, however, most owner-occupied dwellings have generated capital losses, resulting in a decline in the security of housing as assets. A number of homeowners have been tied down with capital loss and the upward mobility within the home ownership sector has been restricted. Such shift has suggested the erosion of the traditional foundations of the housing system that has been oriented towards maintaining the post-war social mainstream (see Chapter 2 for more discussion).

Furthermore, changes in household patterns have led to an increase in those with difficulties in securing adequate and affordable housing. Low fertility, population ageing and low marriage rates are features of post-growth society. There has thus been a decrease in conventional marriage-based households and instead an increase in unconventional households such as single-person, single-parent and elderly-only households. Japan's post-war housing policy has specifically concentrated on encouraging family households to acquire owner-occupied housing while marginalising housing measures for unconventional households. Unlike family households often on middle incomes, unconventional households involve many low-income households. Shifts in household patterns in the post-growth era have therefore meant an increase in those with disadvantages in terms of housing policy and the housing market.

There are an increasing number of single-person households with precarious employment who have harder access to adequate housing. In Japan, marital status is also closely linked to employment status. For example, according to the 2012 Employment Status Survey, the unmarried rate in male regular employees aged 30 to 34 was 39.9 per cent, while the figure for their non-regular counterparts was notably higher at 72.9 per cent. Meanwhile, single-mother households are disadvantaged with regard to employment opportunities and thus housing access. According to the National Survey on Single-Parent Households conducted by the Ministry of Health, Labour and Welfare, among single-mother households the rate of those on public assistance increased from 9.6 per cent in 2006 to 14.4 per cent in 2011 due to their vulnerable employment status in economic downturns. As for older households, there is a gap in the level of home ownership according to household compositions. According to the 2013 Housing and Land Survey, the rate of owner-occupation was high at 88.6 per cent for households with two or more members including those aged 65 or older but the figure was much lower at 64.9 per cent for single-elderly households. The proportion of the number of single-elderly households in the total number of households including older people increased from 15.1 per cent in 1990 to 27.3 per cent in 2015, and the figure is expected to rise even higher (see Chapter 6 for further discussion).

Housing, generation and inequality

Generational fractures

During the period of high economic growth, the housing system oriented towards the mass construction of owner-occupied housing expanded the flow of people ascending the residential property ladder, leading to the construction of a relatively egalitarian society. With the transition into a post-growth era, however, the housing and mortgage markets have begun to shrink and people's upward residential mobility has become stagnant. This has resulted in a compounding of inter- and intra-generational inequalities. The impact of radical social, economic and policy shifts on people's fortunes is not equal across generations but concentrates on the younger generation. Older households have ascended the housing ladder towards home ownership and the accumulation of assets during the growth period with generous state assistance. The younger generation in the post-growth era are, on the other hand, hit by prolonged economic stagnation and diminishing state support in accessing property ownership. An obvious decline in the number of younger people who follow their parent generation in terms of conventional housing paths presents a new challenge to the traditional housing system (Hirayama, 2013).

A remarkable phenomenon relating to the younger generation is the delay in entering the owner-occupied housing market (for a full discussion, see Chapter 4). According to the Housing and Land Survey, the level of home ownership for households with a head aged 30–34 significantly dropped from 45.7 per cent in 1983 to 28.8 per cent in 2013. Less stable employment, reduced real incomes and delayed marriage are some of the explanations for the trend. The gap has been widening among younger people in terms of marital status, employment conditions and housing access. An increasing number of young, unmarried adults on non-regular employment have continued to live in their parents' homes indefinitely, while young one-person households tend to remain in the private rented sector with little prospect of accessing home ownership. Married couples who establish their own independent households have sought to acquire and own their own homes. However, family households with modest incomes who purchased housing have to bear a heavy load of mortgage repayments.

Meanwhile, among the older generation, housing situations are not homogenous but highly differentiated (for a full argument, see Chapter 6). The vast majority of households with older members live in owner-occupied housing. However, older people living in private rented housing in particular tend to suffer from inadequate housing conditions in terms of affordability, amenities and the security of tenure. The rate of private rented housing is particularly high for single-elderly households. The Japanese government has implemented home ownership-centred housing policy, leaving the rented housing sector underdeveloped. It is not clear how housing tenure patterns of households with older members will transform in the future. It is apparent, however, that the rapidly ageing population means a rapid increase in the absolute number of older people living in rental accommodations. Moreover, older homeowners are diverse in terms of property ownership. Elderly households with lower incomes tend to live in properties with low values, while those with higher incomes own houses with higher property values. In addition, high-income older people more often possess additional properties that produce rent incomes (Hirayama, 2010).

Intergenerational family relations

It is salient to examine the role that intergenerational family relations pertaining to housing play in reorganising the structure of social inequalities in the post-growth age. As Piketty's (2014) seminal research on social inequality suggests, in mature economies, as growth slows, and as wealth accumulates, the redistribution of existing family wealth, rather than income flow, becomes more important as a driver of social stratification. Real estate assets generally account for the largest share of family wealth for average families, although financial assets are often larger than housing assets among wealthy families. In developed societies that have a large housing stock, how housing wealth is distributed across generations will increasingly dictate how society is stratified (Forrest and Hirayama, 2017; Forrest and Murie, 1995; Kurtz and Blossfeld, 2004). In Japan, housing policy has not been significantly redistributive: the government has inclined towards promoting middle-class home ownership while residualising low-income housing measures. As a result, most housing wealth is under private ownership and the public sector owns and runs only a very small stock of housing. In addition, the second-hand housing market has remained underdeveloped, reflecting the construction-oriented housing policy system. Therefore, the market is not expected to play a significant role in the redistribution of existing housing. Meanwhile, families have been positioned as one of the most significant keystones of Japan's welfare approach. Consequently, the family system, rather than housing policy and the housing market, plays a particularly definitive role in structuring mechanisms for redistributing housing wealth. Thus, Japan's post-growth society will likely undergo increasing disparities between affluently propertied families that further accumulate housing assets over generations, modest families that have a tendency towards the dissipation of their housing assets accumulated during the growth era, and perpetually renting families that are increasingly being excluded from mainstream society (for a full discussion, see Forrest and Hirayama, 2017).

Within the context of the redistribution of family wealth, it is significant to assess what role property inheritance plays in constituting social inequalities (Izuhara, 2005; Hirayama, 2010). Owner-occupied housing is not only an asset for owner households but can also be transferred to the future generations. Younger cohorts in Japan have experienced a more sluggish economy and faced difficulties in acquiring residential properties by themselves. However, a high level of home ownership among the older generation combined with low fertility means an increased likelihood that the younger generation will inherit residential properties from their parents. In post-growth Japan, the housing and asset portfolio of the younger generation is partly determined by whether their parents own a house and whether they can inherit it. Housing inequalities among the older generation are thus increasingly transmitted to the next generation.

Within the framework of intergenerational family relations, parents' assistance relating to housing, in addition to inheritance, has played an increasingly important role in shaping the housing opportunities of younger generations. This implies that young people's economic independence has tended to decline in the post-growth era. In Japan, together with continuing stagnation and declining real incomes, the availability of family resources has become an incubator in differentiating the fortunes of young people in terms of securing housing and accessing home ownership. Many young, unmarried adults on precarious employment have remained in the parental home instead of acquiring their own independent dwellings. However, not everyone can rely on parents. Married couples who receive financial support from their parents may experience relatively smooth transitions to home ownership, while those without family support have to bear the full cost of purchasing a house. In response to enduring recession, the Japanese government has substantially reduced gift taxes on inter-vivo asset transfers within families when involving children's housing purchase. This measure is expected to help improve the housing conditions of young households and stimulate economic recovery. The policy of promoting inter-vivo asset transfers has, however, exacerbated inequalities among the younger generation in terms of home ownership opportunities according to their parents' resources.

Conclusion

This chapter has articulated the importance of the post-growth context in exploring contemporary housing and social changes. In Japan, the housing and mortgage markets have begun to shrink, while an increasing number of households are now facing difficulties in following the conventional path into home ownership. Such stagnation relating to housing opportunities at both the micro and macro levels poses a new challenge to the housing system that has been oriented towards sustaining the social mainstream.

With the shrinking of the housing market and the associated stagnation of upward residential mobility, housing related social inequalities expand between and within generations. There are increasing disparities between older and younger cohorts in light of access to housing and home ownership. Among young adults, those on precarious employment have found themselves excluded from the housing and mortgage markets, while for older people, economic gaps between the home-owning and the non-owning and between the equity rich and the equity poor have become apparent. Furthermore, we demonstrated the significance of the role played by intergenerational family relations pertaining to housing wealth in reorganising social inequalities. In Japan, as in many other societies, many studies have explored and explained how societies are stratified, placing special emphasis on labour market inequalities in income, class and social status as particularly deterministic key factors. However, in mature economies with lower growth rates and a significant amount of housing wealth, the way in which family properties are distributed over generations will become more significant in reorganising the structure of social stratification.

In post-growth Japan, the population decline as well as subsided urbanisation appears to lessen the demand for dwellings and increase housing surplus. This does not, however, necessarily lead to the improvement of housing conditions. Vacant houses have been increasing in number in rural areas and small towns, where a rise in the vacancy rates does not mean improved housing situations but rather represents declining local economies. As for large cities, disparities in supply-demand relations in the housing markets have expanded between city centres, where the chronic shortage of dwellings has undermined the affordability of housing, and peripheral and unpopular areas, where the outflow of the population has accelerated an increase in deteriorated vacant dwellings. Thus, despite the increase in housing surplus in the society as a whole, supply-demand imbalances in the local housing markets have not necessarily mitigated but rather worsened (for a detailed discussion, see Chapter 3). Moreover, within the post-growth context, precarious employment, reduced real incomes, and an increasing number of unconventional households combine to drive the number of individuals and households who do not have access to adequate and affordable housing. Even if the number of houses has well exceeded that of households, the surplus dwellings are not necessarily distributed to lower class households that aspire to secure housing.

During the past high-growth period, many households had prospects of moving up the home ownership ladder towards entering mainstream society. This translated into a decrease in the extent to which people were conscious of inequalities and thus served to sustain social cohesion. With the entry into the post-growth era, however, an increase in those who have lower expectations of accessing property ownership has begun to unravel the traditional mechanism responsible for social integration. Some young households can achieve home ownership with financial support from their parents but others cannot. Some property-rich elderly households can rent out their additional dwellings to gain rental incomes, whereas low-income elderly people often live in substandard private rented housing, bearing a heavy burden of rent payments. Many people have now begun to perceive social stratification more strongly. Growing inequalities relating to housing and home ownership are thus becoming an important policy issue that should be addressed in the emerging post-growth society.

References

Aalbers, M. B. (2015) The great moderation, the great excess and the global housing crisis, *International Journal of Housing Policy*, 15(1), 43–60.

Crouch, C. (2009) *The Strange Non-Death of Neoliberalism*, Cambridge: Polity Press.

Forrest, R. and Hirayama, Y. (2009) The uneven impact of neo-liberalism on housing opportunities, *International Journal of Urban and Regional Research*, 33(4), 998–1013.

Forrest, R. and Hirayama, Y. (2015) The financialisation of the social project: Embedded liberalism, neoliberalism and home ownership, *Urban Studies*, 52(2), 233–244.

Forrest, R. and Hirayama, Y. (2017) *Late home ownership and social re-stratification*, paper for international conference on *Unreal Estate? Rethinking Housing, Class and Identity*, by Research Committee 43 on Housing and the Built Environment, International Sociological Association, June 18–21, City University of Hong Kong.

Forrest, R. and Murie, A. (eds.) (1995) *Housing and Family Wealth: Comparative International Perspectives*, London: Routledge.

Forrest, R. and Yip, N-M. (eds.) (2013) *Young People and Housing: Transitions, Trajectories and Generational Fractures*, London: Routledge.

Fujita, Y. and Shionoya, Y. (eds.) (1997) *Kigyo nai Fukushi to Shakai Hosho [Employee Benefits and Social Security]*, Tokyo: Tokyo University Press.

Fukao, K. (2012) *Ushinawareta Niju Nen to Nihon Keizai [The Two Lost Decades and the Japanese Economy]*, Tokyo: Nihon Keizai Shinbun Sha.

Fukuda, S. (2015) *Ushinawareta Niju Nen wo Koete [Beyond the Two Lost Decades]*, Tokyo: NTT Shuppan.

Fukui, H. (1992) The Japanese state and economic development: A profile of a nationalist-paternalist capitalist state, in R. P. Applebaum and J. Henderson (eds.) *State and Development in the Asian Pacific Rim*, London: Sage.

Genda, Y. (2001) *Shigoto no Naka no Aimai na Fuan [The Vague Uneasiness of Work]*, Tokyo: Chuo Koron Shinsha.

Harada, S. (1985) Sengo jutaku housei no seiritsu katei [The establishment process of housing laws in post-war Japan], in Institute of Social Science, Tokyo University (ed.) *Fukushi Kokka Vol. 6: Nihon no Shakai to Fukushi [The Welfare State Vol. 6: Japanese Society and Welfare]*, Tokyo: Tokyo University Press, 317–396.

Hirayama, Y. (2003) Housing and social inequality in Japan, in M. Izuhara (ed.) *Comparing Social Policies: Exploring New Perspectives in Britain and Japan*, Bristol: Polity Press, 151–171.

Hirayama, Y. (2010) The role of home ownership in Japan's aged society, *Journal of Housing and the Built Environment*, 25(2), 175–191.

Hirayama, Y. (2013) Housing and generational fractures in Japan, in R. Forrest and N-M. Yip (eds.) *Young People and Housing: Transitions, Trajectories and Generational Fractures*, London: Routledge, 161–178.

Hirayama, Y. (2014) Housing and the rise and fall of Japan's social mainstream, in J. Doling and R. Ronald (eds.) *Housing East Asia: Socioeconomic and Demographic Challenges*, Basingstoke: Palgrave Macmillan, 116–139.

Hirayama, Y. and Izuhara, M. (2008) Women and housing assets in the context of Japan's home-owning democracy, *Journal of Social Policy*, 37(4), 641–660.

Honma, Y. (1996) *Doboku Kokka no Shiso [The Ideology of the Construction State]*, Tokyo: Nihon Keizai Hyoron Sha.

Institute of Social Science, the University of Tokyo (ed.) (1998) *Kaihatsu Shugi [Developmentalism]*, Tokyo: Tokyo University Press.

Izuhara, M. (2005) Residential property, cultural practices and the "generational contract" in England and Japan, *International Journal of Urban and Regional Research*, 29(2), 341–357.

Japan Federation of Employer's Association (1995) *Shinjidai no Nihon teki Keiei [Japanese Business Management for the New Era]*, Tokyo: Japan Federation of Employers' Associations.

Kawano, M., Kinashi, Y. and Shimoyama, E. (1981) *Jukyo no Kenri [Rights to Housing]*, Tokyo: Domesu Shuppan.

Kurtz, K. and Blossfeld, H-P. (eds.) (2004) *Home Ownership and Social Inequality in Comparative Perspective*, Stanford: Stanford University Press.

Miyake, J. (1996) Jinko kazoku no henka to jutaku jukyu [Demographic and family changes and the housing market], in S. Kishimoto and A. Suzuki (eds.) *Kazoku to Jukyo [Family and Housing]*, Tokyo: Tokyo University Press, 205–235.

Murakami, Y. (1992) *Han Koten no Seiji Keizai Gaku [Political Economy of Anti-Classics]*, Tokyo: Chuou Koron Sinsha.

Ohmoto, K. (1985) Fukushi kokka to wagakuni jutaku seisaku no tenkai [The welfare state and housing policy in Japan], in Institute of Social Science, Tokyo University (ed.) *Fukushi Kokka Vol. 6: Nihon no Shakai to Fukushi [The Welfare State Vol. 6: Japanese Society and Welfare]*, Tokyo: Tokyo University Press, 397–455.

Oizumi, E. (2007) Transformations in housing construction and finance, in Y. Hirayama and R. Ronald (eds.) *Housing and Social Transition in Japan*, London: Routledge, 47–72.

Park, B-G., Hill, R. C. and Saito, A. (eds.) (2012) *Locating Neoleberalism in East Asia: Neoliberalizing Spaces in Developmental States*, Oxford: Wiley-Blackwell.

Piketty, T. (2014) *Capital in the Twenty-First Century*, Cambridge: The Belknap Press of Harvard University Press.

Sato, I. (2007) Welfare regime theories and the Japanese housing system, in Y. Hirayama and R. Ronald (eds.) *Housing and Social Transition in Japan*, London: Routledge, 73–93.

Schwartz, H. M. and Seabrooke, L. (eds.) (2009) *The Politics of Housing Booms and Busts*, Basingstoke: Palgrave Macmillan.

Shinkawa, T. (1993) *Nihongata Fukushi no Seiji-Keizaigaku [Political Economy of Japanese-Style Social Welfare]*, Tokyo: San'ichi Shobo.

Streeck, W. (2014) *Buying Time: The Delayed Crisis of Democratic Capitalism*, London: Verso.

Yokoyama, F. (2002) *Sengo Nihon no Josei Seisaku [Public Policy for Women in Post-War Japan]*, Tokyo: Keiso Shobo.

2 Housing in a post-crisis economy

Introduction

Housing systems in post-growth societies are primarily underpinned by unstable economic conditions. The rise and fall of housing bubbles have been closely linked to major economic crises such as the AFC in 1997/98 and the more recent GFC in 2007/08. Over the past few decades, many of the industrialising and post-industrial countries have radically shifted their housing policies to embrace a market-based approach with pervasive and normative neoliberal prescriptions. This is a major cause of fluctuations in housing markets, resulting in housing booms and busts. Such accelerated ups and downs in housing economies have brought about more precarious housing circumstances surrounding households (Forrest and Yip, 2013).

Housing issues in post-growth societies are thus situated within the context of post-crisis economies. This chapter focuses on Japan's 'post-bubble housing' in terms of exploring housing conditions in the era of economic instability. Japan has been experiencing a prolonged economic recession since the burst of the bubble economy at the beginning of the 1990s (see Chapter 1). Reduced real incomes have made it more difficult for many tenants to become homeowners, while a continuous decline in land and housing prices has led to an increase in the number of homeowners with negative equity. Moreover, lower-income households have increasingly been confronted with difficulties in securing affordable housing. The government has re-orientated its housing policy towards emphasising market solutions. Along with the prolonged economic stagnation, the state retrenchment from direct housing provisions and subsidies has further undermined the housing circumstances of many households.

This chapter examines changes in the housing economy, particularly at the household level. It begins with a discussion on the theoretical and social significance of economic bubbles in terms of transformations in housing systems as well as the distinctiveness of the Japanese case in investigating post-crisis housing. This is followed by explorations of the trajectory of Japan's post-bubble housing within the context of economic stagnation and neoliberal policy reforms. Detailed analyses of post-bubble changes in housing affordability and housing assets at the household level are then provided. The housing situations of low-income groups in relation to the policy reform are also examined, and the chapter concludes with an exploration of the implications of post-crisis economies on housing systems in the post-growth era.

Diverging systems and converging trajectories

When investigating the nature of the housing system in post-growth society, it is first necessary to understand post-crisis economic conditions. A key observation is that diverse housing systems in different countries have increasingly converged around similar paths in response to more globalised neoliberal imperatives. Over the past decades, various countries have developed their own distinctive housing system in line with their own social, economic, political and institutional contexts. There have been numerous academic debates to classify housing systems by means of cross-national comparative analyses. For example, various housing scholars have built on Esping-Andersen's (1990, 1999) seminal work on welfare regime typologies in investigating the relationship between housing and welfare approaches (e.g., Balchin, 1996; Barlow and Duncan, 1994; Kurz and Blossfeld, 2004). Kemeny's (1995) classification of rental housing policies is also influential in demonstrating differences in tenure systems across different societies. Such typologies have almost exclusively drawn on experiences of the Western societies. With the economic development of East Asian societies, researchers are now seeking to include this region in the scope and coverage of comparative housing analyses (e.g., Agus et al., 2002; Forrest and Lee, 2003; Ronald, 2007). When it comes to identifying the distinctiveness of housing systems in East Asian nations, many arguments (e.g., Doling and Ronald, 2014; Groves et al., 2007; Lee, 2014) have been made along the line of welfare regime theories including developmentalism (e.g. Wade, 1998; Weiss, 2003) and 'productivist welfare capitalism' (Holliday, 2000).

Developing and critiquing welfare typologies have played a significant role in comparative housing studies over the past few decades (Boelhouwer and Van der Heijden, 1992; Doling and Ford, 2003; Kemeny and Lowe, 1998; Ronald, 2008). With the ascendance and global diffusion of pervasive neoliberalism, however, various countries have begun to undergo similar trends in the transformation of housing system (Aalbers, 2015). Since the 1980s, governments across societies have reformed their housing policy, emphasising the role of the market in facilitating home ownership while significantly reducing state welfare including the direct provision of social housing. Another key feature of the housing reforms was a radical expansion of credit lending that accelerated the financialisation of housing (Aalbers, 2016; Forrest and Hirayama, 2015). The deregulation of financial markets in many societies led to the creation of a more competitive environment for housing loan businesses and thus promoted a variety of mortgage products, encouraging more households to purchase housing. As argued in Chapter 1, the focus of the neoliberal economic policy measures was shifted from government debt to private debt (Streeck, 2014), where individual households instead of governments were encouraged to take on debts to stimulate the economy. Within this context, housing systems were significantly financialised with a notable increase in the number of homeowners with debts. Such housing financing was embedded in the broader framework of growth strategy characterised as 'privatized Keynesianism' (Crouch, 2011) and 'house price Keynesianism' (Watson, 2010).

There are increasingly shared characteristics among different housing systems in terms of the direction of change. For example, the level of home ownership is higher in the UK than in the Netherlands, but both countries have undergone similar growth of the owner-occupied housing sector. Aalbers (2015) argues that various countries began to converge around certain elements in housing system changes and proposed the periodisation of developments in housing structures to distinguish between the pre-modern period, the modern or Fordist period, the flexible neoliberal or post-Fordist period, and the late neoliberal or emerging post-crisis period. Many developed societies with different housing systems tend to undergo a similar shift regarding stages of housing development, although the timeframes of the changes might be different. For example, the UK and the US entered the period of neoliberal reforms earlier than other advanced economies, after which a number of countries then followed suit.

The financialisation of housing combined with increasingly volatile economic conditions has led to intensified housing booms with an unprecedented inflation of house prices followed by tremendous housing busts. The GFC, triggered by the US sub-prime mortgage meltdown, was widespread over many countries, and the excessive collateralisation of real estate resulted in catastrophic financial and economic turmoil. Housing markets across a number of countries were simultaneously entangled in the global crisis, although the extent to and the way in which the crisis affected the national economies as well as housing and mortgage markets varied between countries. Although housing systems in many countries had been orientated towards home ownership, the GFC made it harder for the governments to use the expansion of debt financing as a strategy to implement housing policy. Thus, a number of societies are now facing a common challenge concerning how to reform the housing and mortgage systems in the post-crisis context.

Despite the converging trends, it would be misleading to assume that differences in the housing systems across societies are diminishing. Housing policy and provisions are local in nature, and thus variations exist in housing systems across societies. Similar policy orientations arising from globally prevalent stress on liberalising housing and mortgage markets do not necessarily produce the same outcomes but are mediated by domestic socio-economic, political and institutional contexts and thus produce diverging effects on housing transformations (Forrest and Hirayama, 2009). For example, Schwartz and Seabrooke's (2009) exploration of home ownership and mortgage systems highlighted the variety of 'residential capitalism' types in evidence. It is thus important not to overlook national characteristics within the global shift.

Japan provides an interesting case in terms of exploring post-crisis housing. The country experienced the burst of the property bubble a decade before the AFC and two decades before the GFC. Since then, it has undergone a prolonged, enduring period of economic recession. Japan can therefore be positioned as a preceding exemplar with regard to experiences of post-crisis housing. This is not to say that other post-GFC countries will follow the same trajectory as Japan; rather, insights gained from the Japanese experience will provide valuable lessons for other societies as to the potential trajectories of post-crisis housing and at the same time will stimulate wider debates about housing in the new era of more precarious economic conditions.

Moreover, neoliberal prescriptions have combined with increased economic instability to severely affect the housing conditions of lower-income households (Glynn, 2009; Rolnik, 2013). The 1980 introduction of the 'right to buy' scheme in Britain, in which sitting tenants in council housing were given the right to purchase the property at discounted prices, was symbolic of the beginning of the 'selling the welfare state' project (Forrest and Murie, 1988). Since then, governments in many countries have withdrawn from conventional housing policy, and especially from the provision of social housing. While many governments provided low-income households with rent subsidies, a reduction in social housing units led to the smaller scale of housing policy for low-income households as a whole. Within this context, Japan again occupies a pivotal position regarding difficulties experienced by households on low incomes in securing adequate and affordable housing. The direct state provision of social housing has been traditionally residual, and there has been almost no provision of rental allowances for private tenants. In addition, neoliberal policy reforms have further marginalised low-income housing in Japan (see Chapter 1).

Housing in the post-bubble economic context

The rise and fall of the property bubble

The burst of the bubble economy was a significant watershed in the postwar history of Japan's housing system since it provided a trigger for the fundamental reorganisation of housing policy and the housing market (Forrest et al., 2003; Hirayama, 2007). Prior to the Asian and Global Financial Crises, the burst of the bubble economy in Japan signified the end of the post-war linear growth period and the beginning of the post-growth period of uncertainty and instability in terms of housing and mortgage economies.

It is important to examine how the economic environment surrounding the housing system has transformed since the burst of the bubble economy and how this economic shift has affected housing provision and access.

The bubble economy started emerging in the latter half of the 1980s in Japan. The prices of real estate and stock rose up abnormally, diverging from general price movements that had been relatively stationary. The extreme upsurge in land and housing prices began in the capital city, Tokyo, and then spread to other major cities such as Osaka and Nagoya and eventually all over the country. Changes in the prices of residential land, measured against the previous year, were recorded at 68.6 per cent in Tokyo in 1988 and 56.1 per cent in Osaka in 1990. In the Tokyo metropolitan region, between 1980 and 1990, the average nominal cost of housing rose from 24.8 million yen (198,400 euros [1 euro = 125 yen, May 2017]) to 61.2 million yen (489,600 euros) for a condominium unit and from 30.5 million yen (244,000 euros) to 65.3 million yen (522,400 euros) for a ready-built single-family house, while average price-income ratios increased from 5 times to 8 times for a condominium unit and from 6.2 times to 8.5 times for a ready-built, single-family house (Ministry of Construction, 1996).

The direct cause of the bubble was the deregulation of finance (Muramatsu and Okuno, 2002; Oizumi, 1994). As a consequence of relaxed monetary control, surplus capital was injected into the real estate sector. With the Japan-US trade friction as a backdrop, the Japanese yen immediately appreciated and the interest rate was rapidly slashed after the Plaza Accord in September 1985. The Japanese government was requested by the US to expand its domestic demand and thus augmented expenditure on public works on top of financial deregulations. As argued in Chapter 1, banks, which had mainly been financing investment in the industrial sector, turned towards increasing the amount of finance for real estate as major corporations started placing emphasis on procuring capital from equity finance in the 1980s. Once land and housing prices began to increase, banks, security firms and insurance companies along with many other enterprises poured a significant amount of speculative investment in real estate.

Moreover, housing policy played a crucial role in generating the economic bubble. Housing policy measures in Japan were firmly embedded in the wider framework of economic policy in line with privatised Keynesianism (Crouch, 2011) and house price Keynesianism (Watson, 2010). The government continued to accelerate construction of owner-occupied housing as a propulsion engine for economic growth (see Chapter 1). After the 1973 Oil Crisis, the provision of low-interest loans by the GHLC became one of the key strategies to stimulate the economy. Whenever the country went into recession, the government increased the supply of GHLC loans in order to assist economic recovery. However, house price inflation in the 1970s made it increasingly difficult for households even with reasonable incomes to purchase a house. As a response, the GHLC kept improving the lending conditions (loan limits, repayment periods, etc.) to further facilitate the acquisition of housing.

This stimulated the expansion of demand for owner-occupied housing and the further rise in house prices, prompting the GHLC to yet again improve the lending conditions (see Chapter 1). Thus, the home-ownership-centred housing policy, which continued to drive the construction and acquisition of housing, laid the ground for creating the property bubble.

It was at the beginning of the 1990s that the collapse of the real estate bubble became evident in Tokyo and then spread to other cities. The burst of the property bubble provoked an unprecedented economic turmoil (Muramatsu and Okuno, 2002), signifying the end of Japan's post-war growth period. The unprecedented rise in housing prices during the bubble period discouraged many households from purchasing housing. The government was thus prompted to dissolve the bubble and put a limit on the total amount of real estate financing in 1990. This caused the real estate bubble to immediately burst rather than to gradually dissolve. During the bubble, the continued expansion of credit lending was associated with the excessive collateralisation of real estate. With the abrupt burst of the bubble, therefore, the banking sector was immediately plunged into crisis with a significant amount of bad loans, which led to a chain reaction of the bankruptcies of major banks, security firms and other real estate businesses. The direct impact of the 1997 AFC on the Japanese economy was relatively limited compared to South Korea and Southeast Asian countries, but it provided a catalyst for worsening Japan's financial turmoil. The government delayed investing public funds to address the non-performing loans for fear of the political risk. It was not until 1995 that the government at last began to provide the banking sector with public funds. This delay had the negative consequence of prolonging the crisis.

Post-bubble housing scene

With the burst of the property bubble, radical changes in the housing economy combined with the housing policy reforms have fundamentally reorganised the economic circumstances surrounding the housing system (Hirayama, 2007, 2011). Land and housing prices began to decline immediately after the bubble burst and continued to dive for an extraordinarily prolonged period. Japanese people used to believe the myth of a rapid and perpetual rise in land prices. Therefore, the beginning of the deflation of land and housing prices shocked the nation and challenged the normative expectation of home ownership. In addition, Japan was slower to accept neoliberal imperatives on housing policy compared to its Western counterparts such as the UK and the US. The post-bubble crisis, however, led the Japanese government to move towards adopting a market-based approach: it abolished the GHLC in 2007 while reducing the provision of public rented housing.

Housing prices continued to drop for approximately 15 years until the mid-2000s. Since then, Tokyo has experienced more volatility in house prices, while the prices in provincial regions have continued to decline. Spatial disparities in the patterns of house prices have been a feature of the post-bubble housing market (for further discussion, see Chapter 3). The recession came to an end in 2001, and the price of residential land began to rise in Tokyo and a few large cities in 2006. In Tokyo, as argued in Chapter 3, a rapid increase in property prices even led to the mini-bubble in 2006 and 2007. Residential land prices, however, continued to drop in smaller cities even after the end of the post-bubble recession. The mini-bubble in Tokyo was short-lived. The bankruptcy of Lehman Brothers in September 2008 following defaults in US sub-prime mortgages was a trigger that threw the Japanese and many other economies into crisis-level recession, resulting in the collapse of the Tokyo mini-bubble.

The GFC affected housing and mortgage markets in many countries including Japan (Aalbers, 2012; Forrest and Yip, 2013; Schwartz and Seabrooke, 2009). Since the mid-1990s, up until the sub-prime crisis, many Western societies had undergone a long period of house price inflation (Kim and Renaud, 2009; OECD, 2004). The GFC thus provoked acute downward shifts in housing prices in these countries. Of the advanced economies, Japan along with Germany and Switzerland were an exception to the trends in house prices that many other countries experienced, where housing prices had been almost continually falling since the 1990s. The turmoil of the global economy thus meant an additional blow to the prolonged stagnation in the Japanese housing economy. Defaults in US sub-prime loans were metamorphosed to the GFC, which was mediated by the globalised market of mortgage-backed securities. In many advanced economies, particularly the Anglo-Saxon ones, where policies on deregulating financial markets and forming mortgage-backed security markets have been implemented for a long period, financial institutions were greatly affected by the sub-prime crisis. In contrast, the direct impact of the sub-prime meltdown on the Japanese banking sector was relatively small, implying that Japan delayed introducing a mortgage-backed security system (Forrest and Hirayama, 2009). Nonetheless, Japan's export-based economy was seriously damaged by the global economic downturns, resulting in unprecedented drops in housing construction, property transactions and house prices.

Neoliberal policy reforms have led to substantial reductions in state direct provisions but do not necessarily mean the adoption of a laissez-faire approach and often place emphasis on indirect approaches such as the use of tax and regulatory measures regarding framing market economies. Japanese housing policy had traditionally been intertwined with measures of stimulating the economy. With this as background, the significant downswing in the economy caused by the GFC led the government to launch a series of housing measures to stimulate economic recovery (Hirayama, 2011). The best example was the policy on reducing income tax for home purchasers with mortgage liability to an unprecedented extent. Japan's housing policy in terms of stimulating economic upturn has indeed shifted its central means from the direct provision of the GHLC's mortgages to the indirect and implicit provision of subsidies via the taxation system.

Land and housing prices in Tokyo as well as a few other large cities started to rise again in 2014 for the first time since the Lehman Shock. The LDP, which lost the 2009 national election, returned to power in 2012 with Shinzo Abe as prime minister. The Bank of Japan's policy, which corresponded to the Abe administration's policy that was oriented towards financial deregulation, began to be implemented with unprecedented monetary easing aimed at surfacing from the prolonged economic stagnation. This was reflected in the renewed rise in real estate prices in large cities, particularly Tokyo. However, the prices of land and housing in smaller cities continued to decline. A sharp contrast between Tokyo and provincial regions has thus been created with regard to land and housing price movements (see Chapter 3). The extent to which the unconventional financial policy is effective in coping with the economic stagnation and what risks new policy will bring remain to be seen.

Demographic effects

Finally, it is worth emphasising that demographic changes unique to Japan have combined with unstable economic conditions to accelerate fluctuations in the housing market (Hirayama, 2007, 2011). As Miyake (1991, 1996) argues, while housing scholars tend to place importance on economic factors in explaining changes in the housing market, demographic factors are equally important. Ups and downs in the housing market are certainly driven by economic shifts, but the demographic processes also underpin the economic aspect of housing market movements.

In terms of the housing market trajectory in Japan, it was not only the rise and fall of the economic bubble but also the baby-boomer generation moving up the housing ladder that encouraged the house price volatility. Many baby-boomers, who were born in the latter half of the 1940s, entered the home ownership market by the early 1980s and led a large-scale demand. This subsequently accelerated the rise in house prices during the economic bubble period of the late 1980s. By the early 1990s, many baby-boomers had purchased their own home, which brought the drop in house prices in the post-bubble period. Compared to Western societies, the post-war baby-boom period in Japan was short-lived, lasting only for three years from 1947 to 1949 (Matsutani, 2004). This was due to the anti-fertility legislation being introduced in 1948 to control birth rates in the context of extreme poverty following the Second World War. The implication is that the Japanese baby-boomer generation generated a 'positive demand' and subsequently a 'negative demand' in a short period, which increased the volatility in the housing market (Miyake, 1991, 1996).

The end of the post-bubble recession led to the upward shift in house prices in Tokyo and some other major cities in the mid-2000s. This had again implications in demographic changes (Hirayama, 2011). The second baby-boomer generation, who were born in the first half of the 1970s and included the offspring of the post-war baby-boomers, began to enter the owner-occupied housing market in the early 2000s, underpinning the upturn in house prices in large cities. The direct factor that accounted for the subsequent downturn in the property market was the onset of the GFC. However, an increase in second baby-boomer households who had purchased house resulted in a sharp decline in demand for owner-occupied housing, accelerating the downturn in housing prices.

Moreover, the total population of Japan, which started declining in the mid-2000s, will continue to decline, thereby accelerating societal ageing (see Chapter 1). This will inevitably lead to a decreased demand for housing. If the number of households continues to increase while the household sizes decrease, it sustains the demand for housing despite the decline in the population. It is predicted, however, that the number of households will also begin to decrease in the foreseeable future in post-growth Japanese society. The second baby-boomer generation was the last large cohort of first-time homebuyers and no comparable cohorts that generate large demand for housing are predicted to appear in the future. The Japanese housing economy has long been stagnated since the bubble burst. This is now being combined with demographic changes to bring a further decline in investment in housing.

Post-growth deflation and housing affordability

The rental sector

How have post-bubble economic and policy changes affected housing conditions at the household level? A significant feature of post-bubble housing in Japan has been a decline in affordable housing (Hirayama, 2010a). During the growth period, the inflationary economy accelerated a rise in housing costs, which led to a decrease in the affordability of housing. After the bubble burst, Japan entered a post-growth period associated with deflation or minimal inflation, and housing prices dropped. In theory, house price deflation is expected to improve affordability. In reality, however, the financial pressure of home purchasing did not ease but rather increased due largely to the deflation of real incomes. In other words, there has been a shift from house price inflation to income deflation in terms of the main cause of the decline in housing affordability. In addition, the housing policy reforms with emphasis on market solutions combined with the post-bubble recession to undermine the affordability of housing. Japan's experience suggests that entering the post-growth era does not necessarily alleviate housing affordability issues but rather restructures the mechanisms of determining to what extent housing is affordable.

Post-bubble changes in the economic conditions of the rental housing sector have been characterised by a combination of an increase in the number of low-income households, a reduction in low-rent housing, and a consequent increase in households with heavier burdens imposed by rent payments (Hirayama, 2010a). According to data on tenant households from the National Survey of Family Income and Expenditure, between 1994 and 2009, the nominal monthly disposable income decline from 320,300 yen (2,562 euros) to 291,200 yen (2,330 euros) on average, whereas the average nominal monthly housing cost increased from 42,500 yen (340 euros) to 50,000 yen (400 euros) (see Figure 2.1). As a result, the housing cost-to-disposable income of tenant households, which was 13.3 per cent in 1994, increased to 17.2 per cent in 2009. By 2014, this figure slightly dropped to 17.1 per cent due to a slight increase in disposal incomes but remained at a high level.

The stagnated economy and a decline in real incomes did not lead to lower rents. The main factor behind this is the reduced availability of low-rent housing. The 'decommodified' low-rent housing sector, which is provided not-for-profit outside the market sphere, has consisted of public rented housing and corporate-based employee housing in Japan. However, the neoliberal shift of housing policy has encouraged the further marginalisation of public rented housing that has traditionally been residual, while the provision of employee housing has been decreasing, reflecting the continuous economic stagnation. Thus, there has been a continual decline in the decommodified rented housing sector.

Low-rent accommodations are also provided within the market sector. As the supply of public rented housing and corporate-based rented housing has been limited in Japan, private rented housing occupies the main position in the rented housing sector, accounting for a little more than a

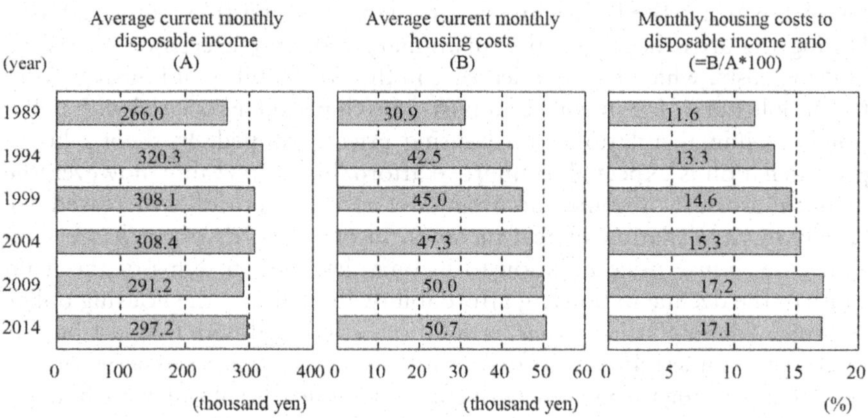

Figure 2.1 Changes in disposable incomes and housing costs of renter households (1989–2014)

Source: Author's calculations from National Survey of Family Income and Expenditure.

quarter of all housing (see Table 1.1 in Chapter 1). Although providing private rented housing was not considered to be particularly profitable, a number of private landlords who held land provided rental units to earn additional incomes without investing in site acquisition (Morimoto, 1994). This made the supply of low-rent accommodations feasible. The rent level of apartment units in wooden structures was particularly set low. Although dwellings of this type were mostly substandard in terms of floor area and amenities, they functioned as low-cost accommodations for low-income households. The number of existing low-rent private dwellings has, however, declined substantially as the units aged and dilapidated.

Moreover, in the late 1990s, the government began seeking to restructure the private rented housing market in alignment with neoliberal policy reforms. The intention was to 'rationalise' the system of financing and providing rented housing while establishing a more 'professional' and profitable market for investments. Under the Land and Housing Lease Act, the security of tenure was highly protected for tenants, and therefore landlords could not easily evict the tenants. This protection was severely criticised by neoliberal reformers as the key factor responsible for hindering market mechanisms, leading to the major 1999 amendments to the act. As a result, it has now become possible for landlords to rent out their properties for a shorter period so that they can estimate their profits more accurately. The outcome of the 'rationalisation' policy is a reduction in the low-rent private rented dwellings that used to accommodate low-income tenants.

The home ownership sector

Housing affordability has been an issue not only in the rental sector but also in the home ownership sector (Hirayama, 2010a). Statistical data on owner-occupier households reveal that the number of outright owners of housing increased significantly from 4,466,400 in 1993 to 22,846,100 in 2013, which reflects societal ageing in Japan with the rapid increase in elderly outright homeowners (see Figure 2.2). Meanwhile, the number of owners of mortgaged housing did not increase but rather decreased from 9,909,800 to 9,319,700 during the same period. This is because the number of households with a head in their thirties and forties, which constitute a main group of first-time homebuyers, decreased between 1993 and 2013 from 6,521,200 to 6,177,500 and from 10,166,200 to 8,297,700, respectively. In addition, a decline in the affordability has discouraged many potential first-time buyers from acquiring housing with a mortgage. As discussed in Chapter 1, within the post-growth context, the housing loan market has arguably been extended to the limit, with a decrease in the issuance of new mortgages. Affordability issues in the home ownership sector are thus related to both the micro (household) and macro (market) levels.

Since the bubble burst, land and housing prices have declined, while interest rates remain at an extraordinarily low level. Nevertheless, the economic

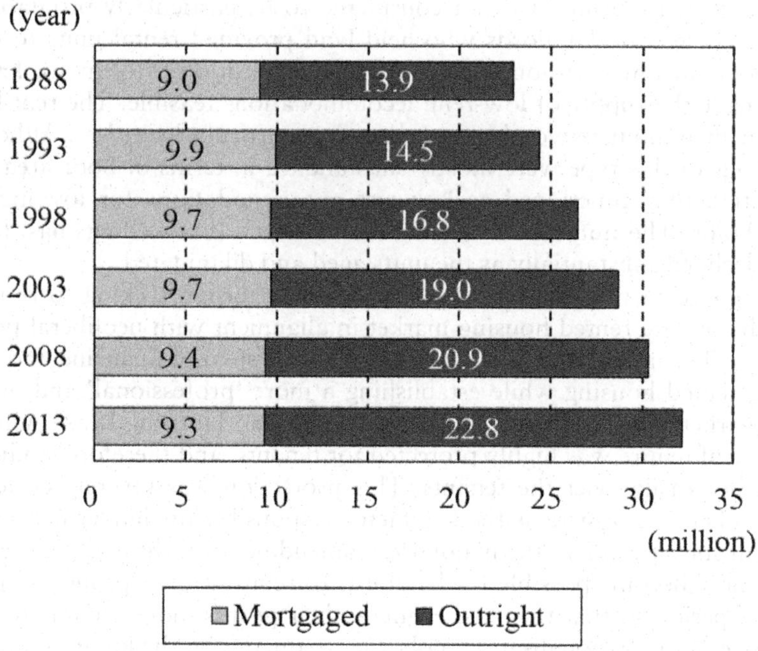

Figure 2.2 Number of owner-occupied households (1988–2013)

Source: Author's calculations from Housing Survey of Japan; Housing and Land Survey of Japan; and National Survey of Family Income and Expenditure.

conditions surrounding households who wish to purchase a property have not been improved. Along with the prolonged post-bubble stagnation, a decline in real incomes and savings has translated into higher loan-to-value ratios due to a smaller deposit with larger mortgage liabilities. The National Survey of Family Income and Expenditure revealed that between 1994 and 2009 among owner-occupied households with mortgage, the nominal monthly disposable incomes on average decreased from 485,600 yen (3,885 euros) to 427,100 yen (3,417 euros), while the average nominal monthly housing cost largely consisting of mortgage repayments increased from 63,900 yen (511 euros) to 80,900 yen (647 euros) (see Figure 2.3). The proportion of housing costs in the disposable incomes therefore increased from 13.2 per cent in 1994 to 18.9 per cent in 2009. This figure slightly decreased to 18.5 per cent in 2014 because of a slight decrease in housing costs but still remained at a high level.

The burst of the property bubble made it harder for many households to obtain a mortgage. However, the government continuously sought to accelerate the acquisition of owner-occupied housing, aiming to stimulate the economy. The supply of GHLC loans was increased to an unprecedented

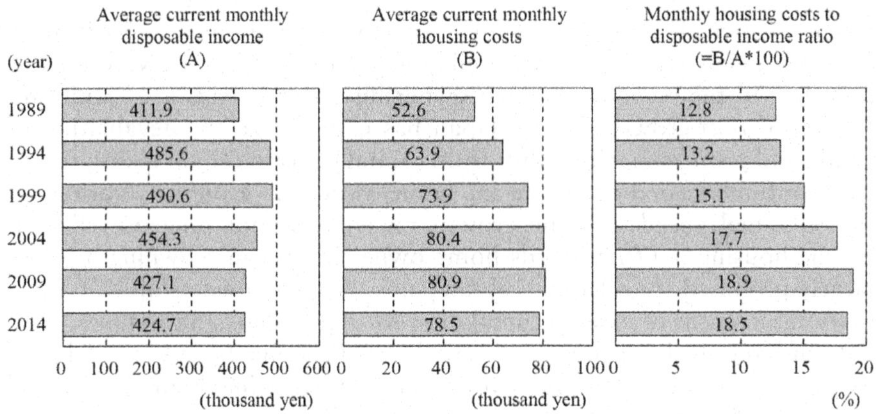

Figure 2.3 Changes in disposable incomes and housing costs of owner-occupied households with mortgage debts (1989–2014)

Source: Author's calculations from National Survey of Family Income and Expenditure.

level in the first half of the 1990s with very low interest rates. The 1994 deregulation on interest rates then accelerated more competition in the mortgage market and resulted in an increase in the supply of high loan-to-value mortgages. As a result of the combination of prolonged economic stagnation and the government policy to encourage home purchase, those who purchase housing with a mortgage have declined in number, while those who acquire mortgaged housing ended up having larger outstanding housing loan debts despite the income deflation.

Furthermore, it is important to examine the extent to which home-ownership-centred housing policy is effective in stimulating economic recovery. During the growth period, the housing system of expanding home ownership was used as an engine for economic growth. With the inflation and real income increase, the value of outstanding mortgage debts was typically lessened in real term. This effectively prevented an excessive decline in disposable incomes after expenditure on housing loan repayments, which had underpinned the buoyancy of the consumption-based economy at that time. Entering the post-growth phase, however, home-ownership-centred housing policy has started to hinder rather than stimulate economic growth. The post-bubble economy with deflation or minimal inflation means the increased real value of outstanding mortgage debts and decreased real incomes. As a result, disposable incomes after mortgage repayments declined sharply. In the era of deflation, owner-occupier households with a larger mortgage but smaller incomes have inevitably become thrifty. A decline in spending power among homeowners with a hefty mortgage is indeed part of the reason for the stagnated economic recovery.

Devaluation of residential properties

Home ownership provides not only security of tenure and social identity but also a basis for asset accumulation over generations. Nevertheless, a decline in the security of home ownership as asset-base is a significant feature of post-growth society. Japan has experienced the devaluation of residential properties with a shift from capital gains to capital losses, resulting in a fundamental change in the home ownership economy. During the period of high-speed economic growth, many households diligently climbed up the housing ladder towards home ownership because owning a house largely promised considerable capital gains. Property ownership was a primary mechanism of asset accumulation for households and families. Tenants entering the home-ownership market as first-time buyers were able to expect an appreciation in the real property values, while homeowners had prospects of trading up their property for further asset accumulation using the existing housing equity as a stepping stone. Capital gains fuelled the system of propelling people towards the top of the housing ladder. In post-growth Japan, however, many residential properties have fallen in value and capital losses for the households have swelled.

Almost all households who purchased a dwelling during the property bubble in the late 1980s have experienced devaluation of their property. The extent of housing depreciation has, however, varied depending on the property type. For example, second-hand properties have lost more value than newly built ones. Condominium owners were also the victims of the substantial capital loss compared to single-family-home owners. The scale of capital losses generated on condominiums has been substantial (Hirayama, 2011): the average price of a newly built condominium unit with a floor area of 70 square meters was 67.2 million yen (537,600 euros) in the Tokyo region in 1991. This fell to 20.3 million yen (162,400 euros) by 2008, generating a capital loss of 46.9 million yen (375,200 euros). In other words, the value of condominium units purchased during the peak of the bubble economy fell sharply by some 70 per cent.

Various institutional and policy factors contributed to the sharp fall in the prices of second-hand condominiums. Housing policy driving mass housing construction as a means of stimulating the economy is one explanation. In response to the post-bubble recession, instead of investing in the existing housing stock to maintain the value of properties, the government continued seeking to expand the production of new owner-occupied homes. This led to the over-construction of new houses and consequently accelerated a fall in the prices of second-hand properties. As for large cities, the government has placed an emphasis on urban regeneration as a key economic policy (see Chapter 3 for more details). This has facilitated the construction of a large quantity of new condominium blocks, resulting in a notable decline in the prices of existing condominiums. Moreover, housing institutions in relation to house purchasing have characteristically been designed to offer advantages to the acquisition of new housing in order to increase the construction of new housing. The GHLC, for example, favoured borrowers who purchased new housing and provided them with mortgage loans under better conditions compared to those who bought a second-hand property. The tax regime advantaged the purchasers of new housing in the same way. Since the 2000s, the government has begun to place more weight on the expansion of second-hand housing transactions. This is due to changes in the condition of the housing market such as the population decline and the rising level of vacant properties (see Chapter 1). However, a considerable amount of time will be required to develop the second-hand housing market, given the legacy of the construction-orientated housing policy.

The extent of the impact caused by the rise and fall of the economic bubble on the asset values of owner-occupied housing also varies between generations. The baby-boomer generation who purchased their homes before housing prices peaked experienced a relatively small price fall. In contrast, the cohorts following the baby-boomers, who often entered the ownership market at the peak of the bubble, were hit the hardest. These post-baby-boomer cohorts experienced house price deflation immediately after their purchase and have subsequently been confronted with a substantial asset loss. Differentiated trajectories in the housing market have thus brought about cohort-based disparities and divided fortunes in terms of housing assets.

The housing asset conditions of homeowners have been exacerbated since the bubble burst. According to the National Survey of Family Income and Expenditure, between 1989 and 2014, among owner-occupier households with two or more members who held mortgage liabilities, the average amount of current outstanding mortgage debts increased from 7.8 million yen (62,400 euros) to 16.0 million yen (128,000 euros), while that of current gross residential property assets decreased from 43.8 million yen (350,400 euros) to 24.5 million yen (196,000 euros) (see Figure 2.4). This meant a sharp decrease in the average housing equity: from 36.0 million yen (288,000 euros) in 1989 to 8.5 million yen (68,000 euros) in 2014. In practice, younger households who purchased expensive housing at the peak of the bubble period without a substantial deposit were particularly confronted with negative housing equity. From 1989 to 2004, of households with mortgage liabilities, those with negative housing equity increased from 5.9 per cent to 23.6 per cent for households with a head aged 34 and younger and from 2.7 per cent to 24.0 per cent for the 35–44 age group (see Table 2.1).

The insecure post-bubble economy translated into an increase in mortgage defaults, heralding the beginning of a new era characterised by higher risks with regard to the maintenance of home ownership (Hirayama, 2011). As mortgage defaults increased, the GHLC was pressed to launch a series of new schemes to assist borrowers who could not repay their housing loans. As a result, increasing numbers of borrowers were permitted to extend their

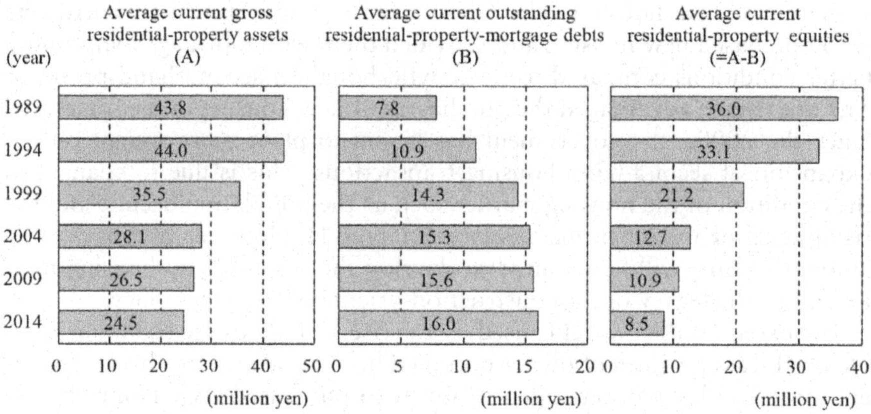

Figure 2.4 Changes in outstanding mortgage debts and gross assets on residential-properties of owner-occupied households with mortgage debts (1989–2014)

Note: Data for households with two or more members.

Source: Author's calculations from National Survey of Family Income and Expenditure.

Table 2.1 Ratios of households with negative housing equity by age of household head (1989–2004)

Age		*1989*	*1994*	*1999*	*2004*
–34	(%)	5.9	8.0	13.6	23.6
35–44	(%)	2.7	4.4	14.3	24.0
45–54	(%)	2.4	1.4	5.3	10.9
55–64	(%)	1.7	0.6	1.3	2.8
65 and over	(%)	1.5	0.2	0.4	0.6
All households	(%)	2.4	2.0	4.9	7.9

Note: Data for owner-occupied households with mortgage debts.

Source: Author's calculations from micro-data on National Survey of Family Income and Expenditure.

mortgage repayment period. The Step Repayment System (see Chapter 1) was a significant measure in the exacerbation of household finances. Households who enrolled in this scheme had to repay at increased levels after the first five years of the low repayment period, even though their incomes did not commensurately increase. The system, criticised for unfairly enticing not only those on middle incomes but also those on lower incomes into buying a house beyond their means, was abolished in 2000. According to data released by the Supreme Court, the number of auctions on foreclosed real estate properties increased from 44,048 in 1991 to 73,537 in 1998 and remained at a high level until the early 2000s. The figure then decreased to 54,920 in 2007 because of the short economic upturn but again rose to 67,201 in 2008 when the GFC began to affect the Japanese economy. The system of non-recourse-type housing loans – in which if the borrower defaults, the issuer can take the collateral but cannot demand any further repayment, even when the collateral does not cover the full value of the defaulted amount – has not yet been developed in Japan, partly due to a long period of house price deflation. Therefore, foreclosures of residential properties with negative equity have resulted in particularly troubling situations where the former owners have lost their home but continued to repay remaining debt liabilities.

The housing policy reforms including the abolition of the GHLC have imposed more risks relating to mortgages on individual households, particularly those with low incomes (Hirayama, 2011). Unlike the government loan corporation, which used to provide every borrower with a mortgage under similar conditions regarding interest rates, loan limits and repayment periods, private banks started to offer a diverse range of mortgage products with various lending conditions. Such private practices allowed housing purchasers on low incomes to take out a riskier mortgage. Some surveys on mortgage borrowers revealed that households on low incomes were likely to choose a variable-rate mortgage over fixed-rate (Japan Housing Finance Agency, 2007). Variable-rate mortgages are often more competitive compared to those of fixed-rate mortgages due to lower initial interest rates, but are accompanied by higher risks in terms of uncertainty pertaining to future interest rates.

Home ownership in contemporary Japan represents no promise of capital gain. People's aspirations to home ownership have not declined significantly but remain strong. According to the 'People's Consciousness about Land Issues' survey conducted by the Ministry of Land, Infrastructure and Transport (2015), the ratio of those who wanted to own land and a house declined from 88.1 per cent in 1996 to 79.2 per cent in 2014, but the fact that most people desired to own a residential property has not changed significantly. Japanese people aspire to own a home for various reasons. The physical characteristics of owner-occupied housing in terms of floor area and amenities are usually much better than that of rented housing. Home ownership is also regarded as a means of ensuring security in old age. However, people no longer purchase housing with any expectation of capital gain. The same survey revealed that the proportion of respondents who agreed that 'land was a more secure asset than saving or stock' dropped from 61.9 per cent in 1994 to 49.2 per cent in 1997 and to 33.2 per cent in 2002 (Ministry of Land, Infrastructure and Transport, 2015). This raises a question as to what home ownership really means in post-growth society.

Housing insecurity and the safety net

Economic decline in post-growth Japan has resulted in an increase in the number of low-income households who cannot secure adequate accommodation. This has raised new policy issues around a housing safety net (Hirayama, 2010b). Until the burst of the bubble economy, poverty was expected to decrease and eventually to disappear, while a 'new middle mass' was predicted to further increase along with growing economic prosperity (Murakami, 1984). In the post-bubble society, however, an increasing number of people are considered to become vulnerable to economic downturn and subsequently fall into poverty. A remarkable increase in the number of homeless people in the early 1990s suggested Japan's entry to a period of social and economic stagnation. The return of poverty is evident as the monthly average number of public assistant recipients under the Living Standard Protection Act had steadily declined from 2.04 million in 1952 to 0.88 million in 1995 until a record high rise back to 2.16 million in 2014.

The ways in which housing insecurity affects households have become more diverse. According to longitudinal surveys on homeless people by the Ministry of Health, Labour and Welfare, the number of rough sleepers in public spaces such as parks, train stations and riverbanks decreased from 25,296 in 2003 to 13,124 in 2010 and then to 6,541 in 2015. This was partly because the 2002 Homeless Independent Living Act together with the more traditional Living Standard Protection Act that was proclaimed in 1950 mediated social assistance to those with housing difficulties. However, rough sleepers who are visible in the streets are not the only ones who cannot secure accommodation (Iwata, 2009). Many low-income individuals have used Internet cafes, capsule hotels and fast-food restaurants as a temporary and low-cost shelter. Due to the economic crisis triggered by the 2008 Lehman Shock, many manual workers who used to live in company dormitories lost both job and accommodation. Rent arrears have increased among those who lost their job. The subsequent forcible eviction of tenants in arrears by landlords and rent guarantor firms started in the late 2000s, provoking a new social problem. Furthermore, in the early 2010s, a number of extremely small accommodations with a floor area of just three to five square meters, which were typically converted from offices and warehouses, began accommodating low-wage earners. Such accommodations are often illegal as they are not zoned as residential spaces. Housing insecurity comes in different forms and now threatens wider segments of post-growth Japanese society.

It was not only economic stagnation but also the introduction of neoliberal prescriptions of deregulation and market-orientation that accounted for increased housing insecurity (Hirayama, 2010b). Prolonged recession has led to an increase in the number of individuals and households who cannot secure housing in the market domain. This prompted the government to provide a housing safety net to those on low incomes, leading to the

2007 establishment of the Housing Safety Act. The application of neoliberal measures in housing policy has, however, meant that state provisions are kept minimal. Despite the implementation of the act aimed at forming a safety net, the social housing sector has been significantly reduced. The government has thus sought to supplement the housing safety net by encouraging private landlords to accept lower-income groups. The scale of such supplemental programmes has, however, been small. There is a clear policy contradiction between the increasing necessity of constructing a housing safety net and restricting the coverage of the safety net to expand the sphere of market-based housing.

The principal measure of the housing safety net is providing low-rent housing. It is thus important to examine the conditions of the low-rent housing sector when assessing the adequacy of the housing safety net policy. There is a tacit assumption that affordable housing for low-income households is provided almost exclusively in the form of not-for-profit 'decommodified' social housing outside the market domain. In reality, however, decommodified housing is not necessarily limited to social housing, and low-rent housing may be supplied within the market sphere. Particularly in countries like Japan, where social housing is residual, some other types of housing have been assumed to supplement the supply of low-income housing. In this sense, the concept of a low-rent housing sector is worth re-examining, and it is necessary to explore the elements that constitute the area of low-rent housing in order to properly understand how housing is provided to low-income households (Hirayama, 2013). In the case of Japan, although public rented housing has been residual, corporate-based employee housing has supplemented the decommodified housing sector, and some low-rent housing has been supplied within the domain of the private market. The provision of corporate-based employee housing and low-rent private housing has been effective in enabling the government sector to avoid having to construct public rented housing sufficient to meet the housing needs of the low-income group. Corporate-based decommodified housing, which is targeted at specific corporation employees, cannot be considered a 'social' housing sector. Many low-rent private dwellings are substandard in terms of physical conditions. Nevertheless, the supply of employee housing as well as low-rent private housing has reduced the demand for low-rent dwellings in the housing market.

The continued implementation of neoliberal policy has led to a substantial decrease in the availability of low-rent dwellings (Hirayama, 2010b). New construction of low-income public housing has almost completely halted, and the reconstruction of public housing developments has increasingly resulted in a reduced number of dwellings (see Chapter 1). The Urban Renaissance Agency has begun to dispose of a considerable number of rental properties. Therefore, the number of public rented dwellings, including both low-income public dwellings and public corporation dwellings, decreased from 3,119,000 in 2003 to 2,814,000 in 2013. Moreover, with an increasingly competitive business environment and the associated weakening of the 'company society', many corporations have begun to unload considerable numbers of properties formerly used as employee housing (see Chapter 1). The number of employee housing units, which was 2,051,000 in 1993, decreased to 1,122,000 in 2013. Consequently, the availability of decommodified rented housing has been significantly reduced: the combined ratio of public rented housing and employee housing in the total rented dwellings dropped from 31.4 per cent in 1993 to 21.3 per cent in 2013. Furthermore, the number of low-rent accommodations in the private rental market has continued to decrease. Many old low-rent accommodations have been demolished due to poor states of repair. Privately rented apartment units of wooden structures, which were low quality but charged low rents, accounted for 18.4 per cent of all rented dwellings in 1993. This figure had decreased to 12.5 per cent by 2013.

The provision of means-tested low-rent public housing for low-income households has been positioned as the core of the housing safety net. As housing policy has been biased towards expanding home ownership, however, public housing has played a limited role in the housing system (Hirayama, 2013). In many developed countries, neoliberal approaches have been increasingly influential in housing policy reforms expanding market-based provision and resulting in the smaller social rented sector (Fitzpatrick and Stephens, 2008). Nonetheless, there are differentiated effects on housing conditions depending on the policy trajectory of different societies. In many European countries, even after reforms, the accumulated large stock of social rented housing continued to play a significant role in providing low-income households with housing opportunities. The level of social rented housing is still considerably high in some European societies: for example, 32 per cent in the Netherlands (2010), 24 per cent in Scotland (2011), 24 per cent in Austria (2012) and 19 per cent in Denmark (2011) (Scanlon et al., 2014). The comparable rate in Japan was 4 per cent in 2013, signifying the limited function of the housing safety net.

Since the mid-1990s, public housing has become more clearly defined as a component of welfare provision. In Japan, as in many other countries, neoliberal imperatives have focused on labour market participation rather than public assistance in addressing social issues pertaining to the economic conditions of low-income households (Saunders, 2005). Special needs groups such as elderly people, single-parent households and people with disability emerged as target groups for public housing. This reflects the principle that a safety net is only applied to households with a low level of employability. Older people and single-parent households are considered to be disadvantaged in the labour market participation and thus considered as priority needs groups for public housing. If individuals and households outside of such welfare categories are assessed to be employable, they are expected to secure housing in the market sphere. Until the 1960s, public housing was aimed at young family households with lower incomes, and they were expected to use it as a stepping stone to move up their housing career into home ownership. Since the 1970s, however, public housing has been removed from the normative housing ladder and been positioned as an isolated sphere where the classes with the lowest income and weakest employability live away from the social mainstream (Hirayama, 2010b). The compositions of public housing tenants and the other households consequently vary widely (see Figure 2.5). There is also an evident decline in residential mobility among public housing tenants (see Figure 2.6).

Conclusion

Backed by post-war high-speed economic expansion, Japan's housing system was instrumental in improving people's housing circumstances and promulgating home ownership among middle-income households. Nevertheless, post-growth Japan has been experiencing economic instability for the third decade, thereby normalising economic insecurity for the current generations. This stagnation and neoliberal policy reforms reorganised the economic conditions of housing. It has become necessary for new homeowners to endure heavier burdens imposed by mortgage repayments. Residential properties in the post-bubble period have been devalued, and an increasing

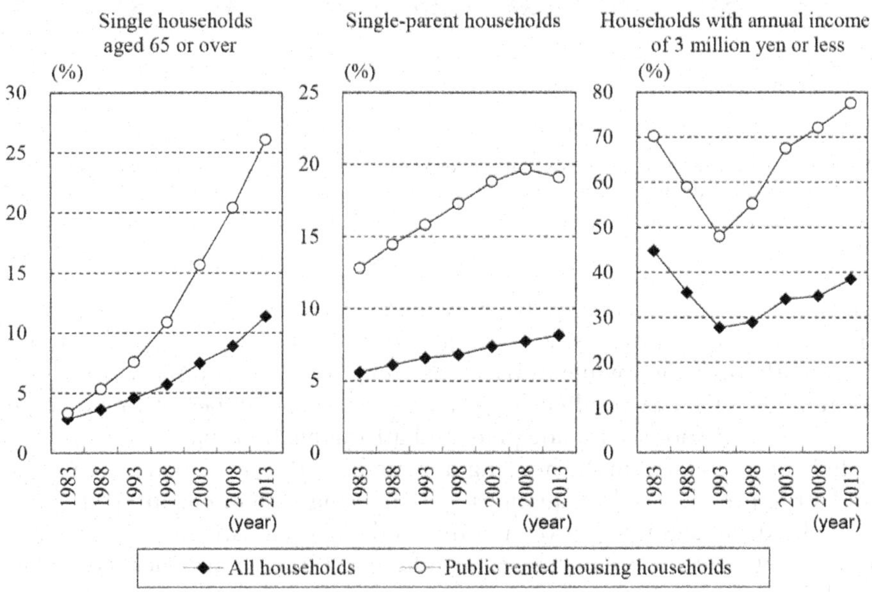

Figure 2.5 Ratios of single-elderly households, single-parent households and low-income households (1983–2013)

Source: Author's calculations from Housing Survey of Japan; and Housing and Land Survey of Japan.

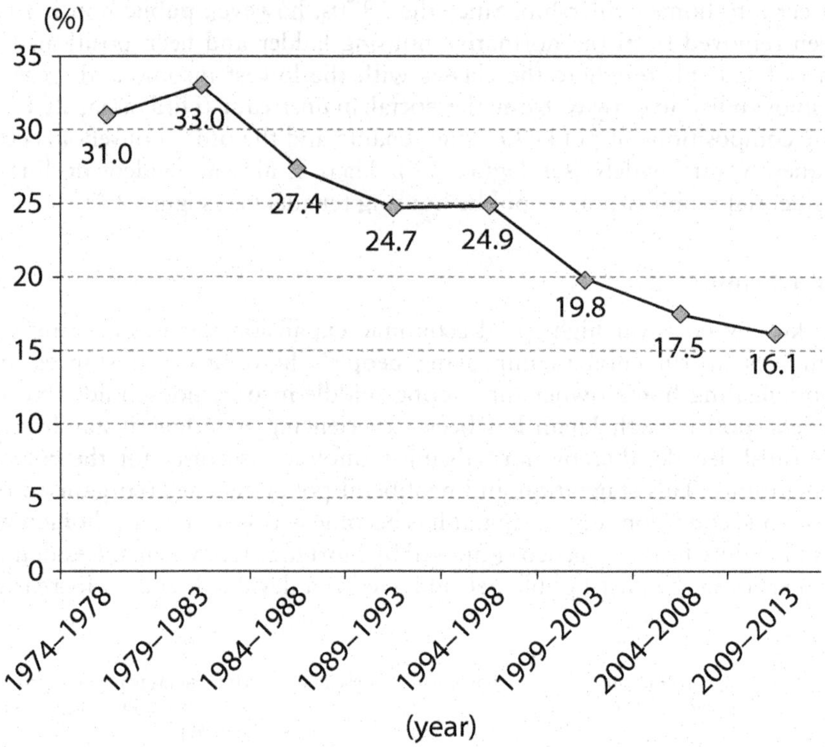

Figure 2.6 Ratio of households who moved out of public rented housing (1974–2013)

Note: Ratio indicates percentage of households who moved out of public rented housing during each period in the total public rented housing tenants at the beginning of the period.

Source: Author's calculations from Housing Survey of Japan; and Housing and Land Survey of Japan.

number of homeowners have been trapped in negative equity. Furthermore, there have been an increasing number of individuals on precarious employment with low wages while low-rent dwellings have substantially decreased in number. This has resulted in an increase in the number of low-income people who cannot secure adequate and affordable housing.

Economic changes in the housing domain have thus reshaped the contour and structure of social inequalities. The housing system encouraged many households to acquire their own homes and enter mainstream society, playing a pivotal role in enhancing social cohesion. It is true that there were inequalities in relation to housing and home ownership, but the housing system provided the large majority of people with the prospect of accessing home ownership. Many tenants were supported by high-speed economic development and government subsidy schemes to enter the owner-occupied housing sector and were thus able to consider themselves as potential members of the home-owning, mainstream society. This effectively reduced the extent to which people were concerned with inequalities and therefore underpinned the foundations of sustaining social integration. Nevertheless, the post-bubble economic stagnation associated with the retreat of the government from housing subsidy schemes has led to an increase in individuals who have no hope of accessing home ownership, and many homeowners have undergone a swell in capital losses in their properties. This has eroded the traditional mechanisms of maintaining social cohesion.

Post-GFC societies have entered a new era characterised by a more precarious economy and the associated vicissitude of housing and mortgage markets while the model of housing inflation-led and mortgage debt-led economic growth has proved to be unsustainable. Housing systems in various countries have maintained distinctive features but are at the same time converging within the context of unstable economic conditions. Japan serves as a significant case with regard to the long-term experience of post-bubble housing situations. Unprecedented phenomena such as an income deflation-led decline in housing affordability and the continuing devaluation of residential properties as well as a notable increase in low-income households with housing insecurity have been observed in post-bubble Japan. Other post-GFC countries may not follow the same path, and will respond differently to the new phase of economic insecurity. An examination of Japan's post-bubble housing situation, however, provides useful insights into potential social processes and presents valuable reference for shedding light on questions as to how housing systems are transformed in the era of economic precariousness.

References

Aalbers, M. B. (ed.) (2012) *Subprime Cities: The Political Economy of Mortgage Markets*, Oxford: Wiley-Blackwell.

Aalbers, M. B. (2015) The great moderation, the great excess and the global housing crisis, *International Journal of Housing Policy*, 15(1), 43–60.

Aalbers, M. B. (2016) *The Financialization of Housing: A Political Economy Approach*, London: Routledge.

Agus, M. R., Doling, J. and Lee, D-S. (2002) *Housing Policy Systems in South and East Asia*, Hampshire: Palgrave Macmillan.

Balchin, P. (ed.) (1996) *Housing Policy in Europe*, London: Routledge.

Barlow, J. and Duncan, S. (1994) *Success and Failure in Housing Provision: European Systems Compared*, Oxford: Pergamon.

Boelhouwer, P. and van der Heijden, H. (1992) *Housing Systems in Europe, Part 1: A Comparative Study of Housing Policy*, Delft: Delft University Press.

Crouch, C. (2011) *The Strange Non-Death of Neoliberalism*, Cambridge: Polity Press.

Doling, J. and Ford, J. (eds.) (2003) *Globalization and Home Ownership: Experiences in Eight Member States of the European Union*, Delft: Delft University Press.

Doling, J. and Ronald, R. (eds.) (2014) *Housing East Asia: Socioeconomic and Demographic Challenges*, Basingstoke: Palgrave Macmillan.

Esping-Andersen, G. (1990) *The Three Worlds of Welfare Capitalism*, Cambridge: Polity Press.

Esping-Andersen, G. (1999) *Social Foundations of Postindustrial Economies*, Oxford: Oxford University Press.

Fitzpatrick, S. and Stephens, M. (eds.) (2008) *The Future of Social Housing*, London: Shelter.

Forrest, R. and Hirayama, Y. (2009) The uneven impact of neo-liberalism on housing opportunities, *International Journal of Urban and Regional Research*, 33(4), 998–1013.

Forrest, R. and Hirayama, Y. (2015) The financialisation of the social project: Embedded liberalism, neoliberalism and home ownership, *Urban Studies*, 52(2), 233–244.

Forrest, R., Kennett, P. and Izuhara, M. (2003) Home ownership and economic change in Japan, *Housing Studies*, 18(3), 277–293.

Forrest, R. and Lee, J. (2003) *Housing and Social Change: East-West Perspectives*, London: Routledge.

Forrest, R. and Murie, A. (1988) *Selling the Welfare State: The Privatisation of Public Housing*, London: Routledge.

Forrest, R. and Yip, N-M. (eds.) (2013) *Young People and Housing: Transitions, Trajectories and Generational Fractures*, London: Routledge.

Glynn, S. (2009) *Where the Other Half Lives: Lower Income Housing in a Neoliberal World*, New York: Pluto Press.

Groves, R., Murie, A. and Watson, C. (eds.) (2007) *Housing and the New Welfare State: Perspectives From East Asia and Europe*, Aldershot: Ashgate.

Hirayama, Y. (2007) Reshaping the housing system: Home ownership as a catalyst for social transformation, in Y. Hirayama and R. Ronald (eds.) *Housing and Social Transition in Japan*, London: Routledge, 15–46.

Hirayama, Y. (2010a) Housing pathway divergence in Japan's insecure economy, *Housing Studies*, 25(6), 777–797.

Hirayama, Y. (2010b) Neoliberal policy and the housing safety net in Japan, *City, Culture and Society*, 1(3), 119–126.

Hirayama, Y. (2011) Towards a post-homeowner society? Homeownership and economic insecurity in Japan, in R. Forrest and N-M. Yip (eds.) *Housing Markets and the Global Financial Crisis: The Uneven Impact on Households*, Cheltenham: Edward Elgar, 196–213.

Hirayama, Y. (2013) Public housing and neoliberal policy in Japan, in J. Chen, M. Stephens and Y. Man (eds.) *The Future of Public Housing: Ongoing Trends in the West and the West*, Heidelberg: Springer, 143–161.

Holliday, I. (2000) Productivist welfare capitalism: Social policy in East Asia, *Political Studies*, 48, 706–723.

Iwata, M. (2009) Jukyo mondai no tayo na hirogari to homuresu monndai no kozu [Diversified housing losses and the framework of homeless issues], *Kikan Shakaihosho Kenkyu [Quarterly of Social Security Research]*, 45(2), 94–106.

Japan Housing Finance Agency (2007) *Jutaku Roon Riyo ni Kansuru Anketo Chosa [Survey on Borrowers of Housing Loans]*, Tokyo: Japan Housing Finance Agency.

Kemeny, J. (1995) *From Public Housing to the Social Market: Rental Policy Strategies in Comparative Perspective*, London: Routledge.

Kemeny, J. and Lowe, S. (1998) Schools of comparative housing research: From convergence to divergence, *Housing Studies*, 13(2), 161–176.

Kim, K. and Renaud, B. (2009) The global house price boom and its unwinding: An analysis and a commentary, *Housing Studies*, 24(1), 7–24.

Kurz, K. and Blossfeld, H-P. (eds.) (2004) *Home Ownership and Social Inequality in Comparative Perspective*, Stanford: Stanford University Press.

Lee, J. (2014) Housing policy and asset building: Exploring the role of homeownership in East Asian Social Policy, in J. Lee, J. Midgley and Y. Zhu (eds.) *Social Policy and Change in East Asia*, Lanham: Lexington Books, 179–197.

Matsutani, A. (2004) *Jinkou Genshou no Atarashii Kousiki [A New Formula for Population Decrease]*, Tokyo: Nihon Keizai Shinbun Sha.

Ministry of Construction (1996) *Shin Jidai no Jutaku Seisaku [Housing Policy for the New Age]*, Tokyo: Gyosei.

Ministry of Land, Infrastructure, Transport and Tourism, Japan (2015) *Tochi Hakusho [White Paper of Land]*, Tokyo: Zenkoku Kanpou Hanbai Kyodo Kumiai.

Miyake, J. (1991) Jinko kozo no henka to jutaku jijo [Demographic change and housing conditions], in K. Hayakawa (ed.) *Jutaku Jinken no Shiso [Thinking on Rights to Housing]*, Tokyo: Gakuyo Shobo, 133–154.

Miyake, J. (1996) Jinko kazoku no henka to jutaku jukyu [Demographic and family changes and the housing market, in S. Kishimoto and A. Suzuki (eds.) *Kazoku to Jukyo [Family and Housing]*, Tokyo: Tokyo University Press, 205–235.

Morimoto, N. (1994) *Toshi Kyoju to Chintai Jutaku [Urban Rental Housing]*, Kyoto: Gakugei Shuppan Sha.

Murakami, Y. (1984) *Shin Chukan Taishu no Jidai [The Era of the New Middle Mass]*, Tokyo: Chuo Koron Sha.

Muramatsu, M. and Okuno, M. (2002) *Heisei Baburu no Kenkyu [Study on the Heisei Bubble]*, Tokyo: Toyo Keizai Shinposha.

Oizumi, E. (1994) Property finance in Japan: Expansion and collapse of the bubble economy, *Environment and Planning A*, 26(2), 199–213.

Organization for Economic Co-Operation and Development (OECD) (2004) *Economic Outlook*, 75, Paris: OECD Publishing.

Rolnik, R. (2013) Late neoliberalism: The financialization of homeownership and housing rights, *International Journal of Urban and Regional Research*, 37(3), 1058–1066.

Ronald, R. (2007) Comparing homeowner societies: Can we construct an East-West model? *Housing Studies*, 22(4), 473–493.

Ronald, R. (2008) *The Ideology of Home Ownership: Homeowner Societies and the Role of Housing*, Basingstoke: Palgrave Macmillan.

Saunders, P. (2005) *Welfare to Work in Practice: Social Security and Participation in Economic and Social Life*, Aldershot: Ashgate.

Scanlon, K., Whitehead, C. and Arrigoitia, M. F. (2014) *Social Housing in Europe*, West Sussex: Wiley Blackwell.

Schwartz, H. M. and Seabrooke, L. (eds.) (2009) *The Politics of Housing Booms and Busts*, Basingstoke: Palgrave Macmillan.

Streeck, W. (2014) *Buying Time: The Delayed Crisis of Democratic Capitalism*, London: Verso.

Wade, R. (1998) *Governing the Market: Economic Theory and the Role of Government in East Asia Industrialization*, Princeton: Princeton University Press.

Watson, M. (2010) House price Keynesianism and the contradictions of the modern investor subject, *Housing Studies*, 25(3), 413–426.

Weiss, L. (ed.) (2003) *States in the Global Economy: Bringing Domestic Institutions Back in*, Cambridge: Cambridge University Press.

3 Running hot and cold in regional and urban transitions

Introduction

In the transition to the post-growth era, the Japanese government has implemented urban regeneration as a key strategy and placed particular emphasis on the redevelopment of its capital – Tokyo (Hirayama, 2009, 2017; Saito, 2003, 2012; Waley, 2007, 2015). In the increasingly globalised economy, international competition in major cities in East Asia as well as in the Global North has markedly intensified. Japan's unstable post-bubble economy has, however, led to the view that the nation's global competitiveness has weakened. Therefore, fueling the restructuring of Tokyo as a lever is considered by the government as a means to revitalise its global competitiveness. Among large cities in Japan, Tokyo has the strongest link to the global economy and thus the extensive redevelopment of Tokyo as a global city has been given top priority in challenging urban competition. Various policy measures including relaxing urban planning regulations, subsidising urban redevelopment projects, and promoting residential purchases have combined to nurture the creation of brand-new landscapes and skylines in the capital city.

The rise of the Tokyo-centred approach represents a shift in the key principle of regional and urban policy from 'development' to 'competition'. Post-war regional policy was embedded in the framework of the developmental state, in which the interventionist government prioritised and pursued economic expansion as a means to maintain state legitimacy and social cohesion (Honma, 1999; Ide, 2011; Murakami, 1992). During the period of high-speed economic growth, regional development played a significant role in improving economic conditions in various regions including not only larger cities but also smaller cities and rural areas. With the post-bubble economic decline, however, intensifying international urban competition has combined with increasingly prevalent neoliberalism to erode the traditional foundation of developmental regional policy. This has led the government to focus on restructuring Tokyo into a more competitive global city. The launch of the novel urban regeneration policy has reflected the state's strategy to create a new direction for the nation in terms of embracing global economic competition.

This chapter focuses on the spatial dimension of housing development in relation to the processes and outcomes of regional and urban policies in the post-growth era. We argue that the new competition-orientated policy has produced economic and spatial disparities between Tokyo and the rest of the country, and within Tokyo itself. In alignment with various policy measures aimed at regenerating Tokyo as a world-class city, a vast amount of investment has been poured into numerous residential projects in the capital city, whereas other regions have continued to suffer from disinvestment. Within Tokyo, real estate investment has increasingly been concentrated in the 'hot spots' in the city centre, promoting housing construction booms. The real estate market in the 'cold spots' at the periphery of the city, on the other hand, has continued to stagnate. The new competition-oriented regional and urban policy has thus led to geo-economic polarisation in Tokyo and in the country as a whole. In this chapter, we begin with examining the concepts of developmentalism and neoliberalism in light of changes in the redistributive aspects of regional and urban policies and then look at the trajectory of policy shifts to the Tokyo-centred approach. This is followed by analyses of the disparities in housing conditions between Tokyo and other regions and between central and peripheral areas within Tokyo. We conclude with an examination of the prospects of housing opportunities in relation to regional and urban transitions in the post-growth era.

Developmentalism, neoliberalism and spatial redistribution

There has been a clear policy shift from a developmental approach to a neoliberal approach in order to deal with urban competition. In exploring the process of this shift, it is necessary to highlight the weakening of the mechanisms of spatial redistribution. With the entry to the post-growth phase, there has been growing economic polarisation both between and within cities. This cannot be considered only a consequence of the economic downturn; it is also an outcome of structural policy changes. The shift to a competition-focused approach by the central government with increasingly uneven resource allocation has eroded the redistributive mechanism of post-war regional and urban policies, resulting in stark spatial disparities within and between cities.

How and to what extent neoliberal prescriptions have replaced the developmental approach in formulating policy in East Asian countries is a matter of considerable debate (Park et al., 2012). Developmentalism has been a dominant ideology in the political economy of East Asia, with advocates asserting that economic progress is best achieved by the state playing a strong role in orchestrating economic development (e.g., Park et al., 2012; Wade, 1998; Weiss, 2003). Neoliberalism is often defined as a political economic ideology proposing that economic progress is best advanced by liberating individual entrepreneurial freedoms within an institutional framework characterised by private property rights and competitive markets (e.g.,

Davies, 2016; Harvey, 2005; Springer et al., 2016). With the globalising economy, a policy shift to neoliberal reforms has been observed in many East Asian countries. It would be, however, misleading to consider that neoliberal policy has replaced developmental state policy entirely. Public policy is path-dependent in nature, while neoliberal prescriptions are influential in reforming the existing policy. Developmentalism and neoliberalism have thus arguably combined to lead to the development of state-guided policies that are oriented towards a market economy. In terms of prioritising economic performance over other social values, neoliberal policy is in fact not much different from developmental policy. Unlike *laissez-faire* liberalists in the past, current neoliberal reformers perceive that markets are not complete in and of themselves but rather framed by state-supervised institutions (Dardot and Lavel, 2013). In this vein, the governments in East Asian societies remain interventionists in managing economic development while increasingly promoting market competition as a key instrument in shaping national policy. For Park and his colleagues (2012), therefore, the ideology behind new economic policies in East Asian countries can be dubbed 'developmental neoliberalism'.

How we understand the relationship between developmentalism and neoliberalism has thus been a matter of debate. There is, however, no doubt that neoliberal reforms have significantly undermined the redistributive mechanism of regional development policy. In the growth period, the Japanese government took the initiative in developing not only large cities but also provincial regions. The equal and balanced development across regions characterised by spatially redistributing resources was the primary focus of the post-war regional policy. The government has paternalistically protected the economy of local communities through the allocation of public works and the system of financial transfers (Honma, 1996, 1999). The state expenditure on public works in Japan has been disproportionally large in comparison to that of Western countries (Ide, 2011). This has underpinned the production and maintenance of employment opportunities in regions where the economy has significantly lagged behind large cities. Using the financial transfer system, the central government provided local governments with grants and subsidies in order to facilitate more even development across the country. In addition, the Comprehensive National Development Plans based on the 1950 Comprehensive National Land Development Act were periodically drawn up as the foundation of regional policy. Such plans consistently stressed the importance of creating balanced regional economies. In terms of the political economy, as discussed in Chapter 1, the Japanese developmental state system was controlled by the 'iron triangle' of the dominant political party (LDP), bureaucrats and the construction industry. A top-down approach was commonly found in the inter-governmental relations, in which the central government used local governments as state agents and governed their policy through a series of regulations and fiscal incentives. In order to rationalise such power structure and to ensure the state legitimacy, the system of geographical redistribution played a crucial role in implementing developmental policy. Moreover, the LDP traditionally had its roots in rural communities and the subsidies to the local economies thus cemented political support for the party.

Nevertheless, with transitions into the post-growth age, there has been a notable decline in spatial redistribution with regard to regional development since the 1990s. The post-bubble crisis in the economy and politics has combined with pervasive neoliberalism to lead to the reorganisation of regional and urban policy with a shift from the balanced development approach to the Tokyo-centric approach (Hirayama, 2009, 2017; Kantor et al., 2012; Saito, 2012). Global economic competition has increasingly intensified and pressured the government to facilitate the restructuring of Tokyo Metropolis into a more competitive global city. Meanwhile, regional policy has been radically reformed towards economic decentralisation, encouraging provincial regions to become more independent and to engage in inter-regional economic competition. This involved a substantial reduction in the allocation of public works and financial assistance to local governments, which implies that the government no longer seeks to protect local economies evenly. Such retreat was accelerated when the public sector fell into an immense fiscal crisis in the 1990s. With continued urbanisation, the ruling party, which had traditionally allocated subsidies to rural regions, shifted its policy towards attracting urban voters in order to remain in power. At the same time, the government promoted mergers of municipalities by providing a series of financial incentives to improve fiscal efficiency. Since small municipalities found it difficult or almost impossible to maintain financial independence, many of them were forced to merge, resulting in halving the number of municipalities in just one decade from 3,232 in 1999 to 1,727 in 2010.

The strategy of the government was to concentrate resources on redeveloping Tokyo as the core of Japan's competitiveness while decentralising the regional policies in a way that required local economies to become more self-sufficient. In 2005, the National Land Sustainability Act, which replaced the Comprehensive National Land Development Act, laid out a new direction of regional decentralisation. This was followed by the introduction of the 2014 Grand Design of National Land for 2050, setting a plan to create the world's largest super-mega-region covering the Tokyo metropolitan region as well as the Tokai and Kansai regions including the major cities of Nagoya and Osaka. The system of traditional regional development has not been dismantled completely owing to the path-dependent nature of government policy. For example, the iron triangle has not unravelled completely and thus the construction industry remains closely associated with some LDP members to push the government to fund public works. Regardless of the extent to which traditional policy has continued, however, the reorientation of regional and urban policies under the influence of neoliberalism has led to a noticeable reduction in spatial redistribution. The economic cleavage within Tokyo and between Tokyo and other regions has deepened, representing not only economic changes but also a shift away from the policy of underpinning balanced regional development.

Towards competition-oriented urban policy

How has the Tokyo-centred, competition-oriented urban policy been developed? This section explores transformations in Japan's regional and urban policies in the post-growth era with particular reference to economic and political pressures imposed on policy making. It was in the early 1980s that the Nakasone Administration originated neoliberal policy reforms, following the lead of Margaret Thatcher in the UK and Ronald Regan in the US. This led to the implementation of flagship projects such as the privatisation of the Japan National Railway (JNR) and the disposition of national land. Neoliberal policy led by Prime Minister Nakasone, however, did not progress significantly but was rather prevented by the power of the 'iron triangle' that was managing developmental policy. The strong economic performance during the 1980s was another reason for the survival of the existing policy. With the perceived success of the developmental state, the LDP, bureaucrats and large corporations continued to play a central role in formulating public policy, seeking to preserve the structure of the 'iron triangle'.

Nonetheless, together with the economic and political crises that followed the burst of the economic bubble at the beginning of the 1990s, intensified global economic competition prompted the government to adopt neoliberal policy reforms (Hirayama, 2017). The Obuchi Cabinet, established in 1998, clearly positioned urban regeneration as a key policy for enhancing the global competitiveness of large cities, especially Tokyo, to address the post-bubble economic decline. The 1999 *Strategy Towards the Revitalization of the Japanese Economy,* published by the Economic Strategy Council (1999), under the prime minister considered 'the revitalization of the large cities' as 'one of the largest frontiers of the 21st century', claiming that the recent critical situation was caused by the decline in the global competitiveness of large cities. The government then launched a series of measures to redevelop Tokyo, including the deregulation of urban planning, the disposal of real estate of the former JNR to private developers, the injection of private funds into the development of public facilities such as government office buildings, and the securitisation of real estate. New policy measures were characterised by 'privatisation', 'deregulation', 'marketization' and 'financialisation' in line with the neoliberal logic.

The significant push to promote the redevelopment of Tokyo came under the government led by Junichiro Koizumi immediately after his inauguration in April 2001 (Igarashi and Ogawa, 2003). Prime Minister Koizumi, who was also the LDP leader, challenged his own political party in disintegrating the traditional developmental system and in progressing neoliberal reforms. The prime minister set up the Urban Renaissance Headquarters in the Cabinet with himself as the chief and all the state ministers as members, asserting urban rejuvenation as the key national strategy. The Urban Renaissance Special Measure Act, which was managed directly by the Headquarters, came into force in 2002 to identify and designate zones that were to be urgently developed, where planning regulations were radically relaxed and government subsidies were provided to private developers.

The Koizumi government deployed a top-down approach in facilitating urban regeneration with an emphasis on the role of the market in expanding private investment in the real estate market. This can be conceptualised as the government-led developmental policy meeting a market-oriented neoliberal approach in the new era of economic competition. Tokyo was once considered a top-class global city along with New York and London (Sassen, 1991), but it was known that the political economy of Tokyo was very different from the other two cities (Hill and Kim, 2000; Saito, 2003; White, 1998; Waley, 2007, 2015). While the relatively liberal economic systems dominated urban transformations in New York and London, the Japanese government played a key role in framing the regeneration of Tokyo. The introduction of a market-orientated approach combined with the interventionist policy is thus now shaping the way in which Tokyo is redeveloped.

The tendency of the government to focus on Tokyo has been evident since the 1980s and was further accelerated in the period of the Koizumi administration (Hirayama, 2009). Within the context of international economic competition, Tokyo was the only city in Japan that had maintained a strong connection with the global economy. Politicians and policy makers thus believed that a rejuvenated and more competitive Tokyo would lead the whole nation to economic recovery. By December 2005, under the Urban Renaissance Special Measure Act, 64 districts of approximately 6,567 hectares across the nation were designated as priority zones for urgent redevelopment. The area designated in Tokyo was by far the largest (2,514 hectares), which was more than double the size in the second largest city, Osaka. In addition, many districts in which regulations on the ratio of building volume could be relaxed were designated in the central area of Tokyo (see Figure 3.1).

The Tokyo Metropolitan Government (TMG), led by Governor Shintaro Ishihara (1999–2012), formulated a policy to transform Tokyo into a more competitive world-class city in line with the urban renaissance policy of the national government (TMG, 2000). Governor Ishihara stressed the importance of the Tokyo-centric approach, asserting that the revitalisation of Tokyo would provide the entire nation with an opportunity for economic recovery. *The Strategic Plan to Overcome Crisis*, published in November 1999, which outlined the policies of the Ishihara Metropolitan Government, stated that 'the success or failure of economic activity in Tokyo has a nation-wide impact and determines the rise or fall of Japan in circumstances where global intercity competition is even more intensified' (TMG, 1999, 12).

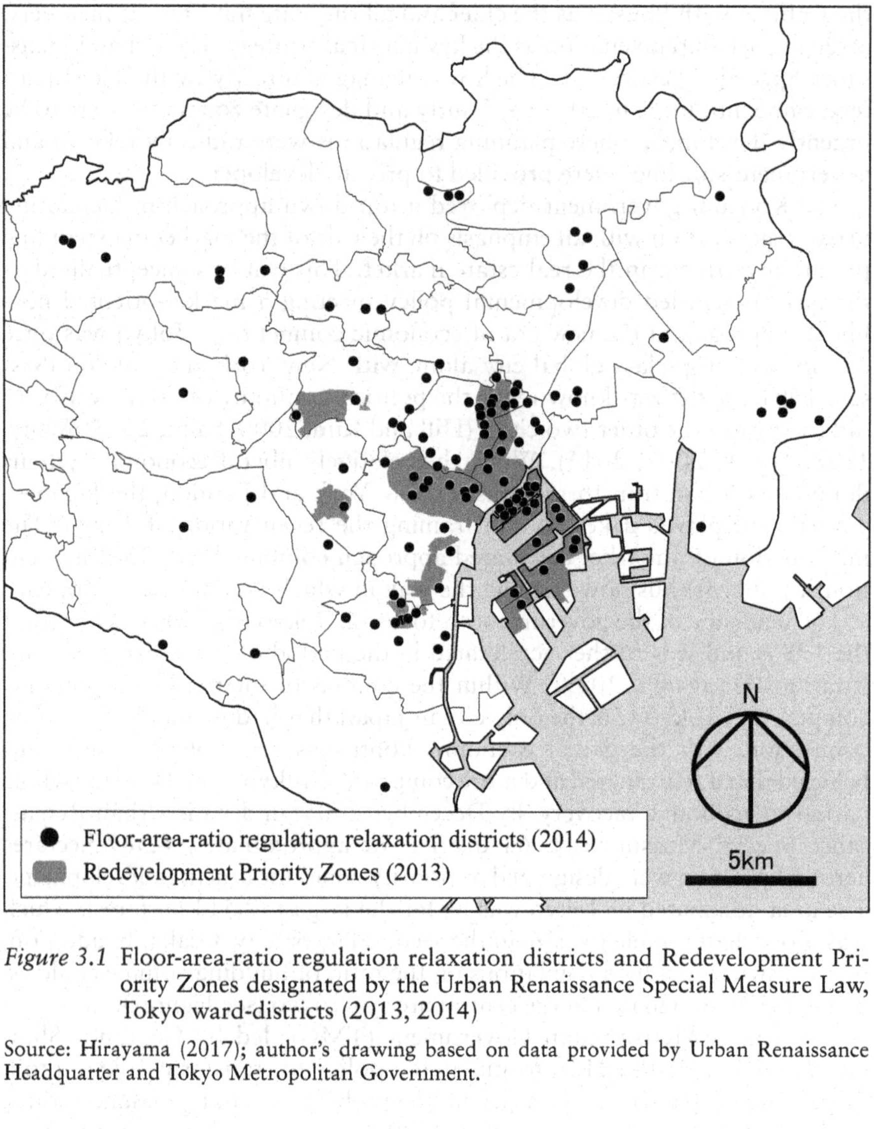

Figure 3.1 Floor-area-ratio regulation relaxation districts and Redevelopment Priority Zones designated by the Urban Renaissance Special Measure Law, Tokyo ward-districts (2013, 2014)

Source: Hirayama (2017); author's drawing based on data provided by Urban Renaissance Headquarter and Tokyo Metropolitan Government.

As the key aspect of the state policy has been shifted from 'development' to 'competition', the government has begun to increase the economic openness of the nation and of Tokyo towards the globalising economy. Japan's economy was previously relatively closed, where inward foreign direct investment was less than outward investment. This partly reflected the legacy of the state's past policy: namely, the government had not lifted control over inward direct investment until the early 1970s for fear of losing control over the Japanese economy to foreign businesses (Suda, 2003). However, since the government led by Ryutaro Hashimoto embarked upon the 'Big Bang' policy in 1996, the deregulation of the financial system has facilitated inward investment in phases. At the same time, the market for securitised real estate started to expand in the early 2000s, together with the 2001 listing of the Japan-Real Estate Investment Trust (J-REIT) and an increase in the number of private real estate funds. This started to encourage transnational as well as domestic investment in the redevelopment of Tokyo.

Such financial liberalisation reflected a fundamental conversion with regard to the view of the property bubble. In the late 1980s when the prices of real estate peaked, many households with even middle incomes could not acquire adequate housing due to the abnormal house price inflation and accordingly the government was pressed to bring an end to the bubble. In contrast, since the late 1990s, the government has looked for measures to create new bubbles. During the post-bubble stagnation, the appreciation of property prices was increasingly considered to be essential in encouraging economic recovery. Financial liberalisation and real estate securitisation, combined with the relaxation of urban planning regulations, were thus expected to expand investments in the property market.

With implementing urban regeneration, the government has stressed the necessity for Tokyo to compete with other global cities, particularly the major cities of East Asia, whose economies have grown at striking paces (Hirayama, 2009; Saito, 2012). After the end of the Second World War, Japan began to catch up with the Western nations in regard to economic prosperity and became the world's second-largest economy in 1968. During the latter half of the 1980s, helped by the peak of the bubble economy, Tokyo was classified as a top-rank global city (Sassen, 1991). Since the burst of the bubble in the early 1990s, however, policy makers have pointed out the stagnated economic conditions of Tokyo compared with the growing economies of East Asian rivals such as Hong Kong, Singapore, Beijing, Shanghai and Seoul. Japan was overtaken by China in 2010 for the position as the second-largest economy in the world. Such changes in Japan's economic fortune thus urged the government to strengthen the nation's global competitiveness and respond to the crisis discourse – namely, that Japan, which once sought to catch up to Western nations, is now being pursued by East Asian nations (Hirayama, 2009).

The economic conditions in Japan have remained unstable. It took more than a decade after the burst of the bubble for the economy to eventually begin to recover in 2002, at which time the government further accelerated the redevelopment of Tokyo. As discussed in Chapter 2, real estate prices in Tokyo consequently started to rise in the mid-2000s, leading to the mini-bubble in 2006 and 2007. Land and housing prices rose only in Tokyo and some other large cities, while the prices continued to fall in smaller cities. The Tokyo mini-bubble in the mid-2000s was short-lived, lasting only until the onset of the 2008 Lehman Shock.

Faced with the challenge of such an unstable economy, the government continued to urge the urban regeneration agenda forward. The Abe Administration, elected in 2012, further drove financial deregulation. In the same vein, the Bank of Japan started to implement unprecedented monetary easing. With unconventional financial measures, real estate prices started to rise again in 2014 in Tokyo and other large cities for the first time since the Lehman Shock, although property prices in smaller cities continued to fall. The Abe Administration followed the previous LDP Administrations in implementing urban renewal policy by facilitating numerous redevelopment projects in Tokyo. Moreover, the successful bid of Tokyo to host the 2020 Olympic Summer Games after losing the previous bid is further stimulating investment in the real estate market with expectations of various large-scale redevelopment projects.

Overall, the attitudes of the government towards urban regeneration have been markedly aggressive. Underlying this has arguably been a feeling of anxiety concerning Japan's entry into the post-growth phase. It is likely that the stronger the feeling of uncertainty grows, the more extremely pro-development the government policy will become. A globalising economy has combined with prevalent neoliberalism to usher in the intensification of intercity competition. Nevertheless, economic decline in Japan has contrasted with the ascending economies of other East Asian nations. Furthermore, Japan's population has been (and will continue to be) decreasing with unprecedented societal ageing. The entry into the post-growth era together with downward demographic and economic transformations has thus brought about pessimistic views on the nation's future. Public policy in relation to challenging urban competition has become increasingly decisive all the more for the feeling of anxiety.

Ups and downs in the Tokyo housing market

Urban regeneration measures have produced new 'hot spots' in Tokyo, especially in the central and waterfront areas, where various redevelopment projects have been implemented. In such areas, the housing market is increasingly active. In contrast, 'cold spots' where the real estate market is persistently inactive have been formed in the suburbs and peripheries. The contrasted fortunes with regard to housing market movements have progressively fragmented Tokyo's urban space. In Tokyo, as in other major cities, the prices of all housing increased during the bubble in the last half of the 1980s and subsequently dropped after the bubble burst at the beginning of the 1990s. There has been, however, the concurrence of hot spots and cold spots within the same city since the mid-2000s, where ups and downs in property values have simultaneously been witnessed (Hirayama, 2005).

This can be explained by the combination of the aggressive competition-oriented urban policy and demographic and economic change in post-growth Tokyo. The population of Tokyo is projected to start declining after reaching its peak around 2020, along with a remarkable increase in the number and proportion of elderly citizens. Economic circumstances surrounding Tokyo have been notably unstable since the bubble burst and the volatility is projected to continue. Therefore, as the urban regeneration measures fuel booms of housing construction in hot spots of the city centre, it leads to the further extension of cold spots in the peripheries with an increasing number of households moving to the city centre. In terms of exploring changes in post-growth Tokyo, thus, it is crucial to examine the role of the urban regeneration policy not only as a means to regenerate the city physically and economically but also as a mechanism in dividing urban space into booming spots and stagnant areas.

Hot spots: creating housing booms

The ascendance of hot spots in the central areas of Tokyo has characteristically been accompanied by the construction boom of condominium towers (see Figure 3.2). In central Tokyo alone, according to research by the Real Estate Economic Institute in 2015, 442 condominium towers of over 20 storeys, consisting of 130,320 units, were constructed between 1997 and 2014. In the greater Tokyo region, which includes Tokyo and the neighbouring prefectures of Kanagawa, Chiba and Saitama, 662 condominium towers, with a total of 193,122 units, were completed during the same period. The number of new projects in the form of super-high-rise condominium blocks, which increased rapidly from the late 1990s when the urban regeneration policy started, decreased sharply in 2008 due to the Lehman Shock and then again started to increase in the early 2010s.

The urban regeneration policy has buttressed the realisation of many mega-complex projects in central Tokyo, which often include super-high-rise residential blocks together with office buildings and commercial facilities. A pair of 47-story condominiums called the Tokyo Twin Parks, which are comprised of 1,000 units, was completed in 2002 in a large-scale redevelopment project of 31 ha in Shiodome, along with many high-rise office buildings. This redevelopment, which was a flagship project symbolising the rejuvenation of Tokyo, was implemented by several private developers using tracts of land previously be owned by the former JNR that were acquired at auction. A 43-story condominium of 650 units called the Shinagawa V Tower was completed along with many office buildings in 2003 in Shinagawa, where private developers acquired 5.3 ha of former JNR land at auction. Twin towers of 58 stories in the Kachidoki district with as many as 2,794 dwellings called The Tokyo Towers were completed in 2008. This large-scale project was accomplished with a new type of redevelopment that gave an eminent position to the private developer.

The accomplishment of various mega-complexes with residential towers has created new, luxurious landscapes and skylines of the central and waterfront areas in Tokyo. Underlying this have been shifts in the strategies

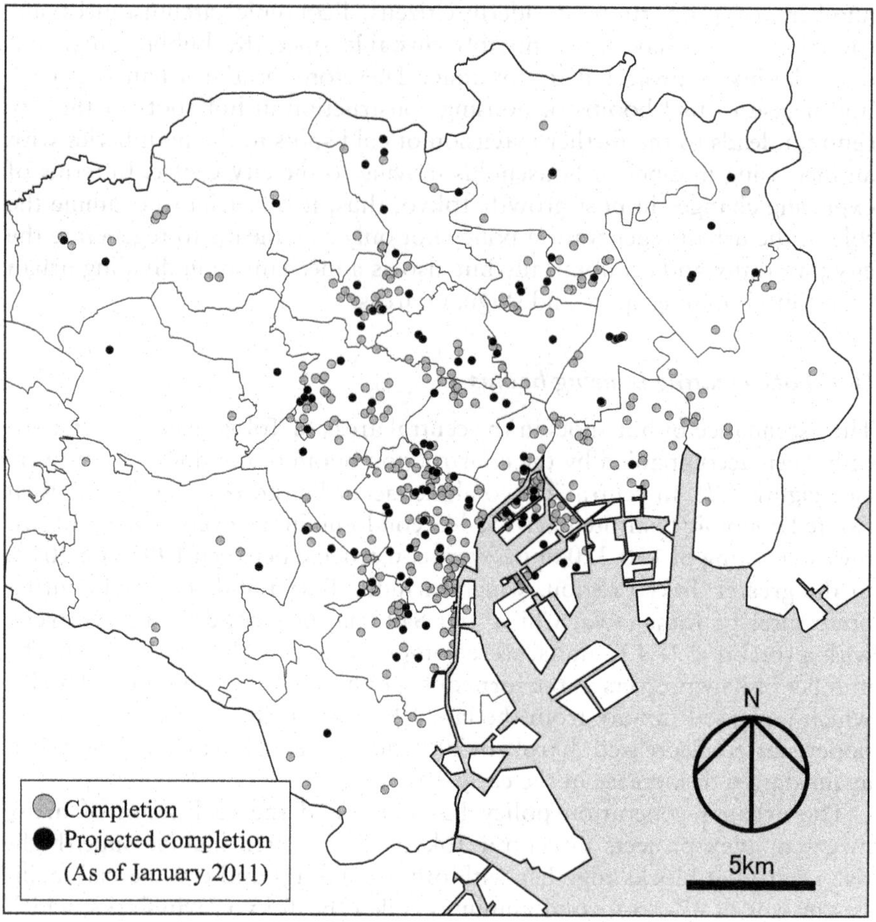

Figure 3.2 Location of high-rise condominium blocks, Tokyo ward-districts (2011)

Source: Hirayama (2017); author's drawing based on data provided by Real Estate Economic Institute.

of urban planning policy (Hirayama, 2009). The government formulated the policy to promote the conglomeration of business, commerce and housing in the urban centre and the TMG presented a plan as a key policy to redevelop the 'centre core area' (TMG, 2000). In the bubble period, the government sector sought to disperse construction works to the peripheries of the city because the concentration of building works in the city centre was considered to inflate real estate prices and cause over-crowding. Since the bubble burst, however, the redevelopment of the urban centre has been intensified to reorganise Tokyo into a more competitive city in response to national economic decline. The government sector also used a strategy to support specific individual mega projects to lead urban reforms rather than organising a more comprehensive redevelopment of Tokyo as a whole. In the central areas of Tokyo, regulations for urban planning were not simply relaxed but rather substantially rewritten for some specific projects. For instance, the maximum ratio of floor space to land plot size for the Shiodome project, which had been 800 per cent, was increased to as much as 1,200 per cent, and from 600 per cent to 950 per cent for the Shinagawa project. At the same time, the government disposed of large plots of national land to private developers, aimed at supporting such mega construction projects.

In addition to urban planning, financial policy has played an essential role in producing hot spots. Within the context of post-bubble stagnation, interest rates have been maintained at extremely low levels and the government helped expand the housing loan market. Private mortgage financing was deregulated in 1994 with regard to interest rates, while the 2007 abolition of the GHLC led to a dramatic increase in the supply of private housing loans. Business circumstances for selling mortgage products have become more competitive, and the subsequent lowering of costs of borrowing has led many households to enter the housing market despite economic stagnation. Such financial policy has underpinned the expansion of the condominium market in the central areas of Tokyo.

With progress on financial deregulation, transnational real estate investments have fuelled housing booms in Tokyo (Hirayama, 2017). It was not only domestic but also overseas investors that provoked the 'mini-bubble' in Tokyo in the mid-2000s. As discussed, the government has re-orientated its policy within the context of intensified international urban competition towards encouraging inward foreign direct investment and expanding the market for securitised real estate since the 1990s. Real estate prices after the bubble burst were considered to have become reasonable for overseas investors, while interest rates continued to be low. As a consequence, real estate investment from overseas, which was mediated by the Japan-Real Estate Investment Trust (J-REIT) and an increased number of private real estate funds, increased to generate the mini-bubble, also known as the 'fund-bubble'. This fund-bubble collapsed due to the 2008 Lehman Shock and overseas investors swiftly abandoned Tokyo. The subsequent monetary easing policy under the Abe administration has, however, facilitated the re-increase of transnational investments into the Tokyo property market. An increasing number of overseas investors, particularly from China, Hong Kong, Singapore and Taiwan, have purchased condominiums in Tokyo hot spots. Along with high-speed economic growth, these East Asian countries have experienced a significant increase in the number of wealthy households who are constantly in search for investment opportunities. Thus, the shift in government policy towards economic openness and monetary easing has linked with an increase in the number of wealthy investors in neighbouring

East Asian countries to provoke the significant expansion of transnational investment in the redevelopment of Tokyo.

An increase in the number of super-high-rise condominiums has resulted in differentiating housing prices both horizontally and vertically. The prices of condominiums located in high-class neighbourhoods are higher than those in ordinary neighbourhoods, leading to the horizontal differentiation of condominium prices. Dwelling prices within residential towers are vertically differentiated. There are lower-priced dwellings on lower floors, attracting middle-income households. The higher the floor on which the dwelling is located, the higher the price becomes. Dwellings on the top floors are for households on high incomes, and the very top floors contain extremely expensive dwellings for the very rich. The vertical differentiation of dwellings in a condominium tower is more noticeable in high-class residential districts than in ordinary districts. Dwelling prices are thus differentiated more in 'the housing market in the sky' than in 'the market at ground level', which reflects the strategy of developers to sell the sky of high-class districts for prestige at extraordinarily high prices. For example, in the case of a 34-storey condominium tower with 314 units, built in Aoyama, one of the most fashionable districts in Tokyo, the floor area of a dwelling is 45–99 square metres and the price of a unit is up to 130 million yen (1,040,000 euros [1 euro = 125 yen, May 2017]) at the highest on the 9th floor or below. For most dwellings on the 24th floor and above, the floor area of a unit is 120 square metres or more and the price of a unit is 100 million yen (800,000 euros) at the lowest. A unit of 240 square metres on the top floor was sold for 710 million yen (5,680,000 euros). Wealthy Japanese families have traditionally preferred to live in large detached houses in a large plot of land. Azabu, Seijo and Den'en Chofu are well-known examples of traditional high-class neighbourhoods with spacious houses where wealthy families have lived over several generations. Luxury dwellings on the top floors of novel condominium towers have thus mostly been purchased by the *nouveau riche*, such as those successful in Internet venture businesses, financial experts in foreign-affiliated companies, and young CEOs in overseas companies.

The luxury appearance of new skyscrapers in the urban centre has been emblematic of rejuvenating Tokyo. To what extent the government's policy to produce and maintain hot spots can be sustainable is, however, another question. Tokyo has entered a post-growth era and is undergoing increasingly unstable economic circumstances, suggesting the fragility of the currently booming hot spots. There are various factors that account for determining how the property market evolves. In Tokyo as well as in many other world-class cities, however, volatile financial flows have become more significant in moving the real estate economy, leading to increased vicissitude in the housing market (Forrest and Yip, 2011). The rise and fall of the mini-bubble and the subsequent boom in the property market have been implicated in restless ups and downs in real estate investments. This suggests that the current housing boom is unlikely to be sustainable due to the volatile financial conditions. The instability of the real estate market will be further amplified with the increasing exposure of Tokyo to the globalising economy. For wealthy investors, distinctions between real estate, stocks and shares as objects of investment have become less important as long as they gain high levels of short-term yields, which leads to a more volatile transnational real estate investment (Forrest and Hirayama, 2015).

Cold spots: deepening housing slumps

As real estate investment is intensified in the urban core, cold spots form in the peripheries, where many homeowners are trapped in negative equity with a continuous decline in the value of their properties (Hirayama, 2005). In particular, suburban condominiums built in the bubble period have been significantly devaluated. In general, the motivation for households who move to the suburbs is to acquire a spacious single-family home. During the bubble period, however, due to the excessive housing price inflation, many households with moderate incomes could only afford a condominium in the suburbs. The marketability of such condominiums in the suburbs nosedived after the bubble burst. The difference in floor areas between condominiums and single-family homes is greater in the suburbs than that in city centres, which has reduced the marketability of suburban condominiums even more. Consequently, residential mobility has been restricted among suburban condominium owners because they have been captured by negative equity and declining marketability.

Moreover, in the peripheries of the Tokyo metropolitan region, an increasing number of heavily discounted second-hand condominiums of less than 10 million yen (80,000 euros) started appearing (Hirayama, 2005). In Japan, as discussed in Chapter 2, where the housing system has encouraged mass construction of new dwellings, the second-hand housing market has inevitably been small. The discounted condominiums are typically small, old and located on the fringes. Another recent trend is the rapid increase in the number of vacant dwellings in the peripheral areas (see Figure 3.3). Vacancy rates are much higher for multi-family housing than for single-family housing, reflecting the fact that the demand for multi-family housing has been in decline, particularly in the fringes. Some discounted second-hand condominium blocks in the cold spots are becoming run-down and rapidly losing market value. This is a cause and a consequence of increases in the rates of vacant dwellings, the number of low-income occupants, and the amount of unpaid management fees.

Demographic transformations will affect all corners of Tokyo but will particularly cast a cloud over the cold spots at the outskirts (Hirayama, 2009, 2017; Luetzeler, 2011). The population will begin to decrease in the near future and the speed of social ageing in Tokyo will be phenomenal. As Tokyo attracts university students and new recruits, the population of the capital

Figure 3.3 Housing vacancy rates in the Tokyo Region (2013)

Source: Author's drawing based on 2013 Housing and Land Survey of Japan.

city has been relatively young compared with that of other regions. However, the overall number of young people will decrease significantly in Japan due to its low fertility rate. The inflow of young people into Tokyo will accordingly decrease and the speed of ageing will not slow. In addition, the rate of baby-boomers is disproportionately high in Tokyo, and they are now ageing *en masse*, accelerating societal ageing (Matsutani, 2004, 2015). In the period of rapid urbanisation and high-speed economic growth of the 1960s and 1970s, a relatively homogenous group of young families purchased homes in expanding suburban communities. Such neighbourhoods are now facing increasing numbers of elderly households and vacant properties. Younger people now seldom return to the parental home in the suburbs, which will further accelerate the shrinking and ageing of suburban communities.

Critically, the cold spots were produced not only by the post-bubble stagnation but also by the formation of the hot spots themselves. The increase in new super-high-rise condominium blocks in the central areas has accelerated the price deflation of suburban condominiums and led to the increase in vacant dwellings in the fringes. The simultaneous rises of hot and cold spots are interlinked and the booming housing market in the hot spots has been created at the expense of the cold spots. Both booming and stagnant spots can therefore be considered as manufactured outcomes of the urban regeneration policy. It is thus reasonable to conclude that competition-orientated policy has not contributed to regenerate Tokyo as a whole but has rather further divided the city.

Contrasting declines in regions

Stagnating local economies

The focus of Japan's post-war regional policy was the equal development of various regions with spatial redistribution. In response to intensified international competition, and within the context of ascending neoliberalism, however, regional policy has been shifted towards placing top priority on the restructuring of Tokyo into a more competitive world-class city. The government has withdrawn from the system of protecting local economies and instead encouraged smaller cities and provincial communities to be more independent and to compete economically against each other. The redistributive functions of the central government have been reduced, creating disparities between the capital city and the rest of the country. Japan has entered a post-growth phase in terms of economic and demographic declines. This has been much more accentuated in smaller cities and rural areas than in large cities. Urban redevelopment projects flourish in Tokyo, while many provincial regions are suffering from disinvestment and associated outflows of the population and employment.

Demographic and economic decline in the provincial regions has been phenomenal. The Japan Policy Council, which is a private organisation consisting of business leaders and academics, published a controversial report in 2014 on a projection of future demographic changes (Masuda, 2014). They presented the dramatic projection that half of all the municipalities in Japan would undergo a serious population decrease within the next 30–40 years – a decline of more than 50 per cent of females aged 20–39, who constitute a key group in terms of maintaining fertility – suggesting that a substantial number of municipalities might disappear. The aim of the report was, however, not to argue the necessity of allocating more resources to the struggling regions but rather to rationalise the government policy to cut back on financial support to local communities. Indeed, a new discourse in post-growth society is constructed around the local economic declines as unavoidable, unrecoverable and thus not worthy of assistance from the central government.

Widening disparities between Tokyo and other regions have provoked a backlash against the Tokyo-centric regional policy. Some scholars heavily criticised the Japan Policy Council because its discourse on 'disappearing local communities' would justify the policy of abandoning provincial economies (e.g., Odagiri, 2014). The government was thus urged to address economic issues facing the declining communities by establishing a new division in charge of regional revitalisation in the Cabinet in 2014. Nevertheless, the Tokyo-centred strategy remains and the policy to encourage local economies to be independent without an increase in assistance from the government is being maintained.

Within the context of inter-regional economic competition, some cities have successfully brought population increase and economic upturns. For example, Fukuoka, the largest city on the island of Kyushu with the population of approximately 1.3 million, absorbed the inflow of people from other prefectures in Kyushu and its population has increased since the early 2000s. With an increase in economic openness, taking advantage of its western location closer to other East Asian countries, Fukuoka has established stronger connections with South Korea and Taiwan for trade and tourism. This demonstrates the possibility of Japanese local cities independently forming cross-border economic relationships with neighbouring cities in East Asia outside of the national economic framework. However, the case of Fukuoka City is exceptionally successful since the rest of Kyushu continues to suffer from the demographic and economic downturn. The relationship between Fukuoka City and the rest of Kyushu indeed mirrors the situation between Tokyo and the rest of Japan.

Devolution and housing

Neoliberal policy reforms have encouraged the devolution of housing policy, resulting in the reorganisation of the local housing systems. Decentralisation of jurisdiction over housing policy has led local governments to devise creative measures to cope with local housing issues. It is now feasible and also necessary for municipalities not to simply accept policies made by the central government but to implement their own ideas fit for local purposes. In many communities, new housing programmes have been developed under collaboration among local governments, citizens' interest groups, non-profit organisations and specialist groups. New schemes may involve renovating the existing housing stock, utilising local housing materials or designing housing estates in harmony with a local landscape.

It is both theoretically and practically next to impossible, however, for local initiatives alone to maintain the low-income housing system (Abe, 2001; Hirayama, 2010). The housing policy reforms oriented towards market solutions meant a further decline in low-income housing, the provision of which by the state sector has been traditionally residual in Japan (see Chapter 2 for more discussion). Regional devolution has further eroded the system of low-income housing. The large majority of the local governments cannot be proactive in providing public rented housing since the financial burden imposed on them is too heavy to construct and maintain such housing. Public housing that serves low-income households does not contribute to the local taxation base but instead pressurises the welfare expenditures to increase. If financial burdens that local governments bear for low-income households exceed a certain level, it may upset middle-class voters and thus risk political instability. Housing policy reforms have given public housing the greater function of welfare provision. This has resulted in a decrease in rent revenues and an increase in rent arrears. There are schemes that reduce or even waive rents for households whose incomes fall due to job loss or illness. However, the local governments have to cover all these costs since such schemes are not financially supported by the central government. In the period between 1966 and 2005, the Housing Construction Plan Act allocated the local governments quotas for the construction of public housing for low-income households, reflecting the top-down approach of housing policy at that time. Without the financial support by the central government, however, local governments are inevitably reluctant to provide public housing. Decentralising housing policy has thus significantly affected the low-income housing system.

Within the context of devolution and economic decline, local governments are now beginning to practice measures to strengthen their competitiveness. There have been wide-spreading views that housing measures aimed at those on low incomes do not enhance but rather hinder local competitiveness. Low-income households are increasingly perceived as non-contributing workers, consumers and taxpayers within the context of neoliberal local economic discourses. Local governments thus tend to favour housing measures that expand the mainstream housing market to attract middle-income residents. Although there is no national cash-based housing benefit except the provision of rent allowances to a very small number of households on public assistance, some local governments in major cities in particular have implemented local rent subsidy programmes. However, such programmes are in general not aimed at low-income households but targeted at newly married young families. This implies the importance of supporting young families for local governments since they are considered as 'productive' citizens who contribute to the revitalisation of the local economy. The rent subsidy programmes are indeed located in the local economic strategy.

Furthermore, the fiscal system has been reorganised to promote decentralisation of housing jurisdiction (Hirayama, 2010). This is best represented by the integration of various national subsidies, including those related to housing, into a 'block grant' package whereby limits to discretionary power of local governments regarding for what and how the subsidies is used are relaxed. It can be assumed that the new fiscal system will lead local governments to adopt more competition-oriented strategies and to further residualise housing measures for low-income households. The 2005 Local Housing Special Law and the subsequent introduction of the Social Capital Block Grant in 2010 systematised a block grant system, providing a basis for further decentralising housing policy and therefore marginalising low-income housing.

Post-disaster housing struggle

An extreme example of the decline in post-growth local economies is observed in the Tohoku region that was hit by the 2011 Great East Japan Earthquake and the associated tsunami (Godzik, 2013; Hirayama, 2011, 2012; Hirayama and Saito, 2013). The human cost was extensive: over 15,800 deaths, over 2,500 people missing and over 6,000 people injured. The damages were also tremendous in the built environment, as 561 square kilometres were flooded, and over 400,000 dwellings were completely or largely collapsed. The earthquake and tsunami caused accidents in nuclear plants in Fukushima, which added complications to the already difficult situation. Before the disaster, many small towns and villages in the Tohoku region were suffering from the post-growth characteristics of declining and ageing of the population as well as the outflow of employment. Since the disaster, demographic and economic changes have been escalated sharply (Hirayama, 2011). Japan has faced a notable increase in major natural disasters, including the 1995 Great Hanshin-Awaji Earthquake, the 2000 Miyake Island Eruption, the 2000 Mount Usu Eruption, the 2004 Chuetsu Earthquake, the 2007 Noto Peninsula Earthquake and the 2016 Kumamoto Earthquake. The Hanshin-Awaji Earthquake hit the conurbation including the large city of Kobe and led to over 6,000 deaths (Edgington, 2010; Hirayama, 2000), while the other disasters struck rural areas, damaging local economies that had already been declining. The impact of the Great East Japan Earthquake on housing indeed provides an extreme case study for uncovering the difficulties experienced by residents in post-growth provincial economies.

How the government and municipalities organise and implement post-disaster housing policy is crucial in terms of whether disaster victims can secure housing to resume their everyday life (Hirayama, 2012). In the Tohoku region as well as in the other disaster-stricken provinces, the dominant tenure of housing is owner-occupation. The majority of disaster-hit households in provincial regions thus wish to reconstruct their own homes. In Tohoku, however, many neighbourhoods were completely washed away by the tsunami and such areas have been designated as unusable for residential sites. The national and local governments have thus offered the victims a series of collective relocation projects in which new housing sites were developed on higher grounds to re-house groups of victim households. Such relocation projects take a considerable number of years, and many people involved have to endure waiting a long time for completion.

In addition, within the post-growth context, meeting the financial requirements to rebuild housing is not feasible for many victim households in Tohoku. Compared to the common insurance against fire, only a small minority of disaster-affected households had taken out housing insurance against earthquake due to the high costs. Financial institutions such as private banks as well as the Japan Housing Finance Agency, the successor to the GHLC, have encouraged victim households to rebuild or repurchase their own homes through providing mortgages. However, many householders who lost their homes were older people and could not be eligible for housing loans. At the same time, young families whose houses had been washed away had, in many cases, not yet completed mortgage repayments and have had to service outstanding debt liabilities for lost properties. With unfavourable economic prospects, such families could hardly afford taking up another mortgage to have their house rebuilt. In addition, the deflationary economy translates into an increase in the real debt burden. Many disaster-affected households have thus been obliged to abandon re-acquiring owner-occupied housing (Hirayama and Saito, 2013).

With the limited effect of the housing loan system in terms of post-disaster housing recovery, the provision of lump sum grants has become more important in leading victim households to have their homes built. In the case of the 1995 Great Hanshin-Awaji Earthquake, there was absolutely no financial support by the government for reconstructing owner-occupied housing, resulting in discouraging many former homeowners from rebuilding their own home. This experience led to the 1998 enactment of the Act on Support for Livelihood Recovery of Disaster Victims, in which Livelihood Recovery Support Grants for Disaster Victims are disbursed to households, whose homes were destroyed in disasters of a certain scale or greater, up to a maximum of 3 million yen. The government initially did not permit public funds to be allocated for the purpose of rebuilding owner-occupied houses because the use of public money for privately owned properties was not considered appropriate (Hirayama and Saito, 2013). However, once it became evident that the housing loan system alone would not support the reconstruction of housing on a large scale, the government in phases started to accept the concept of public funds as a means to encourage housing recovery. Furthermore, in order to facilitate swifter rebuilding of dwellings, many municipalities in the Tohoku region have added extra subsidies to the lump sum grant provided by the act. Thus, reconstructing owner-occupied houses has been a major challenge in the post-growth, super-aged and disaster-stricken areas.

Meanwhile, a number of post-disaster public housing units have been constructed and provided to those who are not able to rebuild their own homes in the Tohoku region, where only a small amount of public housing had existed before the disaster. In the Hanshin-Awaji region hit by the 1995 great earthquake, many post-disaster public housing developments that require large sites were concentrated at the outskirts of the city and separated from other neighbourhoods. This resulted in isolation of residents, particularly elderly people (Hirayama, 2000). In the post-earthquake Tohoku region, therefore, a number of municipalities undertook experimental public housing projects, including small-scale developments, one- or two-storey wooden structures, and estates with a variety of communal spaces. These developments were designed to create intimate neighbourhoods in which disaster-affected people could recover to resume their everyday life. However, many municipalities were urged to construct a large number of public housing units swiftly and thus tended to opt for building standardised concrete apartment blocks. How and to what extent post-disaster public housing can support victims in their livelihood recovery remains to be seen.

Conclusion

When entering the post-growth period under the growing influence of neoliberalism, the Japanese government has shifted the focus of regional and urban policies towards placing particular importance on regenerating Tokyo. In terms of challenging and winning intensified international urban competition, it was assumed to be necessary for Tokyo to be restructured into a more competitive global city. This meant separation from post-war regional policy that was oriented towards the equal, balanced development of various regions across the nation. The extent to which the new approach has replaced the developmental state's approach has been a matter of debate, but there is no doubt that the reorientation of regional and urban policies has resulted in a decline in measures of spatial redistribution.

The competition-oriented urban policy has not only promoted the redevelopment of Tokyo but has also divided Japan into Tokyo and the rest of the country while producing and deepening economic and spatial cleavages within Tokyo. The tendency of economic activity to be gravitated towards Tokyo has been becoming stronger and accordingly smaller cities and rural areas have increasingly been confronted with outflows of capital and labour forces. With a decline in the traditional redistributive system, local governments have been required to be more independent but have largely continued to suffer from sluggish economic environments. Within Tokyo, urban space has progressively been split into hot spots and cold spots, reflecting the polarisation of housing market movements. The government has given priority to creating hot spots in the central and waterfront areas of Tokyo, leading to a construction boom of super-high-rise condominium blocks with extraordinarily luxurious dwellings on the top floors. The real estate market in the cold spots of the peripheral areas has, however, remained stagnant with a number of homeowners trapped in negative housing equity. The new, energetic urban policy has thus created sharp contrasts between Tokyo and other regions, and between central and fringe areas within Tokyo, in terms of economic and spatial disparities.

An examination of transformations in Japan's regional and urban policies demonstrates the increased importance of the spatial dimension in reorganising social inequalities in the post-growth era. The Japanese government's attitudes towards implementing competition-oriented urban policy have consistently been aggressive. Nonetheless, the policy to concentrate resources on the restructuring of competitive cities, particularly Tokyo, is assumed to increasingly face limitations imposed by growing spatial disparities. The regional policy of the latter half of the last century was focused on 'development', which attracted many people and played a key role in integrating and stabilising society. It is not clear whether the policy focusing on international urban 'competition', which is widening economic disparities between and within cities, can be legitimised. With the entry into the post-growth age, the nation has increasingly been encompassed by a feeling of anxiety and threats. This has presumably fuelled the competition-focused, aggressive urban policy even more. However, this energetic policy will in turn exacerbate spatial disparities and therefore produce deterrents to the policy itself.

References

Abe, M. (2001) Jutaku seisaku ni okeru jichitai no yakuwari [The role of municipalities in housing policy], in S. Harada (ed.) *Nihon no Toshi Hou: Vol. 2 [Japan's Urban Laws Vol. 2]*, Tokyo: Tokyo University Press, 299–320.

Dardot, P. and Lavel, C. (2013) *The New Way of the World: On Neoliberal Society*, London: Verso.

Davies, W. (2016) *The Limits of Neoliberalism: Authority, Sovereignty and the Logic of Competition*, Thousand Oaks: Sage Publications.

Economic Strategy Council (1999) *Nihon Keizai Saisei heno Senryaku [Strategy Towards the Revitalisation of the Japanese Economy]*, Tokyo: Economic Strategy Council.

Edgington, D. W. (2010) *Reconstructing Kobe: The Geography of Crisis and Opportunity*, Vancouver: University of British Columbia Press.

Forrest, R. and Hirayama, Y. (2015) The financialisation of the social project: Embedded liberalism, neoliberalism and home ownership, *Urban Studies*, 52(2), 233–244.

Forrest, R. and Yip, N-M. (eds.) (2011) *Housing Markets and the Global Financial Crisis: The Uneven Impact on Households*, Cheltenham Glos: Edward Elgar.

Godzik, M. (2013) Rebuilding housing in Japan's tsunami-hit towns and cities, *International Journal of Housing Policy*, 13(4), 433–445.

Harvey, D. (2005) *A Short History of Neoliberalism*, Oxford: Oxford University Press.

Hill, R. C. and Kim, J. W. (2000) Global cities and developmental states: New York, Tokyo and Seoul, *Urban Studies*, 37(12), 2167–2195.

Hirayama, Y. (2000) Collapse and reconstruction: Housing recovery policy in Kobe after the Hanshin Great Earthquake, *Housing Studies*, 15(1), 111–128.

Hirayama, Y. (2005) Running hot and cold in the urban home ownership market: The experience of Japan's major cities, *Journal of Housing and the Built Environment*, 20(1), 1–20.

Hirayama, Y. (2009) The governance of urban renaissance in Tokyo: Post-urbanization and enhanced competitiveness, in K. H. Mok and R. Forrest (eds.) *Changing Governance and Public Policy in East Asia*, London: Routledge, 303–325.

Hirayama, Y. (2010) Neoliberal policy and the housing safety net in Japan, *City, Culture and Society*, 1(3), 119–126.

Hirayama, Y. (2011) Kiki ha kikai nanoka? Tohoku fukko machizukuri ni mukete [Is the crisis a chance? Towards town reconstruction], *Sekai [The World]*, 820, 67–75.

Hirayama, Y. (2012) Chiiki jizoku wo sasaeru jutaku saisei wo [Housing policy for the sustainability of the region], *Sekai [The World]*, 826, 214–226.

Hirayama, Y. (2017) Selling the Tokyo sky: Urban regeneration and luxury housing, in R. Forrest, S. Y. Koh and B. Wising (eds.) *Cities and the Super-Rich: Real Estate, Elite Practices and Urban Political Economies*, Hampshire: Palgrave Macmillan.

Hirayama, Y., and Saito, A. (eds.) (2013) *Sumai wo Saisei Suru: Tohoku Fukko no Seido Seisak Ron [Rebuilding Housing: Institutions and Policy in Reconstructing Tohoku]*, Tokyo: Iwanami Shoten.

Honma, Y. (1996) *Doboku Kokka no Shiso [Japan's Construction State]*, Tokyo: Nihon Keizai Hyoron Sha.

Honma, Y. (1999) *Kokudo Keikaku wo kangaeru [Reflections on National Development Plan]*, Tokyo: Chuo Koron Shinsha.

Ide, E. (ed.) (2011) *Koyo Rentai Shakai: Datsu Doken Kokka no Kokyo Jigyo [Workers' Solidarity Society: Public Works in the Construction State]*, Tokyo: Iwanami Shoten.

Igarashi, Y. and Ogawa, A. (2003) *Toshi Saisei wo Tou [Denouncing 'Urban Regeneration']*, Tokyo: Iwanami Shoten.

Kantor, P., Lefevre, C., Saito, A., Savitch, H. V. and Thornley, A. (2012) *Struggling Giants: City-Region Governance in London, New York, Paris and Tokyo*, Minneapolis: University of Minnesota Press.

Luetzeler, R. (2011) Left behind in the global city: Spaces and places of ageing and shrinking in the Tokyo metropolitan area, in F. Coulmas and R. Luetzeler (eds.) *Imploding Populations in Japan and Germany*, Leiden: Brill Academic Publication, 473–492.

Masuda, H. (2014) *Chiho Shometsu [Disappearing Local Municipalities]*, Tokyo: Chuo Koron Sha.

Matsutani, A. (2004) *Jinkou Genshou no Atarashii Kousiki [A New Formula for Population Decrease]*, Tokyo: Nihon Keizai Shinbun Sha.

Matsutani, A. (2015) *Tokyo Rekka [Tokyo Decline]*, Tokyo: PHP Shinsho.

Murakami, Y. (1992) *Han Koten no Seiji Keizai Gaku [Political Economy of Anti-Classics]*, Tokyo: Chuou Koron Sinsha.
Odagiri, H. (2014) *Nosanson ha Shometsu Shinai [Villages Do Not Disappear]*, Tokyo: Iwanami Shoten.
Park, B-G., Hill, R. C. and Saito, A. (eds.) (2012) *Locating Neoliberalism in East Asia: Neoliberalizing Spaces in Developmental States*, Oxford: Wiley-Blackwell.
Saito, A. (2003) Global city formation in a capitalist developmental state: Tokyo and the waterfront sub-centre project. *Urban Studies*, 40(2), 283–308.
Saito, A. (2012) State-space relations in transition: Urban and regional policy in Japan, in B-G. Park, R. C. Hill and A. Saito (eds.) *Locating Neoliberalism in East Asia: Neoliberalizing Spaces in Developmental States*, Oxford: Wiley-Blackwell, 59–85.
Sassen, S. (1991) *The Global City: New York, London, Tokyo*, Princeton: Princeton University Press.
Springer, S., Birch, K. and MacLeavy, J. (eds.) (2016) *The Handbook of Neoliberalism*, London: Routledge.
Suda, M. (2003) Kokusai boeki [International trade], in T. Tachibanaki (ed.) *Sengo Nihon wo Kensho Suru [Inspecting Post-War Japan]*, Tokyo: Tokyo University Press, 71–157.
Tokyo Metropolitan Government (TMG) (1999) *Kiki Toppa Senryaku Plan: 21 Seiki heno Daiichi Steppu [Strategic Plan to Overcome the Crisis: The First Step to the 21st Century]*, Tokyo: Tokyo Metropolitan Government.
Tokyo Metropolitan Government (TMG) (2000) *Toshi Hakusyo 2000 [Urban White Paper 2000]*, Tokyo: Tokyo Metropolitan Government.
Wade, R. (1998) *Governing the Market: Economic Theory and the Role of Government in East Asia Industrialization*, Princeton: Princeton University Press.
Waley, P. (2007) Tokyo-as-world-city: Reassessing the role of capital and the state in urban restructuring, *Urban Studies*, 44(8), 1465–1490.
Waley, P. (2015) Pencilling Tokyo into the map of neoliberal urbanism, *Cities*, 32, 43–50.
Weiss, L. (2003) Guiding globalization in East Asia: New roles for old developmental states, in L. Weiss (ed.) *States in the Global Economy: Bringing Domestic Institutions Back In*, Cambridge: Cambridge University Press.
White, J. W. (1998) Old wine, cracked bottle? Tokyo, Paris, and the global city hypothesis, *Urban Affairs Review*, 33(4), 451–477.

4 Young people and the divergence of housing pathways

Introduction

In many homeowner societies, the private ownership of housing provided a material and symbolic basis for securing homes, accumulating assets and maintaining membership in mainstream society. Home ownership thus constituted an essential part of the post-war social contract, promising social inclusion to the majority of individuals and households. In the post-growth era, however, younger cohort households have undergone difficulties in entering owner-occupied housing markets and have increasingly diverged in terms of housing paths. Consequently, the extent to which home ownership-oriented housing systems grant the promise of social inclusion to young people has declined. The shift to the post-growth society indeed highlights inter- and intra-generational fractures in housing pathways and experiences.

Many home-owning societies have evolved around family systems based on independent nuclear households. Young people have thus generally been expected to start leading a conventional adult life-course that progresses from living in the parents' home to securing an independent dwelling, from being single to married, and from tenancy to home ownership. With transitions to the post-growth era, however, an increasing number of younger people have begun to delay this life-stage progression. The extension of adult transitions to full independence has led to the emergence of a new stage of the life-course between adolescence and adulthood (Furlong, 2010; Toivonen, 2013), which Arnett (2000, 2006) calls the 'emerging adulthood' stage and Miyamoto (2004) phrases as the 'post-adolescence' stage. Such delay in life-stage progression among young people may reflect the increased opportunities for some well-off individuals to shape their own distinctive life-courses. At the same time, extended transitions to independence mean that more precarious employment conditions and declines in affordable housing have combined to discourage many struggling individuals from establishing a family and acquiring an owner-occupied house. Moreover, the number of individuals who never get married or access home ownership during their lifetimes is on the rise. Within the post-growth context, changes in young people's life-courses are now raising questions as to the extent to which traditional homeowner societies can be maintained.

Using Japan as a focus, in this chapter, we explore housing pathway divergence in younger generations in post-growth societies. Japan is a primary exemplar with respect to a decline in young people's housing opportunities (Hirayama, 2012, 2013; Hirayama and Ronald, 2008). The chapter begins by introducing the concepts of 'individualisation' and 'familisation' in terms of investigating the diversification of young people's housing trajectories and family formation patterns and then looks at transformations in Japan's family home ownership. We next examine an analytical framework of exploring individual-family relations with particular emphasis on the importance of highlighting both parent-child vertical relations and husband-wife horizontal relations within families. This framework is used in analysing divergence in the housing pathways of younger generations. The chapter further moves on to explore transitions in urban space in relation to young people's diversified housing paths and concludes with examining the implications of changes in young people's housing circumstances for post-growth societies.

'Youth' is usually defined as a period of transition from the dependence of childhood to the independence of adulthood. The age category is often fluid rather than fixed across societies and over time. For statistical consistency, the United Nations defines youth or young people as those aged between 18 and 25. In Japan, 20 years old is the legal coming of age, although the voting age was lowered to 18 in 2016. This chapter, however, predominantly uses the age cohort of 25–34 ('around-30') for the focus of the analysis. Adult transitions to independence in post-growth societies have been extended. Housing-related transitions among young people such as leaving the parental home, moving to better housing and accessing home ownership in response to other transitions including entry into the labour market, career progression and family formation are thus more likely to occur in the late twenties and early thirties. For example, in Japan, according to the Vital Statistics, the average age of first marriage rose to 31.1 for men and 29.4 for women in 2015, while the average age of having a first baby for women increased from 25.7 in 1975 to 30.7 in 2015. This provides a clear justification for the selection of the around-30 cohort as a sample for the analysis.

Individualisation and familisation

In many mature economies, along with socio-economic and policy changes over the past few decades, young people's housing paths and family formation patterns have diverged. This has progressively unravelled the sustainability of societies centred on home-owning nuclear households. In terms of investigating divergence in housing trajectories, we propose here to focus on the 'individualisation' and 'familisation' of people's life-courses (Hirayama, 2017). Some of the literature on housing and family change has highlighted the concepts of individualisation and familisation but has tended to analyse one or the other of these in isolation (Forrest and Hirayama, 2009; Izuhara and Forrest, 2013; Ronald and Hirayama, 2009). We point to the significance of looking at how individualisation and familisation have combined to transform housing conditions.

In Japan, on the one hand, the individualisation of the younger generation has led to an increase in one-person households living in private rented housing, with few prospects of entering the owner-occupied housing sector. On the other hand, a growing number of young households have purchased houses with assistance from their parents. This has been interpreted as an intergenerational familisation of access to home ownership. There has also been an increasing number of unmarried adults who have been living in their parents' homes (Yamada, 1999), which is a development that has reflected the individualisation of younger cohorts and simultaneously the familisation of adult children's early housing careers. Moreover, it has been pointed out that Japan's system of extended family households and the related practice of transferring family properties across generations has not declined significantly but rather has been sustained (Kato, 2009). Individualisation and familisation are opposite forces in transforming individual-family relations but have produced the same consequences with regard to reducing the centrality of property-owning nuclear households in society.

Increased divergence in young people's housing and family patterns cannot only be seen as a consequence arising from changes in personal attitudes and lifestyles but should also be explained by more structural transformations in socio-economic and policy conditions. Transitions into a post-growth society have corresponded with shifts into a post-industrial or post-Fordist society and into a risk society (Beck, 1992), along with a greater level of uncertainty with respect to people's housing and family paths (Beer and Faulkner, 2011; Furlong and Cartmel, 1997). During high growth in the past, young people in many industrial societies were expected to experience conventional life-stage progressions – finding work, leaving the parental home and getting married. Social institutions such as family and company and welfare state policies played a role in protecting young individuals from competitive and relentless market economies. With entering the post-growth period, however, the rise of a risk society combined with increasingly prevalent neoliberal imperatives has led to an increase in the extent to which individuals are exposed directly to volatile, insecure markets, with a decline in various social institutions and state provision.

Both the individualisation and familisation of young people's life-courses have been implicated in socio-economic uncertainty and policy shifts. Within the framework of a post-industrial society, individuals have been progressively removed from traditional social institutions. This has given greater choice of lifestyles to some better-off individuals. They have more leeway in not following conventional life-courses and can afford to spend the 'emerging adulthood' or 'post-adolescence' stage on exploring identity, lifestyle, and educational and occupational career opportunities. However, such de-embedding has exposed many lower-class individuals to increased fluctuations in competitive market economies. A growing number of young people on precarious employment have been at the mercy of insecure economies and consequently been deprived of opportunities to get married and achieve home ownership, which has reflected and accelerated the individualisation of housing pathways. Meanwhile, uncertain economic transitions have increasingly encouraged parents to support their children in securing housing and accessing home ownership. As a reflection of housing-related familisation, many unmarried adults have lived in their parents' house for longer periods, while an increasing number of younger households have achieved property ownership only with financial aid from their parents. This implies a paradox: the rise of a risk society, which has de-embedded many individuals from traditional family institutions, has in turn stimulated the re-embedding of some individuals into reciprocal family systems in new ways. Thus, within the context of a post-industrial or post-Fordist society with the increased exposure of individuals to various risks, socio-economic and policy changes are responsible for both the individualisation and familisation of young people's housing pathways and family formation patterns.

In many countries, transformations in the housing conditions of younger cohorts have increasingly been the subject of academic focus (e.g., Beer et al., 2011; Campos at al., 2016; Filandri and Bertolini, 2016; Forrest and Hirayama, 2009; Forrest and Yip, 2013; Mackie, 2016; McKee, 2012; Mínguez, 2016). Within this context, Japan provides a particularly vivid example in regard to acute changes in young people's housing paths and life-stage progression. In post-war Japan, people's life-courses were highly institutionalised and standardised, with many young people forming home-owning nuclear households featuring 'salary men' and female-homemakers in line with the models of 'male-breadwinner family' and 'company society' (Mathews and White, 2004; Shimazaki, 2008). For men, getting into a better school, and then a better university, and eventually a better company were considered to guarantee security; while for women, marrying a salary man with a stable income was normatively promoted by gendered social institutions (Osawa, 1993; Yokoyama, 2002). Nevertheless, since the beginning of the post-growth period, sharp declines in stable employment, marriages, fertility and affordable housing have combined with the neoliberal reforms of government policies to undermine social and economic environments surrounding young people in terms of following standardised life-courses. The 'company society' model has increasingly unravelled, while the 'male breadwinner family' model has become less pervasive. Many young men have progressively found it increasingly difficult to earn stable incomes sufficient to get married and purchase a house, whilst an increasing number of young women have come to perceive marriage as not as economically secure as it once was. Consequently, the combination of individualisation and familisation has led to a noticeable divergence in young people's housing and family patterns. In Japan, post-growth socio-economic changes and policy shifts have had particularly profound effects on diversifying young people's housing and family paths all the more for the excessive rigidity of institutionalised and standardised life-courses developed in the post-war growth period.

The promise of family-based home ownership

This section looks at changes in housing and family patterns in Japan, with special reference to changing fortunes of the home ownership sector. The expansion of property ownership, which constituted the core of the post-war *Japanese Dream*, was closely linked with the increase of independent nuclear family households in the era of high growth (Hirayama, 2017). This represented a departure from the pre-war social system based on the institution of the patriarchal stem family. Residential property ownership was then considered to be the privilege of the few. Compared to Western discourses such as the *American Dream* and the *Englishman's Castle*, promoting the democratic values through the discourse of the Japanese salary man's dream derived from especially radical social reforms away from the militaristic and patriarchal pre-war social values (Hirayama, 2003). The reorganisation of the housing and family systems after the end of the Second World War was thus expected to nurture the creation of a new, modern society.

The prevalence of nuclear families in the post-war society reflected substantial changes in the family system since the patriarchal family institution was dominant and legally reinforced during the pre-war period. After the defeat in the Second World War, a new Constitution and a new Civil Code were enacted in 1946 and in 1947, respectively. Together with the Family and Inheritance Law in 1948, these new laws replaced the patriarchal family system with a more democratic family system based on the equal rights of family members regardless of gender or birth order. Despite the law defining equal rights between husbands and wives, however, post-war families were constructed around the 'male breadwinner family' model, the same as many other advanced Western economies (Yokoyama, 2002; see also Chapter 5). In Japanese society, the legacy of the traditional family institution continued to define gender roles and patriarchal authority within households. Nonetheless, the legal changes in the family system and the actual increase in the number of nuclear households signified the emergence of modern democracy. According to the Population Census, the rate of nuclear households, which was already considerably high at 54.0 per cent in 1920 in response to the early phase of urbanisation, further rose to 60.2 per cent in 1960 and then to 63.9 per cent in 1975. At the same time, the size of household was shrinking. The average number of members per household decreased from 5.02 in 1920 to 4.56 in 1960 and then to 3.45 persons in 1975, which corresponded to the modern shift to family nuclearisation and low fertility.

Japan's post-war housing system was organised around the 'three pillars' of the government's housing policy in the 1950s (see Chapter 1). This not only played an important role in coping with serious housing shortages in the immediate post-war period but was also expected to create models of 'modern houses for modern families' (Neitzel, 2016; Nishiyama, 1989; Ronald and Alexy, 2011; Waswo, 2002). Before the war, most houses were of a Japanese style, characterised by tatami-matted rooms, a dining room where people sat on the floor, an arrangement of rooms where privacy was not regarded as important, and a drawing room that was considered much more significant than a space for family members to gather. Modern houses built after the war, in stark contrast, were provided for independent nuclear families consisting of parents and children. They introduced a dining kitchen where people sat on chairs to eat, individual bedrooms to secure privacy, and a living room that was more for the family to be together than for guests. Local governments and the JHC developed multi-family housing estates called '*danchi*' mainly for urban salary man families, where concrete structures and open spaces were combined on a large scale. The provision of mortgages by the GHLC led to the creation and expansion of suburban areas with single-family detached homes. The GHLC also developed a standard housing design and distributed it to those who sought to build their own houses, resulting in promulgating modern housing design.

Danchi developments and suburban residential districts were criticised or undervalued for their unified physical forms and monotonous appearances, particularly in the 'post-modern' period of the 1970s and 1980s, when the focus of architectural design was shifted to valuing diversification and differentiation (e.g., Ellin, 1996; Jencks, 1977). It should not be dismissed, however, that standardised modern houses, at least originally, reflected the departure from the patriarchal and hierarchical pre-war social system and the new post-war value system placing special importance on democratic equality (Neitzel, 2016). Nuclear households living in *danchi* estates or suburban residential areas were considered to be independent and equal, and they were hardly asked about which region, which class or which family they came from. This meant separation from the pre-war period when the patriarchal family model was embedded in the hierarchical social system and when people were regarded as a member of a particular family rather than an independent, equal individual. In the production of modern housing for modern families, standardised *danchi* dwellings for salaried workers, and suburban neighbourhoods for nuclear households, housing policy played a crucial role in defining how housing and family in post-war Japan should be.

Meanwhile, Japan's housing system has developed inclusion mechanisms of widening access to home ownership for 'new families'. In a country in which owner-occupied dwellings are designed to offer 'family space', most people do not purchase a house until marriage. According to the 2013 Housing and Land Survey, the rate of owner-occupation, which was 61.7 per cent on average, was 75.0 per cent for couple households with children and 35.5 per cent for one-person households. It was evident that the private ownership of housing provided practical means to securing family homes while symbolically representing their membership in middle-class society. In the growth period, home ownership was thus socially constructed as the ideal housing tenure for 'new families' with positive images of trust, affluence, social inclusion and independence (Hirayama, 2003).

Since the 1990s, however, as argued throughout this volume, socio-economic and policy changes have challenged the conventional post-war home ownership system. Transitions into a post-growth phase of development have been associated with post-bubble continuous economic stagnation, labour market instability with an increase in more precarious employment, a decrease in marriages, house price volatility, and neoliberal reforms of housing and social policies. The security of owner-occupied housing as a real estate asset has been undermined due to house price deflation, while it has become more difficult for many renters to enter the home ownership market because of reduced real incomes. The rise of neoliberal imperatives has led to the retrenchment of the government from housing schemes such as the provision of low-interest mortgages that used to underpin people's housing trajectories towards home ownership. In addition, the decreasing number of conventional family households has translated into a decline in housing purchases. The extent to which family-based home ownership has been prevalent and central in society has thus declined.

The post-growth trend of young people in the housing context is the delay in establishing independent households and entering the home ownership sector. The level of home ownership has decreased significantly among younger age groups. According to the Housing and Land Survey, the sharpest fall of the home ownership rates was observed for the 25–34 age cohort between 1983 and 1993: for households headed by 25–29-year-olds from 24.9 per cent to 13.1 per cent, and by 30–34-year-olds from 45.7 per cent to 31.7 per cent (see Figure 4.1). The property bubble and the associated house price inflation in the latter half of the 1980s comprised one of the main reasons behind the decrease in young homeowners. Even after the bubble burst, the level of home ownership did not recover but decreased further to 11.3 per cent for the 25–29 age group and to 28.8 per cent for the 30–34 age group in 2013. Despite the house price deflation, the shift in the labour market to 'casualisation' and accompanying income instability have placed barriers to marriage and purchasing homes for young people. The decline in the home ownership rates for younger groups has inevitably led to an increase in the proportion of those living in rented housing. As will be discussed, the supply of public rented housing as well as corporate-based employee housing has been reduced. There has, therefore, been a notable and continuous increase in the rates of private rented housing among young households; between 1983 and 2013 from 53.2 per cent to 77.1 per cent for the 25–34 age groups and from 33.5 per cent to 61.6 per cent (see Figure 4.1).

Although the level of home ownership for younger households has declined, the average level of home ownership for all households has hovered

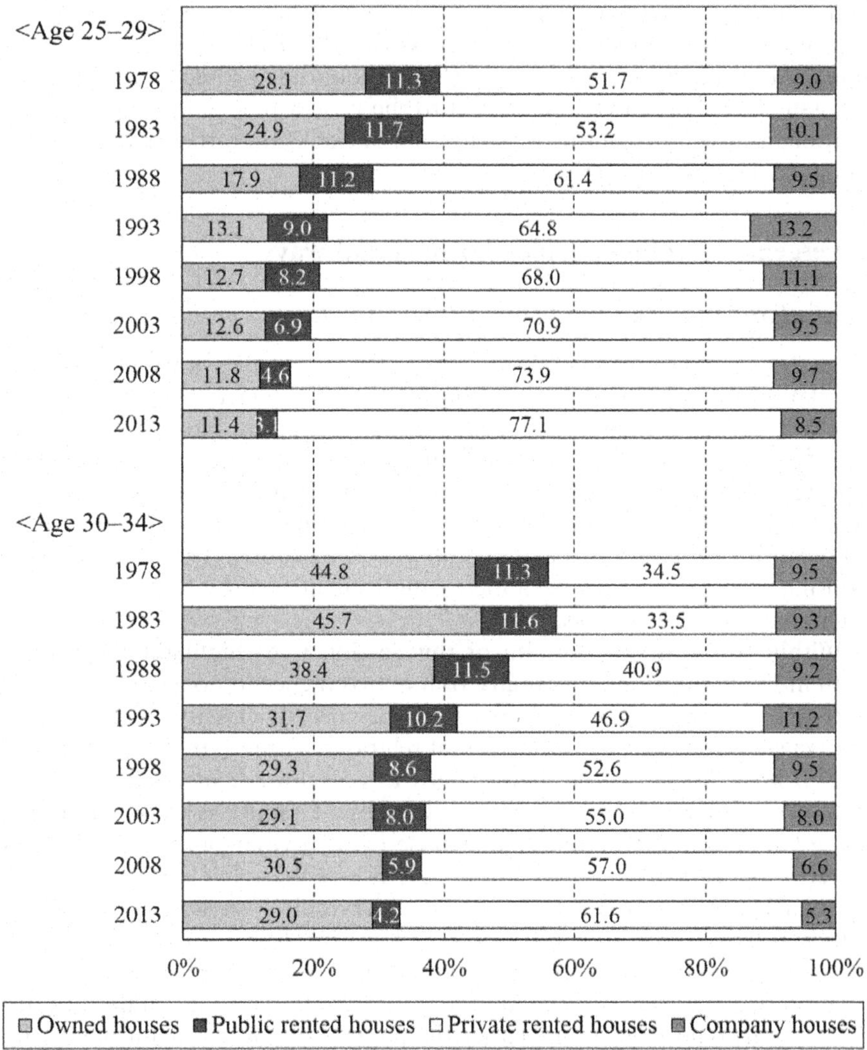

Figure 4.1 Changes in housing tenure by age of household head (1978–2013)

Source: Author's calculations from Housing Survey of Japan; and Housing and Land Survey of Japan.

around 60 per cent. This is because of an increase in the proportion of the older population having higher home ownership levels. Owner-occupation has continued to be the dominant housing tenure, whereas younger groups have been the main casualty of the post-bubble socio-economic downturn in terms of access to home ownership. The post-war housing and family systems that propelled young people to establish an independent household and acquire an owner-occupied house provided them with the promise of entering mainstream society. In other words, the decline in young people's opportunities to attain home ownership has not only brought about a housing issue but also represents a threat to the post-war social promise, where housing is now representing a mechanism of exclusion rather than inclusion in the post-growth society.

Divergence in young people's housing pathways

Vertical and horizontal individual-family relations

Then, how can we examine divergence in young people's housing pathways in relation to changes in mature home-ownership societies? Family-owned housing sectors in many developed countries including Japan have become less dominant, together with a decline in young people's moves towards getting married and accessing home ownership. This has radically reorganised the boundaries separating owning and renting in terms of determining who can access home ownership and who is excluded. The foundation of housing systems has thus been increasingly challenged by fragmentation in young people's life-courses.

Within this context, the aim of this section is to highlight the role of both individualisation and familisation in divergence in housing and family patterns. It introduces an analytical framework of classifying individuals by focusing on vertical and horizontal relations within families (Hirayama, 2017). Individuals can be divided into those who are married and those who are unmarried with respect to horizontal family relations and into those living in parents' homes and those living away from parents' homes in regard to vertical family relations (see Figure 4.2). The family system in pre-war Japan was organised around the hierarchical vertical ties between a father as patriarchal authority and his older son. In contrast, the post-war family institution started to place importance on the horizontal, conjugal relationship between a husband and a wife. Many existing studies of family relations tend to examine either the parent-child dyad or husband-wife relations. What we are interested in is combining the dynamics of horizontal and vertical family relations in exploring family changes. With the classification that we propose here, four distinctive types of individuals are observed: unmarried people living independently, unmarried people living in parental homes, married people establishing their own independent households, and married people co-residing with parents (see Figure 4.2).

Statistical data concerning the composition of individual types for young people aged 25–29 and those aged 30–34 in Japan are illustrated in Figure 4.3. As shown, the largest category is the group of individuals who are married and independent of parents' homes. This reflects the post-war reorientation of the family system in which many people left parental homes and established their own nuclear households. The proportion of married individuals

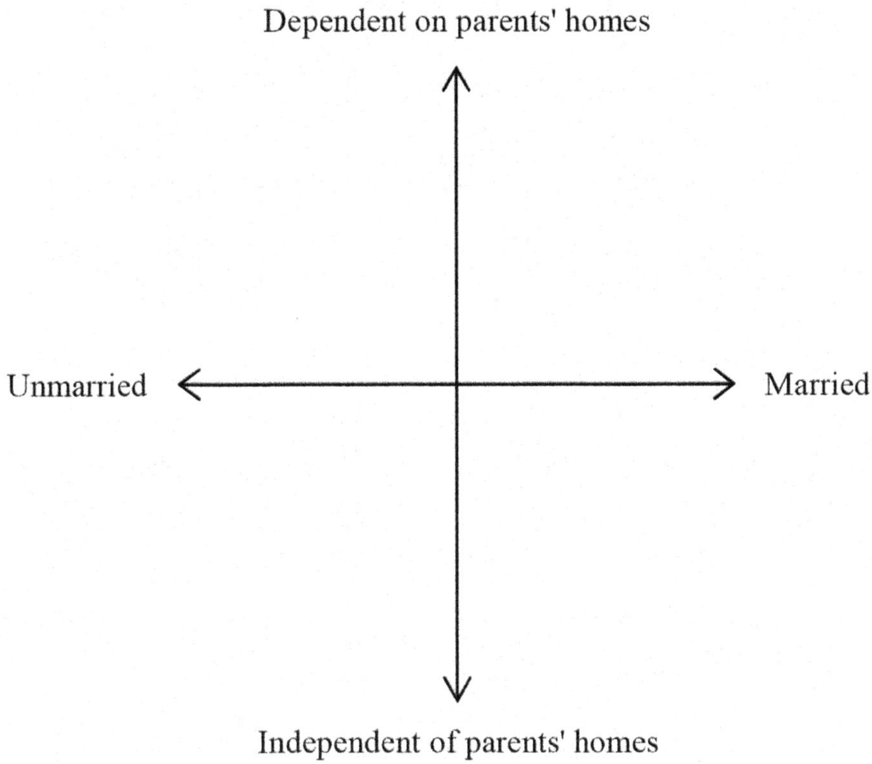

Figure 4.2 Vertical and horizontal individual-family relations

living away from the parental home for the 25–29 age group is much lower than for the 30–34 age group, largely due to the lower marriage rates. Over the decades, the composition of young individuals' types has changed. The percentage of married individuals forming independent nuclear households decreased: from 33.3 per cent to 27.7 per cent for the 25–29 age group and from 53.1 per cent to 48.7 per cent for the 30–34 age group between 1995 and 2010. At the same time, a rise has been witnessed among individuals remaining single. Unmarried people are far more likely to live in the parental home than to live independently. This is particularly noticeable for the late twenties group compared to the early thirties group. Following the classification of individuals with vertical and horizontal family relations as variables, we will explore the housing condition of each individual type in turn.

Explaining parental home dwellers

An increase in parental home dwellers – unmarried adults living in their parental home – has been a new and growing trend in the housing context.

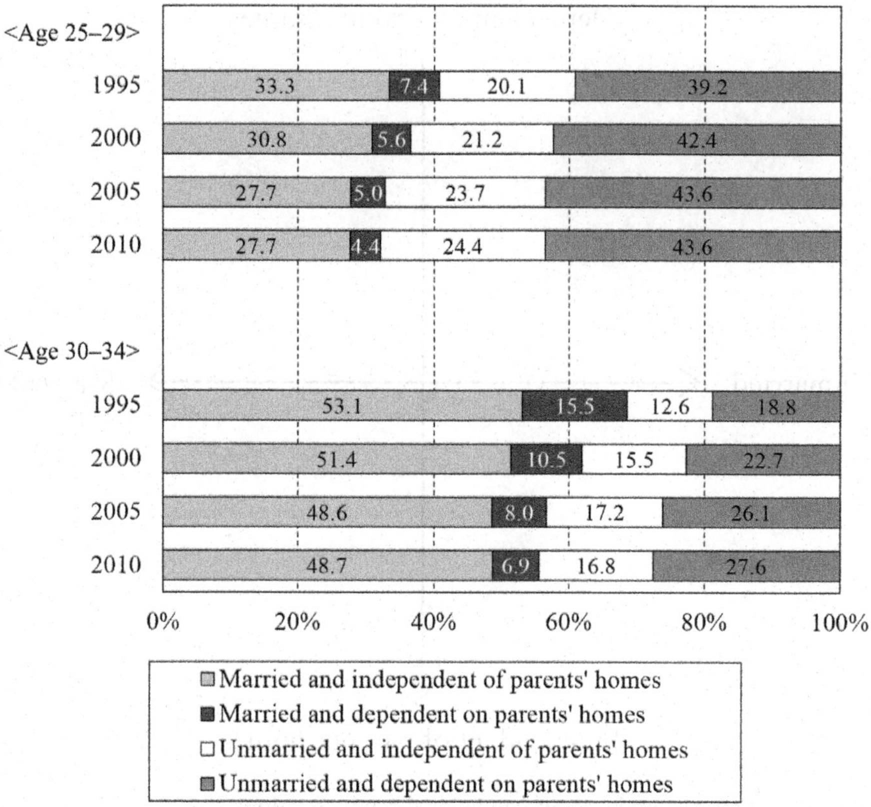

Figure 4.3 Marital status and relationships with parents' homes (1995–2010)

Source: Author's calculations from Population Census of Japan.

The percentage of parental home dwellers increased from 39.2 per cent in 1995 to 43.6 per cent in 2010 for the 25–29 age group. The figure during the same period rose from 18.8 per cent to 27.6 per cent even among older individuals aged 30–34 (see Figure 4.3). The increase in unmarried people dependent on the parental home implies both individualisation and familisation. The formation of the individualised life-course model is reflected in an increase in those who either delay marriage or never get married, while the contrasting force of familisation can be observed in adults' prolonged dependence on parental resources in the form of co-residency.

As the rapid increase in the number of unmarried adults who continue to live in the parental home is a new phenomenon, how to explain it is a matter of debate not only in academic circles but also in the popular discourse. The extension of adult transitions such as remaining in higher education for longer has a knock-on effect on the timing of marriage and subsequent household formation. According to the School Basic Survey, partly reflecting low fertility, over 50 per cent of the current youth population enter higher education and the majority of universities offer four-year degree programmes. In Japan, it is also not uncommon for students to spend extra years preparing to enter a university of their choice. However, the extended period spent on higher education alone does not provide a sufficient explanation for the increase in unmarried adults dependent on their parents' homes. Early research on parental home dwellers in the first half of the 1990s originally highlighted affluent parents over-protecting their adult children (Miyamoto et al., 1997). It was in the period of the aftermath of the bubble economy that initial images of young adults living at the parental home were constructed – including notions of these individuals indulging themselves in the consumption of luxury goods and receiving free accommodation, meals and laundry services without bearing any household expenses. Yamada (1999) labelled parental home dwellers 'parasite singles' and explicitly highlighted their dependent behaviours. This label was rapidly popularised and provided a trigger provoking 'parasite bashing' in popular discourse in which young adults, often university graduates, living in parental homes were reproached for their dependency (Kitamura, 2001).

In the late 1990s when the post-bubble recession had deepened, the labour market deregulation started in alignment with the introduction of neoliberal policy. This resulted in the casualisation of the employment market, particularly affecting younger groups. Within this context, the instability of socio-economic and policy circumstances surrounding younger people became a subject of research, and many scholars launched into more evidence-based explanations for the youth dependency (for example, Nagase, 2002; Miyamoto, 2004; Shirahase, 2005). A survey on young adults living in their parents' homes conducted by the National Institute of Population and Social Security Research (2001) found that many parental home dwellers were neither idle nor lazy; rather, their wages were insufficient to establish an independent household. Various surveys on unmarried adults also revealed that the rates of non-regular employees were much higher among those who lived with parents than for those who lived independently (Iwagami, 1999; Ohishi, 2004; Hirayama and Kawata, 2015). In the period of high growth, those on employment seldom fell into poverty. Since the 1990s, however, along with economic downturn and the deregulation of employment practices, the 'working poor' has increased in number since the 1990s, which has been especially noticeable for younger groups (Goishi, 2011). Even Yamada (2004), who originally introduced the term 'parasite singles' and emphasised their reluctance to become independent, started arguing the importance of economic stagnation to explain young people's delay in leaving home. The extension of adult transitions is indeed not only attributed to the personal preferences of individuals but also to the structural transformation of social, economic and policy conditions.

The delay by younger generations in starting their own independent households has been assumed to derive from shifts in people's attitudes towards marriage. According to a survey periodically conducted by the NHK Broadcasting Culture Research Institute, the rates of those who answered 'it is a matter of course to get married' and 'it is a matter of course to have children' decreased from 45 per cent and 54 per cent in 1993 to 33 per cent and 39 per cent in 2013, respectively (Takahashi and Aramaki, 2014). The rates were much lower for younger respondents. It is necessary, however, to look at not only the change in people's attitudes towards marriage but also the economic condition when examining factors behind the increase in parental home dwellers. The Employment Status Survey in 2012 revealed that the percentage of unmarried men aged 25–34 in regular employment was 52.1 per cent, while the figure for those in non-regular employment was much higher at 79.9 per cent. Regardless of young people's attitudes, financial and psychological barriers are often imposed on those on precarious non-regular employment in regard to getting married and establishing an independent household.

Some researchers have attempted to explain the 'parasite' phenomenon as a reflection of a cultural value unique to Japan. It is not unusual for parents to provide well for their children, which in turn hinders their transitions to independence (Miura, 2005; Yamada, 1999). However, increases in the number of parental home dwellers are seen not only in Japan but also in many other countries (Forrest and Yip, 2013; Holdsworth and Morgan, 2005; Newman, 2012). East Asian countries have commonly undergone notable increases in the number of unmarried adults living in parental homes. The rates of parental home dwellers in southern European countries have been much higher than those of Japan and are increasing even more, while in Western European countries and Anglo-Saxon societies, where only a small number of parental home dwellers have traditionally existed, the numbers have more recently started to rise. In many societies, neoliberal policy reforms and the associated deregulation of labour markets have commonly undermined the economic security of younger generations, resulting in the increases in unmarried adults who have delayed leaving home. It is thus reasonable to attribute the increase in Japanese parental home dwellers to the broader global economic transformation rather than to domestic cultural specificity.

Furthermore, Japan's tenure-biased housing policy, which has concentrated on driving the growth of home ownership, has accounted for the increase in parental home dwellers (Hirayama, 2012). For Mulder (2006), home ownership oriented housing systems tend to delay marriage and the establishment of families. It is likely that young individuals who wish to leave home to establish their own households need affordable rented housing before entering home ownership markets. The housing system that focuses on expanding owner-occupied housing sectors, however, tends to neglect developing other tenure sectors. In Japan, the limited number of public rented dwellings available for young households without priority need, the generally low quality of private rental housing in terms of floor space and amenities, and the high rents for privately rented dwellings have effectively combined to discourage young people from leaving their parents' homes. Moreover, the retrenchment of housing policy in line with neoliberal prescriptions has meant less public assistance for younger cohorts to acquire housing. Many young people have sought to secure housing in the private rented housing market only to find it difficult to access adequate and affordable accommodations to live.

Young adults living in the parental home have rested on a particular form of intergenerational family reciprocity. The reorientation of labour and housing policies towards a neoliberal course has particularly affected younger cohorts in terms of securing employment and housing. Meanwhile, within the framework of post-war housing policy with emphasis on promoting home ownership, the current parents' generation has acquired their own relatively spacious homes, enabling the younger generation to live with them. In addition to an increase in unmarried adults who have continued to live in the parental home for long periods, there has also been an increase in 'returners' who could not sustain their independent household due to job loss or income reduction and then returned to the parental home (Hirayama, 2013). As Furlong and Cartmel (1997) suggest, movements in adult transitions typically go back and forth between dependent and independent status. The parental home thus plays a role in anchoring, protecting and providing for adult children in their transitions.

The Big Issue Japan Foundation, a non-profit organisation that helps homeless people rebuild their lives, collaborated with housing researchers in conducting a 2014 survey on 1,767 unmarried individuals aged 20–39 with very low incomes (below 2 million yen (16,000 euro [1 euros = 125 yen, May 2017]) annually) (Hirayama and Kawata, 2015). The findings revealed that parental homes sheltered a number of young people who could not live independently. Of respondents living in the parental home, the percentages of unemployed people, those with a history of mental illness, and those who do not expect future marriage were 42.8 per cent, 28.5 per cent, and 93.0 per cent, respectively. The survey also revealed that 18.0 per cent of the respondents were 'returners'.

Beck (1992) argued that risk societies tend towards individualisation in welfare provision by weakening the role of family institutions. The increase in the number of unmarried adults living in the parental home has, however, implied that parent generations have increasingly supported offspring generations suffering from unstable employment conditions in terms of securing housing. Paradoxically, the individualisation of young people on precarious employment has stimulated the familisation of providing them with places to live. Such vertical family reciprocity based on home ownership has arguably functioned as a buffer against a decline in social stability (Hirayama, 2013). With neoliberal policy reforms, a notable decline in secure regular employment for younger people has been perceived as a potential factor for social destabilisation. However, intergenerational support relations, which have protected unmarried individuals, have mitigated the influence of policy changes on younger cohorts. In other words, family resources linked to home ownership have assumedly underlain and underpinned the implementation of the neoliberal measures, substituting for the regulatory and provisional state functions for the labour market and housing.

Exploring one-person households

An increase in the number of unmarried people living on their own demonstrates more structurally proceeding individualisation in adult transitions. This is a smaller group compared to parental home dwellers, but another category in which an expansion has been observed. Between 1995 and 2010, the percentage of unmarried people independent of parental homes increased from 20.1 per cent to 24.4 per cent for the 25–29 age group and from 12.6 per cent to 16.8 per cent for the 30–34 age group (see Figure 4.3). The figure is higher for men than for women, reflecting the gender-based difference in marriage rates.

This group of unmarried people living away from parents' homes consists mainly of single people who form one-person households. Within the framework of the home-ownership-centred housing policy, single people have been consistently disadvantaged and marginalised in the housing system (Hirayama, 2003, 2012; Hirayama and Izuhara, 2008). The government has explicitly encouraged family households to secure housing and access home ownership while mostly excluding one-person households (see Chapter 1). The eligibility for low-interest loans provided by the GHLC was not extended to include single-person households until the 1980s. One-person households have not been a client group for public housing. Taxation, social security and corporate welfare systems have also been structured around the 'male breadwinner family' model, effectively marginalising unmarried individuals. The neoliberal policy reforms have particularly affected the housing circumstances of single people. The 2007 dissolution of the GHLC has forced many housing purchasers to procure mortgages from private financial institutions. Unlike the government, which excludes one-person households through housing policy measures, the private mortgage lenders do not discriminate against single people. Nevertheless, marital status is clearly correlated with credit status in post-growth Japan. Many family households on stable employment and with secure incomes have access to the housing-loan market, whereas an increasing number of low-income single people on unstable employment cannot enjoy the benefits of the more open mortgage market.

As argued, the level of private rented housing among younger groups has markedly increased. This is particularly noticeable for one-person households. According to the 2013 Housing and Land Survey, the percentage of private renting among one-person households aged 25–34 was very high at

83.8 per cent. Dwellings of this type have often been considered temporary places for young people before they move up their housing careers. Therefore, the government has not invested significantly in improving the private rental sector. Nevertheless, increasing numbers of people who remain single continue to live in private rented housing for longer periods. Home ownership is closely linked with marriage in Japan, while those who continue to be unmarried tend not to be on stable employment. Many single people therefore have almost no prospect of moving up a housing ladder to achieve home ownership.

It is also important to look at gender-based differences in housing preferences among unmarried people. Of unmarried individuals, women are more likely to be parental home dwellers compared to men. According to the 2010 Population Census, the proportion of the number of unmarried parental home dwellers to that of unmarried people forming one-person households for those aged 25–34 was 1.79 times for men and 2.55 times for women. This suggests that unmarried women tend to continue to live in their parents' homes until marriage; i.e., they do not tend to leave home to become independent singles. This tendency has often been regarded as culturally 'natural'. In addition, young females are more often employed if they agree to commute from their parental home. This reflects and reinforces the tendency by unmarried women to remain as parental home dwellers. However, economic reasons behind the gendering of housing preferences should not be overlooked. The incomes of single female households are considerably lower than those of single men largely due to their labour market status. Nevertheless, single women tend to pay higher rents than single men in private rental situations (Hirayama, 2012). This suggests that single women in urban areas place importance on central locations for short commutes, crime-free environments and high-quality amenities. Therefore, it is assumed that single women, who require dwellings that meet particular conditions and have higher rents despite lower incomes if they choose to become independent, tend to remain in the parental home. This arguably accounts for the difference in the proportion of parental home dwellers to one-person households between genders.

Nuclear families purchasing housing

Individuals who left the parental home and established their own independent households have traditionally occupied the dominant position in society but have been decreasing in number (see Figure 4.3). A couple with dependent children used to be regarded as a 'standard' family type in post-war Japanese society. With the rapid transformations in household patterns, however, the ratio of single-person households had already exceeded that of standard nuclear family households by the mid-2000s (see Chapter 1). This raises critical questions about whether such nuclear family households can still be considered 'standard' in post-growth society, and whether and how the link between the standard family and home ownership can be maintained.

Unlike their single counterparts, young individuals who have established nuclear households are more likely to ascend the housing ladder towards home ownership. However, economic burdens imposed by purchasing housing have become heavier within the context of post-bubble economic decline (for a full discussion, see Chapter 2). As a result, the means of nuclear family households to access home ownership have become more diversified. In many cases, male incomes alone are no longer sufficient to purchase a family home in the post-growth society, which has clearly undermined the sustainability of the 'male breadwinner family' model. Accordingly, an increasing number of married couples have begun to form a dual-earner household in order to enter the owner-occupied housing market. Alternatively or alongside, many households increasingly receive financial support from parents in purchasing a first home. This means that both horizontal and vertical family relations have begun to play a more important role in responding to the changes in the home ownership economy. Contemporary nuclear households are noticeably different with regard to the way they finance home ownership (Hirayama, 2017; see also Chapter 5 for more discussion).

The participation of married women in the workforce is an increasingly pervasive household strategy in accessing home ownership (Hirayama and Izuhara, 2008; Izuhara 2016). The 'male breadwinner family' model was pervasive in post-war society. However, the continued economic stagnation has weakened the stability of male employment, and this has consequently promoted a decrease in household incomes and a resultant increase in the number of married women entering the paid workforce. As the economic burdens of purchasing housing have become heavier, many women have increasingly been expected to earn substantial incomes. Transformations in the home ownership economy have thus made it more rational for married couples to form horizontally cooperative dual-earner households so that they can acquire owner-occupied houses. In addition, the income levels of both husbands and wives have become determinants of whether the household can enter the home ownership market and whether they can purchase a quality accommodation. Households with a husband on high income and a full-time working wife are most likely to be able to purchase high-class housing in terms of size and specs, whereas households with couples both in non-regular employment are likely to acquire dwellings at low prices or to remain in the rented sector for longer periods.

Inter-vivo asset transfers also provide important means for encouraging married adult children to enter property ownership (Hirayama, 2013). Although nuclear family households are independent in appearance, in fact they have been increasingly dependent on parental financial support in purchasing houses. The current older households had become considerably wealthier than their previous or subsequent cohorts (see Chapter 6 for more details), whereas younger cohorts are facing more stagnated economic conditions. Many families have thus become more concerned with strategies of accumulating and managing assets across generations (Izuhara and Forrest, 2013). Moreover, the government explicitly facilitates intergenerational asset transfers with the intention of stimulating the economy through tax concessions. In response to the economic downturn caused by the 2007/08 GFC, gift tax in cases where parents financially assist their children in purchasing and renovating housing were substantially reduced. The housing conditions of young households in the future will thus be partly determined by the parental resources. This indicates that owner-occupied housing no longer represents the rite of young people's passage to complete independence gained fully by their own incomes. Access to home ownership has increasingly become a family project rather than a project of independent nuclear households.

Rediscovering extended families

Family change in post-war Japan was primarily characterised by an increase in nuclear family households and a decrease in extended family households. Following the fundamental reform of various family-related laws, the increase and dominance of nuclear households symbolised the democratised family system (Matsubara, 1969; Morioka, 1993). This has corresponded to a decline in co-residency, i.e., a living arrangement where elderly parents typically live with the oldest son and his family. The percentage of married people who lived in parental homes decreased between 1995 and 2010 from 7.4 per cent to 4.4 per cent for the 25–29 age group and from 15.5 per cent to 6.9 per cent for the 30–34 age group (see Figure 4.3).

However, an increase in the number of nuclear households did not necessarily mean a decline in the institution of the stem families (Ando, 2004; Ito, 1994; Ochiai, 1994). Many people who were born in the 1920s and 1930s had a considerable number of siblings. They moved from rural areas to large cities immediately after the end of the Second World War and then established their own independent households because conventionally only one child, often the eldest son, was able to succeed the family. Urbanisation and the traditional family system were thus the reasons behind the expansion of nuclear households in urban areas. Despite the persistence of the institution of stem families, the system of nuclear families appeared to replace it. For Ochiai (1994), the actual increase in the number of nuclear households did not mean any significant change in the family system but rather effectively concealed the sustainability of the institution of the stem families.

Moreover, Kato's research (2005, 2009) on changes in Japanese families demonstrated that during the post-war period the system of extended families did not decline substantially. Young married couples tended to live away from parents' homes immediately after they got married, which was statistically evident (see Figure 4.3). According to Kato's analysis, however, when couples became older, some of them chose to return to live in parental homes. From the end of the Second World War to the period of high-speed economic growth, the decrease in the rate of young married couples who lived in parental homes prompted many researchers to highlight the rise of the post-war nuclear family system. This reflected not only statistical evidence but also many post-war scholars' aspirations to a democratic, modern society. However, Kato emphasised that the rate of middle-aged couples who lived together with their ageing parents has been sustained at a certain level and argued that the traditional family norms had not necessarily declined. The rate of married people who live in the parental home has decreased among younger age groups but has hovered at around a little less than 20 per cent for middle-aged people (Hirayama, 2017).

Forming an extended family household is practical in terms of intergenerational succession of family residence. Kato (2009) pointed out that the main reasons for a considerable number of middle-aged couples to live in parental homes are to care for elderly parents and also to inherit land and housing from them. Older households maintain home ownership partly to bequeath the assets to their children. According to the Survey on People's Attitudes towards Land Issues conducted by the Ministry of Land, Infrastructure and Transport in 2008, approximately half of the respondents who wished to own land and housing expressed the intention to bequeath assets to their offspring as the main reason. Meanwhile, it has become more difficult for the younger generation to acquire home ownership due to the potential financial burden imposed by mortgage repayments. This has led a considerable number of children who reached middle-age to move back to their parents' homes with the prospects of inheriting properties. The system of late-forming extended families has thus been closely connected to the system of housing inheritance.

In addition to co-residency, near-residency, where elderly people live in close proximity to their adult children, now represents another version of the preservation of the traditional stem families (Ohtsuki, 2014). In many cases, co-residence and living nearby provide a structure to facilitate informal care exchange between the generations. Unlike co-residency, which is mostly formed between elderly parents and their oldest son (and his family), near-residency arrangements can be observed between older parents and their daughter (and her family). There is an emotional advantage in forming parents-daughter near-residency, as young mothers find it easier to rely on their own parents than in-laws for help with childcare and other domestic chores. It is assumed that many young couples prefer near-residency to co-residency as a contemporary inter-generational living arrangement, avoiding any conflicts while maintaining privacy and lifestyles. As elderly parents become older and frailer, however, near-residency arrangements, particularly between parents and their oldest son, may switch to co-residency by the son's family moving into his parents' house.

The Japanese government, which has been led by the LDP during most of the post-war period, has tended to encourage the maintenance of extended families (see Chapter 5 for more detailed discussion). Many conservatives consider the institution of stem families to be essential in preserving the nation's social, cultural and value systems. The policy to facilitate co- and near-residency has more recently been further strengthened within the context of the super-ageing population and falling fertility rates. This arguably reflects, not necessarily directly, the concept of the 'Japanese-style welfare society' in the late 1970s, where family reliance with property ownership was expected to play a key role in developing Japan's welfare approach (see Chapter 1). The growing elderly population and lowered birth rates have prompted the government to expand various social policies to sustain older people's livelihood and recover fertility. The government's fiscal conditions have, however, deteriorated to an unprecedented crisis level. Therefore, the LDP and government bureaucrats have increasingly encouraged vertically cooperative relations within families in caring for elderly people and children.

Young people and urban change

Divergence in young people's housing pathways and family formation patterns has not only facilitated changes in their life-course but also increasingly accelerated divisions in urban space (Hirayama, 2013). In post-war Japan, as in many other developed societies, urban planning reflected the 'male breadwinner family' model and drove the development of suburban residential estates for emerging nuclear families (Miura, 1999). With the home-ownership-centred housing system, young people were expected to form an independent nuclear household and to eventually acquire a single-family home, often in a suburban 'new town' (Sumita, 2015). During the period of high-speed economic growth, there were strong aspirations for young families to follow the conventional life-course. Within this context, the landscape of suburban single-family housing estates was a symbol of the post-war mainstream society. However, with entering the post-growth phase of development, the life-course of young people has been increasingly diversified with a decline in marriages and thus in the number of conventional nuclear households. The fragmentation of urban space is another outcome of the shift in family patterns, weakening the foundation of post-war urban planning.

Both parental home dwellers and single people forming one-person households are unmarried individuals, but their residential locations are completely polarised, which has accelerated divisions in urban space and in their lived experiences (see Figure 4.4). An increase in the number of parental home dwellers has been observed in fringe areas in particular (Hirayama, 2013). In the urban peripheries, employment opportunities and rental housing properties are scarce, whereas owner-occupied homes owned by older parents are relatively spacious. This has accounted for high rates of parental home dwellers in the peripheries. In various 'parasite bashing' discourses, unmarried adults living in parents' homes were assumed to be the best customers for trendy boutiques and expensive restaurants, since they were considered able to spend all their disposable income on themselves (Miyamoto et al., 1997; Yamada, 1999). However, such perceptions were not evidence-based. Many unmarried adults who continue to live in parental home are casual workers with low wages. Moreover, in peripheral and suburban areas where parental home dwellers tend to reside, the everyday landscape can be far from fashionable.

In contrast to single parental home dwellers, many single-person householders live in central urban areas. The extent to which residential locations concentrate on specific areas is much higher for single-person households than for single parental home dwellers. Most young singles place importance on central locations for convenience and short commutes when making their residential choice. As a result, single-person households tend to be concentrated in urban centres. In addition, city central areas are more likely to offer rental accommodations suitable for single occupancy, which acts as a magnet to attract young singles.

Young single households are, however, not necessarily welcomed by local municipalities and long-term residents who have firmly established their roots in the neighbourhood (Hirayama, 2013). In Tokyo, for example, an increasing number of ward municipalities have begun to impose restrictions on the development of *one-room mansions* (medium-rise complex consisting of one-room studio flats) with the intention of controlling the supply of such compact units attracting single residents (Kinoshita et al., 2008). A considerable number of single people who move into metropolitan wards do not register themselves in the ward office and thus the ward municipality cannot levy the resident tax on them. In some wards where the percentage of single-person households is extremely high, local municipalities seek to shift the composition of household-types to achieve a healthy balance. Many municipalities in fact prefer owner-occupied families to single renters in light of maintaining quiet, safe and cooperative communities. These are some of the reasons behind the ward municipalities' policy to restrict the further construction of *one-room mansions*. In Toshima Ward, one of the eight central wards in the Tokyo Metropolitan area, where one-person households account for more than half of all the households, the municipality started to tax multi-family housing blocks comprised of small size dwellings in 2004, aiming to reduce the provision of units to single people. Moreover, behind the restrictive policy there is an implicit or even explicit prejudice against single-person households. Residents in *one-room mansions* are often assumed to have irresponsible behaviours in terms of controlling noise and litter despite little evidence to support such claims. There has been, however, a continuous increase in single-person householders moving into central city neighbourhoods. Although the new development of *one-room mansions* is being restricted, a large number of existing rental properties still accept single-person households.

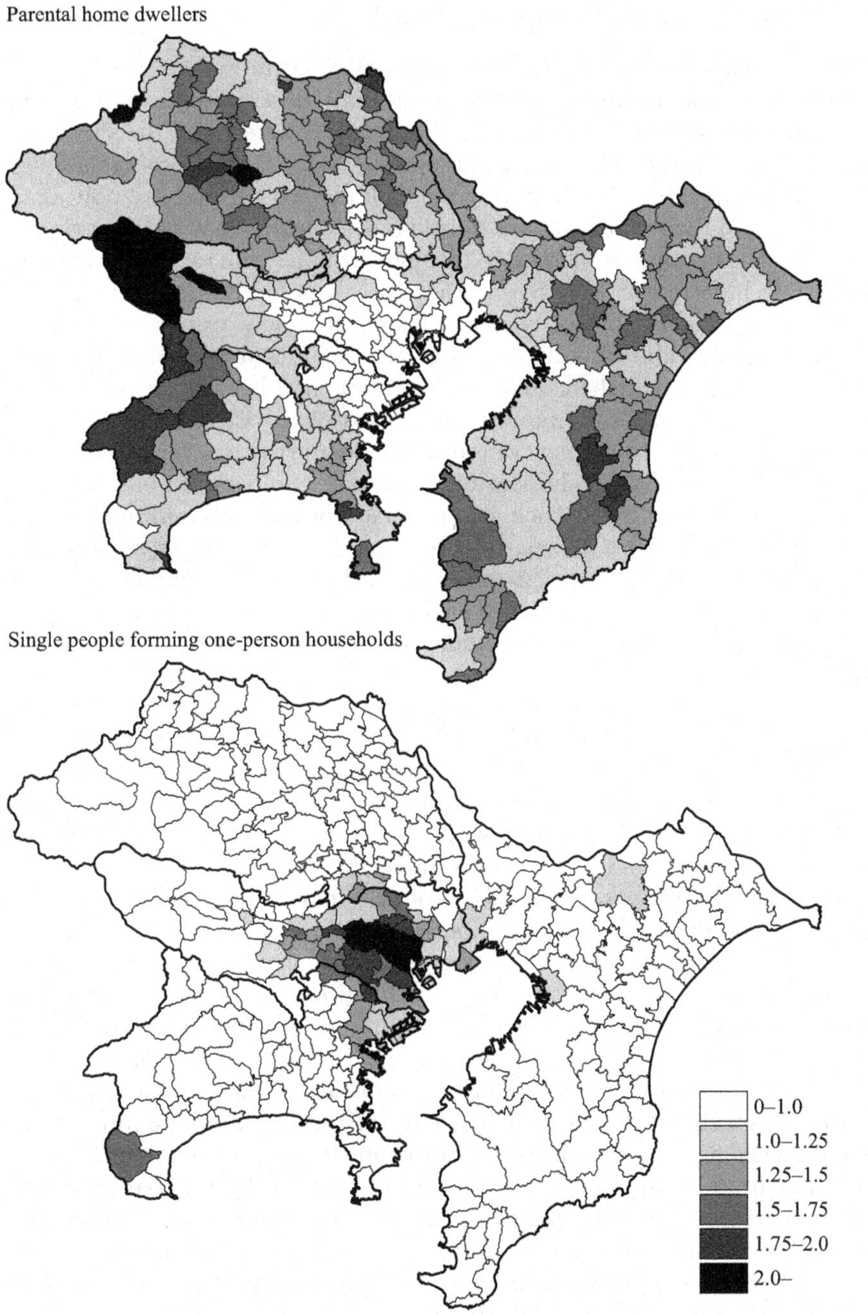

Figure 4.4 Specialisation coefficient of parental home dwellers (aged 25–34) and single people (aged 25–34) forming one-person households, Tokyo Region (2005)

Note: Specialisation coefficient is calculated by dividing the share of a given group of a given group of a given municipality by the share of the group of the whole Tokyo region.

Source: Author's drawing based on 2005 Population Census of Japan.

The suburbs were developed for nuclear families in the era of economic growth. With the beginning of the post-growth phase, however, the decline in the formation of new nuclear families has translated into the shrinking and ageing of these suburban communities. Many baby-boomer families who moved into the suburbs during the high growth period have now aged *en masse*, and their children have moved out. As a result, while the proportion of elderly people is increasing throughout cities, the rate of increase is noticeably high in the suburbs. Furthermore, a notable increase in vacant houses and vacant plots of residential land is a new feature of changes in suburban neighbourhoods (Kubo et al., 2015; Miura, 2012; Yoshida, 2010). Owning a detached, single-family home had been the aspiration of many salary men and their families in the post-war society (Miura, 1999), but for the current young generation in the post-growth society, such aspirations do not exist strongly because increasing numbers of households of more contemporary types (such as one-person households and dual-earner households) tend to prefer apartments located in city centres to detached houses in the suburbs. The demand for suburban single-family homes, and thus suburban residential estates as a whole, is therefore predicted to decline even more, further shaking the foundation of Japan's post-war mainstream society.

Conclusion

The housing system in post-war Japan led many nuclear families to acquire their own homes, underpinning the creation and maintenance of a home-owning democracy. With the transition to the post-growth era, however, socio-economic changes, along with neoliberal policy reforms, have encouraged divergence in young people's housing and family patterns. This chapter looked at the role of the combination of individualisation and familisation in dividing housing paths and family formation patterns into unmarried parental home dwellers, single people living in private rented dwellings, nuclear households purchasing houses, and parent-child co- or near-residency. This disparity among younger generations in terms of shaping life-courses has resulted in a new challenge to the traditional foundation of the home-ownership society centred on independent nuclear households.

Fragmentation in young people's housing and family patterns has reshaped the contours of social inequalities by reorganising boundaries separating owning and renting in terms of helping determine who can acquire owner-occupied housing and who cannot. An increasing number of those remaining unmarried whose employment and income are unstable are not likely able to enter the owner-occupied housing market, while even married couples who purchase houses, unless they earn high incomes, are confronted with heavy burdens imposed by mortgage repayments. Moreover, the housing and asset conditions of younger households will partly be determined by whether their parents own residential properties, whether they can inherit the parental home, and whether they can receive financial support from their parents in purchasing a house. This means that younger generations in the post-growth age are less independent in regard to acquiring home ownership and accumulating assets. As discussed in Chapter 1, the way in which family wealth is distributed over generations has become more definitive in expanding inequalities in the post-growth era. The housing system during the high-growth period was a mechanism of granting the promise of home ownership and associated social inclusion. However, this is no longer the case in the new era of the post-growth society. Post-war social contracts centred on property ownership are thus now under threat.

Finally, it is important to look at government responses to changes in young people's housing conditions. The combination of individualisation and familisation has accelerated divergence in housing pathways. However, housing policy is noticeably biased, where various measures supported familisation but not individualisation. The government has increasingly encouraged parents to financially assist their children in accessing property ownership while seeking to maintain the system of extended families by facilitating co- and near-residency. There is a growing ideological view that the familisation of housing issues is rational in sustaining a post-growth society: specifically, by stimulating the economy, supporting young people in securing housing, improving older people's living conditions, and alleviating the decline in fertility (see Chapter 5 for a full discussion). On the other hand, government policy that has been discriminately inclined towards familisation is expected to further expand social inequalities. Single-person householders are remaining in private rented housing with little expectation of improving their housing situations, while parental home dwellers on low or no incomes have almost no prospects of leaving home and acquiring independent housing. Individualisation and familisation in younger generations combined with the government's characteristically biased responses are thus restructuring social inequalities.

References

Ando, Y. (2004) Kazoku to raifukosu no henka [Changes in the family and life-courses], in H. Shimizu, K. Mori, M. Iwagami and M. Yamada (eds.) *Kazoku Kakumei [Family Revolution]*, Tokyo: Kobundo, 76–85.

Arnett, J. J. (2000) Emerging adulthood: A theory of development from the late teens through the twenties, *American Psychologist*, 55(5), 469–480.

Arnett, J. J. (2006) Emerging adulthood in Europe: A response to Bynner, *Journal of Youth Studies*, 9(1), 111–123.

Beck, U. (1992) *Risk Society: Towards a New Modernity*, London: Sage.

Beer, A. and Faulkner, D. (2011) Housing over the life course: Housing histories, careers, pathways and transitions, in A. Beer, D. Faulkner, C. with Paris and T. Clower (eds.) *Housing Transitions Through the Life Course: Aspirations, Needs and Policy*, Bristol: The Policy Press, 15–37.

Beer, A., Faulkner, D., with Paris, C. and Clower, T. (2011) *Housing Transitions Through the Life Course: Aspirations, Needs and Policy*, Bristol: The Policy Press.

Campos, B. C., Yiu, C. Y., Shen, J., Liao, K. H. and Maing, M. (2016) The anticipated housing pathways to homeownership of young people in Hong Kong, *International Journal of Housing Policy*, 16(2), 223–242.

Ellin, N. (1996) *Postmodern Urbanism*, Cambridge: Blackwell.

Filandri, M. and Bertolini, S. (2016) Young people and home ownership in Europe, *International Journal of Housing Policy*, 16(2), 144–164.

Forrest, R. and Hirayama, Y. (2009) The uneven impact of neo-liberalism on housing opportunities, *International Journal of Urban and Regional Research*, 33(4), 998–1013.

Forrest, R. and Yip, N-M. (eds.) (2013) *Young People and Housing: Transitions, Trajectories and Generational Fractures*, London: Routledge.

Furlong, A. (ed.) (2010) *Handbook of Youth and Young Adulthood: New Perspectives and Agendas*, London: Routledge.

Furlong, A. and Cartmel, F. (1997) *Young People and Social Change: New Perspectives* (2nd edition), Buckingham: Open University Press.

Goishi, N. (2011) *Contemporary Poverty: The Working Poor*, Tokyo: Nihon Keizai Shinbunsha.

Hirayama, Y. (2003) Housing and social inequality in Japan, in M. Izuhara (ed.) *Comparing Social Policies: Exploring New Perspectives in Britain and Japan*, Bristol: Polity Press, 151–171.

Hirayama, Y. (2012) The shifting housing opportunities of younger people in Japan's home-owning society, in R. Ronald and M. Elsinga (eds.) *Beyond Home Ownership: Housing, Welfare and Society*, London: Routledge, 173–193.

Hirayama, Y. (2013) Housing and generational fractures in Japan, in R. Forrest and N-M. Yip (eds.) *Young People and Housing: Transitions, Trajectories and Generational Fractures*, London: Routledge, 161–178.

Hirayama, Y. (2017) Individualisation and familisation in Japan's home-owning democracy, *International Journal of Housing Policy*, 17(2), 296–313.

Hirayama, Y. and Izuhara, M. (2008) Women and housing assets in the context of Japan's home-owning democracy, *Journal of Social Policy*, 37(4), 641–660.

Hirayama, Y. and Kawata, N. (2015) Jakunen, mikon, teishotokuso no kyoju jittai ni tsuite [Housing conditions of young, unmarried, low-income people], *Nihon Kenchiku Gakkai Keikakukei Ronbunshu [Journal of Architecture and Planning]*, 80(716), 2303–2313.

Hirayama, Y. and Ronald, R. (2008) Baby boomers, baby busters and the lost generation: Generational fractures in Japan's homeowner society, *Urban Policy and Research*, 26(3), 325–342.

Holdsworth, C. and Morgan, D. (2005) *Transitions in Context: Leaving Home, Independence and Adulthood*, Berkshire: Open University Press.

Ito, T. (1994) *Seikatsu no Nakano Jinkogaku [Demographics and People's Lives]*, Tokyo: Kokon Shoin.

Iwagami, M. (1999) Niju-dai, sanju-dai mikonsha no oya tono dobekkyo kozo [The research about unmarried people in their twenties and thirties co-residing with own parents in Japan], *Jinko Mondai Kenkyu [Journal of Population Problems]*, 55(4), 1–15.

Izuhara, M. (2016) Towards individualising couple finance: Women's housing assets and housing decisions in Japan, *Gender, Place & Culture*, 23(7), 1003–1016.

Izuhara, M. and Forrest, R. (2013) 'Active families': Familisation, housing and welfare across generations in East Asia, *Social Policy and Administration*, 47(5), 520–541.

Jencks, C. (1977) *Language of Postmodern Architecture*, London: Academy Editions.

Kato, A. (2005) "Chokkei kazoku kara fufu kazoku he" ha honto ka [Is "from stem families to couple oriented families" true?], in S. Kumagai and K. Okubo (eds.) *Kohoto Hikaku niyoru Sengonihon no Kazokuhendo no Kenkyu [Comparative Cohort Analysis on Family Changes in Postwar Japan]*, Tokyo: Nihon Kazokushakai Gakkai Zenkoku, Kazoku Chosa Iinkai [Committee on National Family Survey, Japan Society of Family Sociology], 130–154.

Kato, A. (2009) Chokkei kazoku no genzai [Contemporary stem families], *Shakaigaku Zassi [Journal of Sociology]*, 26, 3–18.

Kinoshita, R., Ohtsuki, T. and Fukami, K. (2008) Tokyo niju-san ku ni miru wan rumu manshon mondai to taiou sesaku no hensen ni kansuru kenkyu [One-room mansion problems and policy responses in Tokyo twenty-three ward municipalities], *Nihon Kenchiku Gakkai Keikakukei Ronbunshu [Journal of Architecture and Planning]*, 73(624), 263–270.

Kitamura, A. (2001) Seijin mikonsha no rika to oyako kankei [Unmarried adults, home leaving and family relations], *Life Design Report*, 7, 22–45.

Kubo, T., Yui, Y. and Sakaue, H. (2015) Aging suburbs and increasing vacant houses in Japan, in M. Hino and J. Tsutsumi (eds.) *Urban Geography of Post-Growth Society*, Sendai: Tohoku University Press, 123–145.

Mackie, P. K. (2016) Young people and housing: Identifying the key issues, *International Journal of Housing Policy*, 16(2), 137–143.

Mathews, G. and White, B. (2004) *Japan's Changing Generations: Are Young People Creating a New Society?*, London: Routledge.

Matsubara, H. (1969) *Kakukazoku Jidai [The Era of Nuclear Families]*, Tokyo: Nihon Hoso Kyokai [Japan Broadcasting Corporation].

McKee, K. (2012) Young people, homeownership and future welfare, *Housing Studies*, 27(6), 853–862.

Mínguez, A. M. (2016) Economic crisis and the new housing transitions of young people in Spain, *International Journal of Housing Policy*, 16(2), 165–183.

Miura, A. (1999) *Kazoku to Kofuku no Sengoshi [Post-War History of Family and Happiness]*, Tokyo: Kodansha.

Miura, A. (2005) *Karyu Shakai [Low Class Society]*, Tokyo: Kobunsha.

Miura, A. (2012) *Tokyo ha Kogai kara Kieteiku [Disappearing Suburbs in Tokyo]*, Tokyo: Kobunsha.

Miyamoto, M. (2004) *Posuto Seinenki to Oyako Senryaku [Post-Youth Period and Family Strategies]*, Tokyo: Keiso Shobo.

Miyamoto, M., Iwagami, M. and Yamada, M. (1997) *Mikonka Shakai no Oyako Kankei [Family Relations in Unmarried People Society]*, Tokyo: Yuhikaku.

Morioka, K. (1993) *Gendai Kazoku Hendo Ron [Contemporary Family Change]*, Kyoto: Mineruva Shobo.

Mulder, C. (2006) Home ownership and family formation, *Journal of Housing and the Built Environment*, 21(3), 281–298.

Nagase, N. (2002) Jakunenso no koyo no hiseikika to kekkon kodo [Marriage timing and the effect of increase in non-standard employment among the youth in Japan], *Jinko Mondai Kenkyu [Journal of Population Problems]*, 58(2), 22–35.

National Institute of Population and Social Security Research (2001) *Setai nai Tanshinsha ni kansuru Jittai Chosa [Survey on Parental Home Dwellers]*, Tokyo: National Institute of Population and Social Security Research.

Neitzel, L. (2016) *The Life We Longed for: Danchi Housing and the Middle Class Dream in Postwar Japan*, Portland: Merwin Asia.

Newman, K. S. (2012) *The Accordion Family: Boomerang Kids, Anxious Parents, and the Private Toll of Global Competition*, Boston: Beacon Press.

Nishiyama, U. (1989) *Sumai Kokon Gaku [Contemporary Housing History in Japan]*, Tokyo: Shokokusha.

Ochiai, E. (1994) *Nijuisseiki Kazoku he [Family Change Towards the 21st Century]*, Tokyo: Yuhikaku.

Ohishi, A. (2004) Jakunen shugyo to oya tono dobekkyo [Young people's employment and their living arrangements with parents], *Jinko Mondai Kenkyu [Journal of Population Problems]*, 60(2), 19–31.

Ohtsuki, T. (2014) *Kinkyo [Near-Residency]*, Kyoto: Gakugei Shuppansha.

Osawa M. (1993) *Kigyo Chushin Shakai wo Koete [Beyond the Company Society]*, Tokyo: Jijitsushin.

Ronald, R. and Alexy, A. (eds.) (2011) *Home and Family in Japan: Continuity and Transformation*, London: Routledge.

Ronald, R. and Hirayama, Y. (2009) Home alone: The individualisation of young, urban Japanese singles, *Environment and Planning A*, 41(12), 2836–2854.

Shimazaki, N. (2008) *Raifukosu no Shakaigaku [Sociology of Life-Courses]*, Tokyo: Gakubunsha.

Shirahase, S. (2005) *Shoshi Korei Shakai no Mienai Kakusa [Invisible Inequalities in Low Fertility, Aged Society]*, Tokyo: Tokyo University Press.

Sumita, S. (2015) *Gendai Nihon Haujingu Shi: 1914–2006 [Modern Housing History in Japan: 1914–2006]*, Kyoto: Mineruva Shobo.

Takahashi, K. and Aramaki, O. (2014) Nihonjin no ishiki, yonjunen no kiseki [The trajectory of Japanese attitudes over forty years], *Hoso to Chosa [Broadcasting and Research]*, July, 2–39.

Toivonen, T. (2013) *Japan's Emerging Youth Policy: Getting Young Adults Back to Work*, London: Routledge.

Waswo, A. (2002) *Housing in Post-War Japan: A Social History*, Richmond: Curzon Press.

Yamada, M. (1999) *Parasaito Shinguru no Jidai [The Time of Parasite Singles]*, Tokyo: Chikuma Shobo.

Yamada, M. (2004) *Parasaito Shakai no Yukue [The Future of Parasite Society]*, Tokyo: Chikuma Shobo.

Yokoyama, F. (2002) *Sengo Nihon no Josei Seisaku [Public Policy for Women in Post-War Japan]*, Tokyo: Keiso Shobo.

Yoshida, T. (2010) *Kogai no Suitai to Saisei [The Decline and Rejuvenation of the Suburb]*, Kyoto: Koyo Shobo.

5 Fertility and housing

Policy rhetoric and reality

Introduction

Women are one of the central concerns of post-growth society. In many ways, the role of women in contemporary societies is fluid and tends to shift in response to the transformation of existing socio-economic systems. For example, in terms of labour market participation, women have been considered particularly useful to capital as a 'reserve army of labour'. In times of economic boom and labour shortages, women were often brought in to fill the gap and then become subsequently disposable during a period of economic downturn, compared to their male counterparts (see Bruegel, 1979). Such labour market approach is indeed highly linked to both family system and welfare regime. In many developed economies during the early post-war period, for example, the social system and the labour market were organised around the male-breadwinner family model (Lewis, 2001; Blossfeld and Drobnič, 2001). Japan was not an exception in this approach (Osawa, 2007; Kumazawa, 2000). The role of women was defined predominantly in the private sphere of families, while the male heads of household were engaged in paid work outside the home and earned the 'family wage' (Land, 1980).

In the current post-growth climate, the Japanese government is now promoting the discourse of '100 million all active society'. In order to maintain the population of 100 million for the next 50 years and thus to boost the nation's stagnated fertility rates, the policy rhetoric is to encourage 'everyone' – implicitly and explicitly referring to women – to be *active* in all spheres of the family, workplace and community. It was in the early 1990s when the burst of the bubble economy triggered redefining the role of women. Under this discourse, however, their role is inevitably further stretched. Women are now expected to participate in both private and public spheres, in particular, paid work, reproduction and care for dependent children and older family members as counter measures to the downward economic and demographic trends.

One of the critical issues associated with post-growth society is very low fertility. Japan as well as many other East Asian societies including Singapore and South Korea is at the forefront of such global demographic phenomenon. The decline in fertility shocked Japanese society in the mid-1970s, recording a total fertility rate (TFR) of 1.58, which was lower than the historically low rate in 1966, the year of *hinoeuma* [Fire Horse] driven by the superstition based on the horoscope (considered bad luck for girl babies born in that year) (Sato, 2008). Since then, a slow but steady decline has been recorded reaching as low as 1.26 TFR in 2005, which is significantly lower than the population replacement rate of 2.1. Under the current Administration, a strategy to tackle such very low fertility is strongly featured in their official documents (for example, *Shoushi-ka taisaku taikou* [The outline of the countermeasures for low fertility society] (Cabinet Office, 2015). The key words in the policy document emphasise the promotion of 'marriage', 'reproduction', 'child-friendly' as well as 'child-rearing-friendly' society, and it proposes a holistic approach to tackling the issues involving different sectors of society (the state, companies, communities and individuals) and addressing in the different stages of people's life-course.

This chapter uses housing as a lens to explore women's issues, especially issues emerging from their multiple roles of work, reproduction and care in the post-growth society. Housing and gender are a relatively under-explored field of social policy compared to other social policy areas such as social security, social care, employment and education (Kennett and Chan, 2011). Housing policy itself is often considered as a 'wobbly pillar' of the welfare state in home-ownership societies like Japan and the UK since housing is more likely to be provided in the private domain (see Torgersen, 1987). Gender issues tend to be absent or concealed in the contemporary housing debates in terms of access, affordability and asset level because it is often 'households' not 'individuals' which are used as a unit of measurement in statistics (Hirayama, 2014; Izuhara, 2015). The activities of the heads of the households usually matter, and they are not always but often men.

In Japan, women's access to housing is indeed typically sought through the male heads of household, as described in the traditional saying '*On'na wa sankai ni i'e nashi*' [Women do not own a house across their three-life stages], indicating their lack of rights and status as a daughter, a wife and a mother. Such gendered social norms translate into gendered institutional structures, which in return influence and constrain women's choice and access to housing. In this context, women are often treated as dependent: once married, they become part of the husband household; and if unmarried or divorced, they remain or revert back to the original (parental) household. Therefore, women appear in housing statistics and debates only if they are the heads of household. This explains why contemporary housing debates involving women are dominated by issues of single-female households such as lone-mothers' housing poverty; single career women purchasing a condominium unit alone; and care and housing for older widows (e.g. Ronald and Nakano, 2013). In order to fill the gap in knowledge and understanding, this chapter instead explores housing issues of partnered women of reproductive age.

The aims of this chapter are two-fold: First, post-growth society is typically a divided society. Many spheres of society (by employment status, income levels and marital status) are now partly polarised and increasingly unequal between households. It is thus to examine how post-growth social characteristics have produced new and differentiated processes and outcomes of women in housing situations. Second, it investigates to what extent policy rhetoric around housing in the post-growth context are effectively addressing the nation's fertility agenda in relation to reconciling family and work. Many of the discussions to follow in this chapter are concerns of women in their reproductive age. This is an important stage in their life-course when a significant expansion of home ownership traditionally occurs with increasing real incomes and seniority in the work place. It is also a period in which other key life-course transitions such as family formation and transition to parenthood may occur, which will require major housing decisions. The chapter begins with locating women in the family and welfare systems in order to ascertain how the women's housing situations have derived. It then moves on to examine the relationship between work, family and housing in women's life-course. The main part of the chapter investigates the link between fertility and housing and how current (housing) policy attempts to address fertility issues. The analysis of alternative approaches to address gender issues in housing will conclude the chapter.

The family model and the myth of housewifery

The transformation of the marriage-based family system is a cause and a consequence of post-growth society characterised as a decline and delay in marriage, low fertility and societal ageing. The male-breadwinner family model based on marriage and clear gender roles within the family and society was promoted in the post-war period. In post-growth Japan, however, the shift away from the conventional family model can be explained as both structural constraints and women's increasing agency. While women have become freer from traditional expectations of the gender roles in contemporary society, it is also evident that the labour market structures and income insecurity in the current economic climate place significant barriers in front of young adults' prospects for family formation. Such shifts have remarkable implications on women's housing choice and access.

What has underpinned the patterns of marriage and female employment is the gendered welfare state based on the 'family as a unit'. The male-breadwinner family model is typically described as 'standard male employment trajectories, offering high replacement benefit rates with marriage-based benefits for women' (Ostner, 2003). Institutionalised gender roles in the family and society have thus a major influence on the status of women as individuals. Under the family-as-a-unit system, strong norms in the social contract involving rights and responsibilities were conjugal collectivity rather than individual autonomy (see Izuhara, 2016). Considering the advantages which were brought to women, the strong notion and values of housewifery had been developed in post-war Japan. Housewives, compared to single women or working mothers, had a high status in the economic growth period. Social security and fiscal policy provided married women with financial protection and certain advantages. Class 3 state pension category is a case in point since it benefits housewives without any additional contributions by themselves or their employed husbands. In the corporate-centred society, the male income alone was also sufficient to support the nuclear family households. Emphasising the role of women as a wife and a mother, the traditional value of '*ryōsai kenbo* [good wife, wise mother]' is still alive and well in contemporary Japanese society more than Chinese societies in the region influenced by the Confucian doctrine. Compared to Japan, for example, rates of female labour participation are higher in Hong Kong and Taiwan among women of reproductive age (see Figure 5.1). Koyama (2013) argues, however, that the notion of 'good wife, wise mother', which is often considered to be the traditional Confucian value, is in fact a modern construct. According to Koyama (2013), the ideology has a European root based on the new role of women in the second half of the nineteenth century, which made a notable contribution to the formation of the modern state. Unlike the common understanding, the concept was therefore associated with views of the qualities desirable in women in 'modern' Western societies.

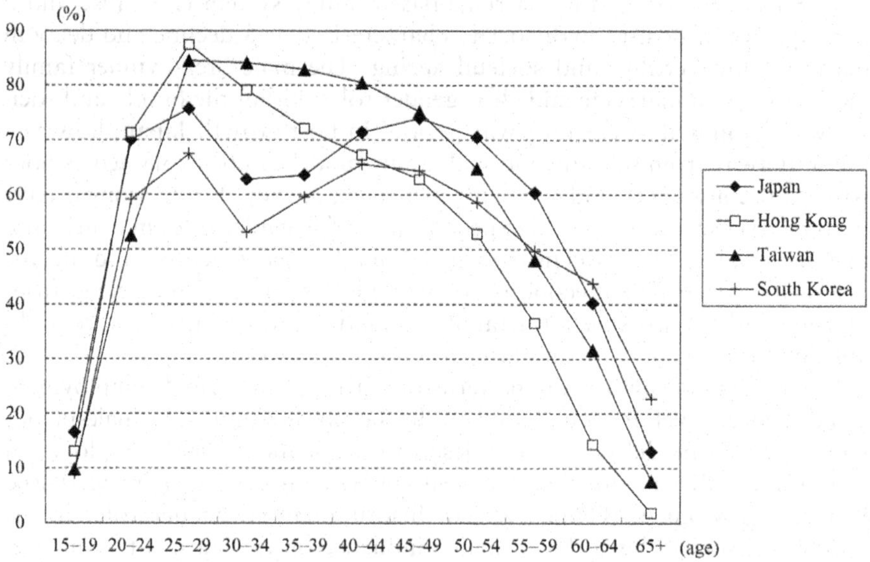

Figure 5.1 Female labour force rates by age in East Asia (2006)

Source: Ministry of Health, Labour and Welfare, World Health, Labour and Welfare 2009.

Such a value of being a housewife still remains strong among some younger women in post-growth Japan, despite the diversification of the female life-course and growing opportunities. According to the panel data on the attitudes of unmarried women aged between 25 and 34 towards work, marriage and reproduction, for example, Tanaka (2015) observed the mixed responses of women regarding their career and marriage prospects. There were strong divides in their views according to four different clusters: (1) clerical employees; (2) family-focused/housewives; (3) career/professional orientation and (4) non-regular/service employees. It is somehow predictable that aspiration for housewife is strong among working women in clerical position (*ippan-shoku*) compared to those on the management track (*sogo-shoku*). Their choice of employment in the first place could be a reflection of their aspirations towards home or career under the dual employment systems in Japan. Such job categories for women themselves are peculiarly Japanese, dividing women into different career trajectories since the mid-1980s. In order to eliminate gender-based discrimination in the workplace and to promote women's social participation, 'Equal Employment Opportunities' first came to effect in 1986 with subsequent revisions in 1997 and 2007. Differentiated job categories were then created by corporations to provide a small number of women with more opportunities to progress their career, while retaining the majority in supplementary (clerical) positions. At the same time, a series of deregulations were introduced to the then paternalistic Japanese labour market, allowing more flexibility and diversification of the workforce. With a combination of further industrial restructuring and the prolonged recession placing significant pressure on male job security and incomes, such reforms promoting women's equal employment opportunities have therefore resulted in drawing women into the increasingly casualised labour market as the non-regular workforce (Kumazawa, 2000). For example, although the bottom of the classic M-curve (the lower rates of employment participation among women in their thirties) has risen from 58.8 per cent in 2000 to 67.6 per cent in 2010 for women aged between 30 and 34, however, more than a half (54.7%) of all female employees were concentrated in non-regular employment (Ministry of Internal Affairs and Communications, 2010) (see Figure 5.2). Such stratification in female employment leads to income and wealth divisions between households, resulting in differentiated housing outcomes (see for example, Tachibanaki and Sakoda, 2013).

The existing male-breadwinner family model in relation to collective and conjugal solidarity and gender divisions of labour, however, increasingly contradicts with wider socio-economic changes and the reality of families in post-growth Japan. According to a recent National Fertility Survey, there was a widening gap in the views among young single women between their 'ideal' life-course and the 'likely' life-course. While 19.7 per cent of the female sample still aspired to follow the conventional 'housewifery' life-course model, however, only 9.1 per cent thought that they would realistically

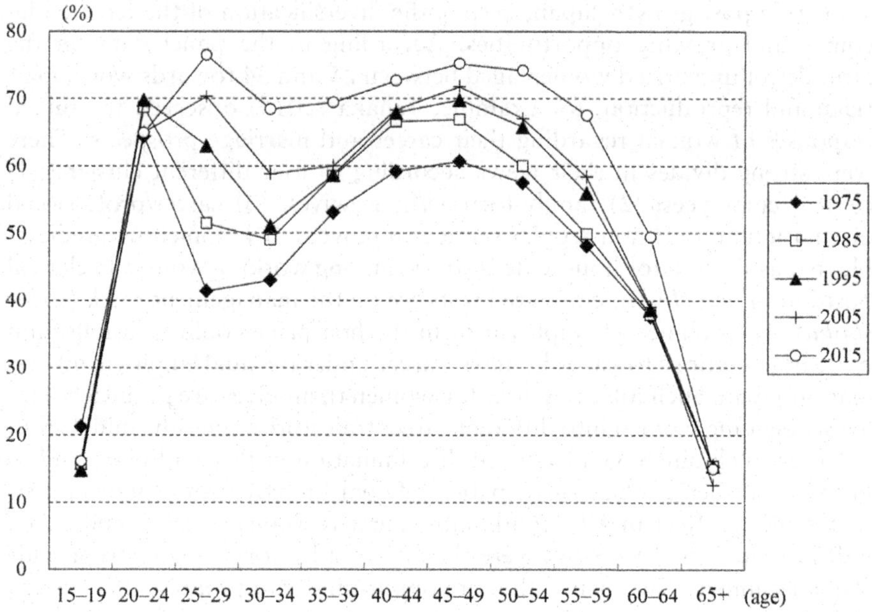

Figure 5.2 Female labour force rates by age in Japan (1975–2015)

Note: Labour force rates = proportion of employees and completely unemployed in the total population aged 15 and over.

Source: Author's calculations from Labour Force Survey.

be able to achieve it (National Institute of Population and Social Security Research, 2011). Instead, over a third of the sample predicted that their life-course would be more like the 'return-to-work' model, resuming paid employment often after their youngest child reach the school age. A considerable proportion (17.7%) of the female sample thought that, although a small minority (4.9%) aspired to the ideal, they would continue to work without getting married, reflecting the current demographic trends. A significant demographic shift taking place therefore suggests that the conventional system is no longer realistic or sustainable to support women's lives. Moreover, Shimazaki (2008) argues that there still exists a salient paradox between such demographic shift and a rigid conformity of the social systems to realise a true diversification of the women's conventional life-course model. For example, many people no longer form a conventional family household at an expected point in their life-course. According to the Population Census, 34.5 per cent of women aged 30 and 34, 23.1 per cent aged 35 and 39, and 10.6 per cent aged 50 and over remained unmarried (including divorced and widows) in Japan in 2010 (See also Chapter 1). Almost a third of those unmarried women aged between 25 and 34 were living with their original family in 2010 and this rate had doubled from 15 per cent in 1980 (Ministry of Internal Affairs and Communications, 2010). Some 70 per cent of unmarried women in their early thirties lived with their parent(s). High educational attainment and labour market participation among women are considered to have increased their capacity to live without a male breadwinner, while reducing the available pool of appropriate partners for marriage (Raymo and Iwasawa, 2005; Shirahase, 2007). More recent research, however, found that high-earning potential of women with post-secondary education acts as an advantage for marriage (Fukuda, 2009).

The nexus of marriage, work and home ownership

Before we examine the link between housing and fertility, it is worthwhile investigating women's life-course in post-growth society. While marriage and subsequent family formation are likely determinants for the entry to the home ownership sector, becoming a homeowner tends to push women out to the labour market. When their entry to home ownership coincides with a period of child-rearing, it results in women in taking up multiple roles in 'the family, workplace and community'.

Since neoliberal policy trends have become particularly influential in reshaping work and housing systems and opportunities in post-growth Japan, the state places even more emphasis on individual and family to be responsible for many spheres of their lives including housing access and child care (see for example, Forrest and Hirayama, 2009). What is highly relevant to such post-growth characteristics is that women and marital status represent another dimension of widening social inequalities. In the recent economic climate, full-time employment is an important variable for men to get married, while married households are more likely to be able to access better quality housing and home ownership. Also, partnering of those with similar status is increasingly the case at both high- and low-income groups. This is a clear departure from the stable male breadwinner with full-time housewife model. Although a small minority, men in high income brackets are more likely than men on low income to marry women equally in high income brackets, which further contributes to a widening of income inequality among households (Otake, 2000). Such double income couples can inevitably access home ownership earlier compared with unmarried individuals or couples with unstable employment and low incomes. Securing home ownership then often leads to having the first and subsequent children.

The home ownership rates of women are strongly linked to their marital status in Japan. It is partly because marriage often represents household stability in employment and income. However, it is also largely policy driven since the post-war housing policy has consistently been targeted to new 'families', supporting nuclear families to access home ownership through low-interest, long-term loans provided by the GHLC and public housing provided by the JHC, as discussed in Chapter 1. In the era of economic growth, new families took advantages of the policy measures as stepping stones to achieve home ownership. Single people have been largely excluded from such state initiatives. The eligibilities for the government housing loans were extended to include single households over the 1980s and 1990s, while such eligibilities for public housing units started including single-elderly households in 1980. However, in reality, mortgage provisions to single people had been limited before the closure of the GHLC. Social housing still tends to exclude single people apart from single older persons.

Married women are more likely to live in an owner-occupied house, although tenure and legal ownership are not necessarily in concert (Izuhara, 2016). Limited data are available on women's tenure patterns and housing asset levels as individuals, not at the household level. For example, the survey of women and material assets (based on 2,205 female sample aged between 25 and 54) in the mid-2000s revealed a very conservative picture that marriage provided women with a strong advantage to access home ownership (Institute for Research on Household Economics, 2006; Hirayama and Izuhara, 2008). Married women were more likely to live in an owner-occupied house compared to their unmarried counterparts. The average rate of home ownership was 55 per cent for married women across all age bands, while the rate was as low as 8 per cent among unmarried women. The home ownership rates increased with age, which was in line with the national trend. The home ownership rates were 52 per cent for women aged 35 and 39 and went up to 65 per cent among those aged 45 and 49; while rates were 12 per cent and 17 per cent for unmarried women in the respective age bands. It is thus evident that marriage largely buys women a residential home and women climb up the housing ladder through marriage, not as individuals (Hirayama and Izuhara, 2008).

When you observe the relationship between home ownership and patterns of female labour market participation, owner-occupied women are more likely to have paid employment. For the current reproductive generation, incomes earned from the labour market are still important means to access home ownership in Japan. In the advanced post-growth society, however, it is predicted that intergenerational transfers of housing assets may contribute more substantially to wealth acquisitions of the future generations (see Chapter 6). Current homeowners are in general much more likely to have purchased their residence or had their house built with their own incomes using housing loans rather than to acquire it through inheritance. For married couples who have been the dominant clients in the housing market, 'using their own means' is usually meant through 'male' incomes. According to the survey which distinguished wives' contributions from their household finance, the male heads of households were often identified as ones who financed their home purchase. For example, while the majority (96%) of households who purchased or had their house built used mortgages, housing loan repayment was almost exclusively the responsibility of husbands

(90%) (Institute for Research on Household Economics, 2006; Hirayama and Izuhara, 2008). The financial credibility based on regular employment has been the key to access the mortgage market and such financial credentials were usually granted to regular male workers. There are many cases where wives contributed to mortgage repayment as the secondary earner of households, but they tend not to be formally responsible for a mortgage due to their lack of financial credibility (Izuhara, 2016).

Employment status of wives can also determine home ownership rates as owner-occupied women are more likely to be working (Hirayama and Izuhara, 2008). In the current post-growth economic climate, the working generation is on average experiencing a decline in real income, job security and thus heavier financial burdens compared to the previous generations in terms of the proportion of mortgage repayment from their disposable income. Many married women have been thus drawn into the labour market to boost their household income or to supplement the decline in male incomes. Mizutani (2013), for example, demonstrates the relationship between women's labour market participation and their housing tenure and the size of their mortgage. Rates of labour market participation by wives were higher among women in their thirties who owned a mortgaged house than those who rented. Among women aged between 35 and 39, employment rates of wives were 16 percentage points higher in the highest quarter group (based on the proportion of husband's income in mortgage repayment) (66.6%), compared to the lowest quarter group (50.2%). It is not conclusive whether the size of the mortgage was the determinant to draw wives into the labour market since the existence of young children tends to keep women away from paid work. However, the data revealed the prominence of financial contributions by wives to access home ownership in the current post-growth economic context.

Moreover, the ownership of individual assets within households can have significant impact of the autonomy and well-being of women, maintaining power relationship between couples as well as promoting individual agency within households. The ownership of assets by women can be important not only in case of divorce, protecting them financially, but also in order to influence household decisions in marriage (Deere and Doss, 2006). Considering the importance of female contributions to the mortgage repayment, however, the situation is often that married women live in a dwelling owned by their husband. Women's financial contributions are not necessarily reflected in the ownership. There are a few explanations for this gendered situation. First, historically, family households have collective attitudes towards home ownership in Japan. Such notion has been carried over from the pre-war patriarchal system as the ownership of land and intergenerational transfers of assets were firmly gendered in line of the first-son succession and organised around the continuation of family. Partly due to the recent trend of low fertility, more opportunities will be created for daughters to acquire assets through inheritance, if social norms do not supersede the legal definitions in practice regarding their rights to inherit an equal share. Second, there are institutional mechanisms which may deter women from having a share of home ownership (Izuhara, 2016). In the Japanese system, there is a clear link between regular earning, housing loans and legal ownership of properties. The practice of lending institutions expect a clear line of financial responsibility by individuals and thus requires a strict match, sole or proportioned, of mortgage holder with their property ownership. Proportions of financial contributions, either cash or loans, directly translate to the shares of property ownership. Any deviations are considered a gift which is subject to taxation. There are, therefore, interesting divides between the main income responsible for mortgages and supplemental incomes which tend to be spent on supplementary expenses such as children's extra curricula and holidays (Izuhara, 2015).

While marriage benefits women with their tenure patterns, another notable trend is the increasing number of unmarried women over the past decades. This is an important factor to analyse when we consider the role of housing in fertility patterns, given the emphasis of marriage in the female life-course. This provides another explanation why the standard family model in housing policy and provision is no longer relevant or applicable to a growing number of individuals. According to the Population Census, the proportion of conventional nuclear households, consisting of a married couple and their children, decreased from 40 per cent in 1985 to 26.9 per cent in 2015. Between 1980 and 2015, the rate of unmarried women instead rose from 24 per cent to 61 per cent for the 25–29 age group, and from 9.1 per cent to 34.67 per cent for the 30–34 age group, respectively (see also Figures 1.3 and 1.4 in Chapter 1). The ratio of unmarried women at the age of 50, who are defined as 'life-long never-married' in the Japanese statistical term, increased to 14.2 per cent by 2015. Such changes are particularly noticeable in urban areas. For example, in Tokyo in 2005 the rate of unmarried women was 43 per cent for the 30–34 age group; the rate of life-long never married women was 13 per cent; and the percentage of nuclear households was as low as 26 per cent. As a result, the combination of the family-orientated housing system and the increasing number of unmarried women has led to an inevitable increase in female individuals who struggle to make housing-related life-course transitions.

Since marriage and the formation of a new household are strongly connected in Japanese society, the decline in marriage often means a decline in new household formation. Some scholars (see Yamada, 2004) argue that the stagnated growth of new households among younger people is one of the reasons for the shrinking economy. Single women tend to remain residentially dependent on their parents, if not financially, in the form of co-residency. Intergenerational relations are complex in co-residency as flows of support are not necessarily one way from one generation to another but often reciprocal and mutually dependent. However, it is indeed the Japanese characteristic that unmarried individuals tend to remain at their parental home rather than forming an independent household in the private rental or home ownership sector (Hirayama, 2012; also see Chapter 4). An international comparison by Kawata and Hirayama (2010) highlight the tendency of unmarried women aged between 25 and 54 to live with their parents (60.3%). The equivalent rate was less than 10 per cent for Northern European societies such as 6.3 per cent in England and 4.4 per cent in Sweden. Even in the familial state of Italy, the rates were less than 50 per cent.

The role of housing in boosting fertility?

The previous sections clearly identified what marriage brings to women in terms of housing access and finance. This section considers what role housing can play in influencing women's fertility decisions. The analysis of the relationship between low fertility and socio-economic status of individuals and households is a common approach. Population studies tend to look at indicators such as educational attainments, employment status and incomes. For example, job insecurity and low pay often have negative effects on couples who wish to have a first or subsequent child in a period of recession. However, little is known or discussed about the link between housing policy and fertility (see, for example, Bernardi, 2005) including the role of housing in supporting or hindering fertility decisions of individuals and households. Demography interacting with housing is a two-way process: changing families such as household size create different demands for housing, while available housing stock and affordability issues in society or localities could dictate people's housing choices and thus facilitate or constrain their opportunities in family formation (see Mulder, 2006).

The availability of suitable and affordable housing can influence young people's transitions in the life-course, which include fertility decisions. It is well known that home ownership is connected to family formation as it tends to provide security and stability of home for families. In some Western European contexts, couples may feel it is important to secure housing of a 'certain quality' before they have children. Such quality often means single-family home and/or home ownership, as couples are more likely to have children after a move to such housing (Feijten and Mulder, 2002). An Italian case study, which is a society with a high rate of home ownership but with very low fertility, demonstrates a positive link between housing security and fertility intention. The more couples felt secure about their housing situation, the more likely that they positively considered having a first child (Vignoli et al., 2013). Tenure security can indeed increase chances of couples having children, especially in societies with a lack of regulations in the private rented sector and thus with high risks of eviction since owner-occupiers can control their housing conditions more easily.

Social norms appear to influence household decisions. In some cultures such as the familial home-owning regime of Italy, there is a perceived necessity to become a homeowner before forming a family. In Japan, taking one step backwards, home ownership is first and foremost connected to marriage; or, as discussed earlier, marriage almost acts as a prerequisite for people to access home ownership as evident in the fact that the home ownership rate among unmarried people are extremely low for men and women. Therefore, home ownership has been firmly embedded in the conventional family life-course as marriage tends to lead to children followed by home ownership, while becoming a homeowner leads to parenthood in societies such as Germany and the Netherlands (Mulder and Wagner, 2001). In this scenario, the low fertility can be a by-product of the stagnated entry to home ownership by the 30-something households. In Japan, however, marriage is a prerequisite of parenthood and having a first child may increase the probability of becoming a homeowner. In such cases, the stagnated entry to home ownership may not be a direct cause of the fertility decline. Instead, the stagnated rise of home ownership rates among the reproductive age group can be explained as the decline in people forming partnership leading to marriage as marriage and fertility are very strongly linked, together with insecurity in employment and income. These are clearly the drivers of low fertility.

Moreover, owner-occupied housing is often considered to be more suitable for families as it is often larger in size and in better quality than private or public rental accommodations. However, home ownership can decrease couples' chances of having a first or subsequent children due to the cost. In societies where parenthood comes after home ownership, households of the reproductive age may need to weigh their expenses across housing cost and the cost of having children among other competing financial pressures. Considering the limited financial resources, decisions over housing (mortgaged home ownership) and fertility (having children) may compete, especially in countries where access to high-quality housing in other sectors is not easy to achieve. For example, home ownership was associated with lower fertility in Britain in the 1990s (Hakim, 2003) and in France (Courgeau and Lelièvre, 1992). Indeed, home ownership is attached to key financial determinants such as housing price, income level and access to mortgage when home ownership provides stability in family life backed up by stable employment and income in the post-growth context. Dettling and Kearney (2014) estimated that a 10,000 US dollars increase in housing prices lead to a 5 per cent increase in fertility rates among homeowners as opposed to a 2.4 per cent decline among tenants in the US. Both becoming a homeowner and becoming a parent are not necessarily irreversible but require a long-term financial commitment with significant cost attached to it (see Mulder and Billari, 2010). It may be thus easier for younger families to have children in the social housing regime. However, in the post-growth context with widening inequality between haves and have-nots, financing home ownership and the cost of child-rearing are not necessarily mutually exclusive. It is more likely that those who can afford home ownership are likely to afford the cost of having children.

Women's income can also influence fertility decisions. Using the evidence from Hong Kong, for example, Yi and Zhang (2010) demonstrate rising male incomes have a strong positive effect on fertility, while rising female incomes have mixed outcomes – negative substitute effect and positive income effect on the demand for children. Among OECD countries, in Japan along with South Korea, gender wage gaps are the highest while the fertility rates are the lowest. There exist contested arguments whether rising female wage relative to that of males may encourage fertility (Apps and Rees, 2004). Women's high income indeed could affect fertility decisions in two opposite ways: increasing female incomes could raise the opportunity cost of working mothers leaving their employment to look after babies, while if it is high enough, they could purchase child care services in the market. However, within the East Asian region, it is puzzling that the gender pay gaps in countries such as Hong Kong and Singapore are level with those of developed Western societies but those countries are equally suffering from the very low fertility (Mryskyla et al., 2011). The level of disposable income appears to be an important variable for fertility decisions but not the only or the most important determinant.

As McDonald (2008) suggests, countries where home ownership is difficult to attain have the lowest fertility. Such micro-level personal decisions in households are usually shaped by the macro-societal-level factors including access to both housing market and financial market, the availability of social housing and the affordability in the private rented sector. Mulder and Billari (2010) define the 'difficult home ownership regime' as a combination of a high share of home ownership with low access to mortgages. In such regimes as Italy, Spain and Greece, access to home ownership may be constrained as households need to depend on personal savings and intergenerational asset transfers. When there is the lack of affordable, good quality rental accommodations, fertility rates tend to remain low. In Japan, and many other East Asian societies, access to home ownership has been difficult for the younger generation, although the fertility decisions among Japanese households may not rest predominantly on the access to home ownership as mortgage products are widespread and act as the major source of financing.

It is not just housing itself but the location and neighbourhood that also matter for young families. It may not be the sole reason to dictate the fertility decisions of households, but housing choice of households with children is often influenced by the built environment and the accessibility to relevant services. In order to raise the quality of life of young families, it is usually essential to choose appropriate environment to meet the needs of different stages in their life-course. According to a survey conducted among the thirty-somethings households with young children (Ministry of Land, Infrastructure, Transport and Tourism, 2008), there are a number of key indicators young families place importance upon: only 7.8 per cent of the respondents mentioned the size or layout of housing itself, while 24 per cent for safety and security measures at and around their house. While 11.6 per cent mentioned that access to kindergarten and primary schools was important, 10.5 per cent on interaction with neighbours and community. Other key elements included the availability of parks and spaces where children could play (8.9%) and good quality pavements (8.9%).

A gap between policy rhetoric and the reality

Despite the complex and multiple needs of young working women, the current housing policy measures by the Japanese government to boost the nation's fertility is firmly 'familial' – indeed the maintenance or revival of the traditional Japanese family model in housing and living arrangement. There is an importance of marriage as conjugal solidarity, which housing policy has promoted as women's access to home ownership in the post-war period. For boosting fertility in the contemporary post-growth society, policy is explicitly targeted at the promotion of co-residency, drawing on the intergenerational support of extended families to realise the national fertility agenda. Such policy initiatives, manifested in the neoliberal policy discourse of self-help and individual responsibility, are set to meet the dual purposes of utilising family support to care for children and ageing parents as well as encouraging female labour market participation. In this vein, there are a series of policy incentives at different levels, providing subsidies and tax incentives for those forming three-generation households and/or two households (older parents and their adult children) moving to live close to each other. For example, from 2016, the Ministry of Land, Infrastructure and Transport specifically promoted extended family living arrangements through subsidies and tax concessions for building or renovating eco-friendly accommodations suitable for the needs of contemporary multi-generation living. The Urban Renaissance Agency (former Urban Development Corporation providing public housing and new towns) started providing rent subsidies in 2013 to encourage family generations to reside nearby. There are plenty of other examples that exist in smaller scales at the local government level. The city of Kobe, for example, introduced a programme in 2013 to subsidise the cost of moves to form extended family living or living nearby.

Housing policy focussing exclusively on family resources especially in the traditional multi-generation living arrangements, however, may not produce positive outcomes for boosting fertility for a number of reasons (Hirayama, 2016). There is a significant implementation gap between the family-centred policy ideology and the reality of everyday life of contemporary families. First, family nuclearisation has been a long-term trend over the post-war period, partly instigated by home-ownership-centred housing policy. Three-generation households were partly a mode of survival in the past and once the society became more affluent with rising incomes and social security including pensions, nuclear family living gained in popularity. The number and proportion of elderly-only households have been steadily increasing.

According to the National Basic Life Survey, for example, over a half of the households with older members aged 65 and over were elderly-only households in 2013 (31% for elderly-couple households and 25.6% for single-elderly households). Second, the pro-family policy is not evidence-based as the attitudes of both younger and older generations tend not to express preferences of the revival of extended family living. An opinion survey on child-rearing in the family and communities, conducted by the Cabinet Office in 2013, for example, revealed that only 20.6 per cent of respondents mentioned three-generation co-resident as an 'ideal type of living arrangement'. Such rates were low at 14.9 per cent among male respondents in their thirties and even lower at 10.7 per cent among female respondents in the same age group. Instead, more positive attitudes were observed among thirty-something men and women in terms of living nearby their parents: 50 per cent of the male sample and 48.5 per cent of the female sample expressed their preference to live near their parents while maintaining their own household.

Furthermore, the evidence used to develop such familial housing policy often comes from particular regional contexts. Fukui is a rural prefecture located in the Chubu region on Honshu Island facing the Sea of Japan. Fukui has distinctive patterns of high proportions of multi-generation households, high female labour participation rates and high fertility rates. Such combination is labelled as the 'Fukui model' and has become a model to underpin some fertility policy initiatives (see, for example, Fujiyoshi, 2015). In Fukui, housing policy has long promoted co-residency and living nearby between family generations. According to the 2010 Population Census, the prefecture had the second highest rates of three-generation co-residency (17.6%), while unmarried rates of women at the reproductive age of 30 and 34 was the second lowest (28.4%) in the country. Given the high marriage rates, the fertility rates are one of the highest in the nation (1.63 in Fukui compared to the national average of 1.46 in 2015). Across the regions, significant disparity can be often observed in female labour force participation partly due to the availability of formal and informal childcare support and services (see Cabinet Office, 2016). Fukui has the national highest female labour participation (76%), which was approximately 10 percentage points higher than prefectures with lower rates such as Nara, Hyogo and Osaka. The Cabinet Office report also identified that one of the characteristics dividing female labour participation rates across the regions is the availability of public childcare services. The childcare spaces per women at the reproductive aged of 25 and 49 was, for example, 0.24 in Fukui, which was three times higher than prefectures with the low female participation rates such as Nara (0.09). It is often considered that the traditional co-residency could be the major reason behind the highly productive female population in the prefecture. It is, however, also driven by the social norms of agricultural-based economy and the high prevalence of manufacturing industry which push women out to the labour market. Although there exists a strong correlation between co-residency, fertility and female labour participation, what is equally evident is that working mothers in Fukui are highly stretched with the multiple roles of paid and unpaid work. The 2015 Fukui Statistics Report shows that working women in Fukui spent on average 32 minutes longer (7 hours 52 minutes) than the national average (7 hours 20 minutes) in total on paid and domestic work including care. Such discrepancy was only 7 minutes among males.

Due largely to the demographic patterns, people's attitudes and the existing housing stock, what works in Fukui is not necessarily transferrable to large cities such as Tokyo. Low fertility is much more prevalent in large cities such as Tokyo (1.17) because of the low marriage rates. The existing housing stock and high housing prices also challenge the feasibility of promoting co-residency. Housing is on average much smaller in size in Tokyo, which is evident in its low rates of three-generation households (only 2 per cent). The intention of promoting co-residency is implicitly or explicitly expecting grandparents to provide informal child care. However, those who are married tend to have children and the issue is an increasing number of women not having any children because they remain single as the marriage and child-birth is still strongly associated in Japan. Housing solutions to address the issues associated with low fertility need to support younger people in their transitions to adulthood and form an independent household away from their parents.

Conclusions

It is increasingly understood that housing, especially home ownership, is important in influencing women's life chances, social participation and well-being, but at the same time, there has been widening social divisions between those who can access housing and those who cannot. We can observe more concentration of wealth and resources in post-growth society such as the contrasts discussed between Tokyo and disappearing regions in Chapter 3. Such divisions also place women into winners and losers in a housing term as a gap between well-resourced couples with two high incomes and those without secure employment has been widening. Compared with popular discourse on class divisions and intergenerational justice over housing wealth and welfare, however, the gender dimension of housing inequalities has been under debated. It is largely because the institution of marriage based around the conjugal collectivity has often concealed gender differences in household finance and asset portfolio. The issues in relation to gender inequalities and power relations derived from their financial positions may be less apparent in many societies due to the conventional perception of housing and home ownership based on households. A significant demographic change, however, meant that many people no longer form a conventional married household and thus remain outside of the standard family model. Such trends have started jeopardising the existing housing and family systems.

The role of women is increasingly promoted in the current economic and political context. For a privileged few, there are increasing opportunities in the labour market, promotion, income and asset accumulation, while many female homeowners have to take multiple roles of paid and unpaid labour with the expectation to contribute to a mortgage repayment. This could be a double-edged sword, putting more pressure on women to take up responsibilities especially under the national fertility agenda.

Policy influences practice since the current housing situations of women are the products of post-war social institutions such as housing policy, the family and labour market systems. In the Japanese context, those who are not supported by the institution of marriage thus tend to be particularly disadvantaged. In post-growth society, however, the life-course of women has been much more diversified, and an increasing number of women are outside of the conventional married households. Yet, policy measures are still confined to support only those who fit in the particular family model. Post-growth responses to housing and fertility exhibit clear contradictions. Re-familisation is an institutional framework in the housing context, which does not support women regardless of their marital status. The idea of safety nets continues to be located in extended families, who tend to absorb new social risks of divorce, mental illness or job loss. Fertility politics would not be effective to address the nation's stagnated fertility by encouraging co-residency of those who have already formed their own family (married households). Policy measures in areas such as social security, employment or housing are required to treat women as individuals instead of dependents of husband or parents; and supporting women to become independent and sustain their independent living could be a more effective means to address the fertility crisis in the long term.

References

Apps, P. and Rees, R. (2004) Fertility, taxation and family policy, *Scandinavian Journal of Economics*, 106(4), 745–773.

Bernardi, F. (2005) Public policies and low fertility: Rationales for public intervention and a diagnosis for the Spanish case, *Journal of European Social Policy*, 15(2), 123–138.

Blossfeld, H. P. and Drobnič, S. (eds.) (2001) *Careers of Couples in Contemporary Society: From Male Breadwinner to Dual-Earner Families*, Oxford: Oxford University Press.

Bruegel, I. (1979) Women as a reserve army of labour: A note on recent British experience, *Feminist Review*, 3, 12–23.

Cabinet Office, Government of Japan (2015) *Shoushi-ka taisaku taikou [The Outline of the Countermeasures for Low Fertility Society]*, Tokyo: Cabinet Office.

Cabinet Office, Government of Japan (2016) *Chiiki no Keizai 2016 [Regional Economies 2016]*, Tokyo: Media Land.

Courgeau, D. and Lelièvre, E. (1992) Interrelations between first home-ownership, family constitution and occupation, in J. Trussel, R. Hankinson and J. Tilton (eds.) *Demographic Applications of Event History Analysis*, Oxford: Oxford University Press, 120–140.

Deere, C. D. and Doss, C. R. (2006) The gender asset gap: What do we know and why does it matter? *Feminist Economics*, 12(1–2), 1–50.

Dettling, L. and Kearney, M. (2014) House prices and birth rates: The impact of the real estate market on the decision to have a baby, *Journal of Public Economics*, 110(C), 82–100.

Feijten, P. and Mulder, C. H. (2002) The timing of household events and housing events in the Netherlands: A longitudinal perspective, *Housing Studies*, 17(5), 773–792.

Forrest, R. and Hirayama, Y. (2009) The uneven impact of neoliberalism on housing opportunities, *International Journal of Urban and Regional Research*, 33(4), 998–1013.

Fujiyoshi, M. (2015) *Fukui Model: Mirai ha chihou kara hajimaru [Fukui Model: Future Begins With a Region]*, Tokyo: Bungei Shunju.

Fukuda, S. (2009) Shifting economic foundation of marriage in Japan: The erosion of traditional marriage, *MPIDR Working Paper* WP 2009-033, November.

Hakim, C. (2003) A new approach to explaining fertility patterns: Preference theory, *Population and Development Review*, 29(3), 349–374.

Hirayama, Y. (2012) The shifting housing opportunities of younger people in Japan's home-owning society, in R. Ronald and M. Elsinga (eds.) *Beyond Home Ownership: Housing, Welfare and Society*, London: Routledge, 173–193.

Hirayama, Y. (2014) Jutaku seisaku to jenda [Housing policy and gender issues], *Jutaku Kaigi [Journal of Japan Housing Council]*, 91, 4–9.

Hirayama, Y. (2016) Sansedai doukyo sokushin no jutaku seisaku wo dou yomuka [How to assess housing policy promoting three-generation living], *Sekai*, April (880), 107–118.

Hirayama, Y. and Izuhara, M. (2008) Women and housing assets in the context of Japan's home owning democracy, *Journal of Social Policy*, 37(4), 641–660.

Institute for Research on Household Economics (2006) *Josei no Raifu Kosu to Jutaku Shoyu [Women's Life-Course and Home Ownership]*, Tokyo: Institute for Research on Household Economics.

Izuhara, M. (2015) The life-course diversity, housing choices and constraints for women of the 'lost' generation in Japan, *Housing Studies*, 30(1), 60–77.

Izuhara, M. (2016) Towards individualising couple finance: Women's housing assets and household decisions in Japan, *Gender, Place and Culture*, 23(7), 1003–1016.

Kawata, N. and Hirayama, Y. (2010) Housing conditions of single people in Japan: A cross-national perspective, *Journal of Architecture and Planning*, March, 75(649), 681–689.

Kennett, P. and Chan, K-W. (eds.) (2011) *Women and Housing: An International Analysis*, London: Routledge.

Koyama, S. (2013) *Ryōsai Kenbo: The Educational Ideal of 'Good Wife, Wise Mother' in Modern Japan*, Boston: Brill.

Kumazawa, M. (2000) *Josei Rōdō to Kigyō Shakai [Women's Work and Corporate Society]*, Tokyo: Iwanami Shoten.

Land, H. (1980) The family wage, *Feminist Review*, 6, 55–77.

Lewis, J. (2001) The decline of the male breadwinner model: Implications for work and care, *Social Politics*, 8(2), 152–169.

McDonald, P. (2008) Explanations of low fertility in Asia, in P. Straughan, A. Chan and G. Jones (eds.) *Ultra-Low Fertility in Pacific Asia: Trends, Causes and Policy Issues*, London: Routledge.

Ministry of Internal Affairs and Communications, Japan (2010) *Rōdōryoku Chōsa [Labour Force Survey]*, Tokyo: Statistics Bureau.

Ministry of Land, Infrastructure, Transport and Tourism, Japan (2008) *White Paper on Land, Infrastructure, Transport and Tourism in Japan 2008*, Tokyo: Gyosei.

Mizutani, N. (2013) Mochi ie to josei no shugyo [Home ownership and women's labour market participation], *Japanese Journal of Research on Household Economics*, Autumn (100), 42–51.

Mulder, C. H. (2006) Population and housing: A two-sided relationship, *Demographic Research*, 15(13), 401–412.

Mulder, C. H. and Billari, F. C. (2010) Home ownership regimes and low fertility, *Housing Studies*, 25(4), 527–541.

Mulder, C. H. and Wagner, M. (2001) The connections between family formation and first-time home ownership in the context of West Germany and the Netherlands, *European Journal of Population*, 17(2), 137–164.

Myrskyla, M., Kohler, H. and Billari, F. (2011) *High development and fertility: Fertility at older reproductive ages and gender equality explain the positive link*, PSC Working Paper Series 10-3-2011, University of Pennsylvania.

National Institute of Population and Social Security Research (2011) *The National Fertility Survey*, Tokyo: National Institute of Population and Social Security Research.

Osawa, M. (2007) *Gendai Nihon no Seikatsu Hosho Shisutemu [The Social Security System in Contemporary Japan]*, Tokyo: Iwanami Shoten.

Ostner, I. (2003) 'Individualisation' – the origins of the concept and its impact on German social policies, *Social Policy & Society*, 3(1), 47–56.

Otake, F. (2000) *Churyu sou no houkai ha konkyo toboshii [Lack of evidence in the breakdown of the middle class]*, *Nihon Keizai Shinbun*, February 29–March 7.

Raymo, J. M. and Iwasawa, M. (2005) Marriage market mismatches in Japan: An alternative view of the relationship between women's education and marriage, *American Sociological Review*, 70(5), 801–822.

Ronald, R. and Nakano, L. (2013) Single women and housing choices in urban Japan, *Gender, Place and Culture*, 20(4), 451–469.

Sato, R. (2008) Nihon no chou shoushi ka – sono gen'in to seisaku taiou wo megutte [Very low fertility in Japan: Causes and policy responses], *Journal of Population Problems*, 64(2), 10–24.

Shimazaki, N. (2008) *Life Course no Shakai Gaku [Sociology of the Life Course]*, Tokyo: Gakubun sha.

Shirahase, S. (2007) Women's economic status and fertility: Japan in cross-national perspective, in F. M. Rosenbluth (ed.) *The Political Economy of Japan's Low Fertility*, Stanford: Stanford University Press.

Tachibanaki, T. and Sakoda, S. (2013) *Fufu Kakusa Shakai [Unequal Society of Married Couples]*, Tokyo: Chuo Koron Shinsho.

Tanaka, K. (2015) Jakunen mikon josei no shigoto, kekkon, shussan no kibou pattern [Patterns of aspirations for work, marriage and fertility among young unmarried women], *Japanese Journal of Research on Household Economics*, Autumn (108), 6–17.

Torgersen, U. (1987) Housing: The wobbly pillar under the welfare state, *Scandinavian Housing and Planning Research*, 4(1), 116–126.

Vignoli, D., Rinesi, F. and Mussino, E. (2013) A home to plan the first child? Fertility intentions and housing conditions in Italy, *Population, Space and Place*, 19, 60–71.

Yamada, M. (2004) *Parasaito Shakai no Yukue: Data de Yomi Toku Nihon no Kazoku [Directions of Parasitic Society]*, Tokyo: Chikuma Shobo.

Yi, J. and Zhang, J. (2010) The effect of house price on fertility: Evidence from Hong Kong, *Economic Inquiry*, 48(3), 635–650.

6 Super ageing, widening inequalities and housing asset-based welfare

Introduction

Ageing of the population is one of the most prominent post-growth characteristics in society. Housing needs are likely to change throughout the life-course often in relation to other life-course related changes such as household formation and dissolution following marriage or divorce, parenthood as well as retirement and ill health. The meaning of home to individuals and families also changes following changes in their abilities and needs in later life. As people age, what important or key functions in their housing are likely to change and their home may acquire a new or different meaning. At the same time, their home may lose some functions in order to compensate for the reduced functional capacity of ageing (Rowles and Chaudbury, 2005). For example, older people tend to spend more time at home compared to their younger counterparts, and thus the immediate home environment becomes their primary living space, which increases attachment and importance to their housing, emphasising the use value of housing (Rowles and Chaudbury, 2005). Affordability usually becomes important as people's income tends to be reduced in post-retirement. So does accessibility since mobility may become restricted when people advance in age. Moreover, their changing health status and household compositions bring different housing needs to older households. In this context, housing could serve adaptive functions and people would place more emphasis on maintaining and enhancing control and comfort over their home and the neighbourhood. At the micro level, therefore, people tend to 'consume' housing differently in different stages of their life-course. Affordable, accessible and adequate housing is indeed critical to support older people in their 'third' and 'fourth' age, emerging life stages of maturity and dependence as a result of increased longevity (see Laslett, 1996; Heywood et al., 2002; Evans, 2009).

At the macro level, one of major housing questions in 'super-aged' Japanese society lies how social stratification in housing which has existed earlier in people's life-course is translated and accentuated in their later life. In the Japanese context, post-war baby-boomers who were born between 1947 and 1949 have already reached their retirement age *en masse*, accelerating the societal ageing. Due to the large size of the cohort, the baby boomer generation has constantly influenced policy agenda in the post-war growth period with their employment, housing and welfare needs as they move on through the stages of their life-course. Now as the cohort has reached post-retirement age, it is interesting to observe whether and how this ageing baby-boomer cohort would influence (housing) policy and initiatives as they did to the long-term care debate in the 1990s. The baby-boomers are often considered to be the beneficiaries of post-war economic growth and the generation of homeowners. Thus, a critical question can be posed as to what housing equity and equality mean to this generation, many of whom acquired home ownership through state and company assistance. In Japan, the home ownership rate among older people is particularly high at over 80 per cent compared to the national average of approximately 60 per cent. There is, however, a stark difference in the wealth level between older homeowners and tenants as well as among homeowners themselves. Moreover, there is an important element of home ownership as material assets in old age. Home ownership is a long-term accumulation of assets which, under the right circumstances, may act as an additional income source in later life for those who own their own property. In policy terms, an inevitable increase of care need has arisen from extended life expectancy in many mature societies and poses a significant challenge to the state and families. As it is well debated in the Western academic circle (see, for example, Elsinga et al., 2007; Doling and Ronald, 2010; Watson, 2009), home ownership could be considered as an asset base for older people to generate an income in old age or to fund their own health and long-term care need only if the existing institutions and market can support such equity release mechanism.

After examining the meaning of home and housing in later life, the main aims of this chapter are to explore the divisions which exist in housing tenure, conditions and asset levels among older people and how post-growth characteristics such as asset volatility and deregulation contribute to widen such inequalities. The chapter then moves on to explore the role of housing and housing wealth in later life, the mechanisms of asset transfer and its implication in post-growth society which is rapidly ageing. The feasibility of the housing asset-based welfare approach in the Japanese context will be examined. By doing so, the chapter attempts to bring housing issues into the area of welfare debate, which are often missing in the Japanese as well as other East Asian policy context.

Demographic change, ageing society and housing

Increased longevity and the speed of societal ageing are some of the major drivers leading to post-growth society. Many East Asian societies enjoy the highest rates longevity in the world for both men and women, and Japan is at the forefront of such phenomenon (see Chapter 1 for more details of the demographic change). In 2015, life expectancy in Japan had reached

87.05 years for women and 80.79 years for men which was extended approximately five years from 81.9 years and 75.9 years, respectively, since 1990. As the post-war baby boomers who were born in the latter half of the 1940s had already reached the retirement age of 65, Japan is now the most aged society globally with the world highest percentage of older people in its total population. According to the Population Census, 26.7 per cent of its population was aged 65 and over in 2015. Post-growth societies are indeed 'mature' societies in demographic terms. Therefore, debates such as productivity versus dependency and thus policy options of 'workfare' (e.g., job creation, in-work benefits) versus 'welfare' (e.g., social protection) are highly relevant in this social context.

Increased longevity has meant that post-retirement years have become extended for many individuals. People tend to formally retire at the retirement age of 65 in Japan although the practice of post-retirement employment was common in earlier economic growth periods, while extending working life in the current post-growth economic climate may become a notable trend. In this vein, housing will become more critical in people's everyday life as they spend more time at home in their prolonged post-retirement years. While environmental psychology thesis emphasises the critical importance of housing, home and the immediate home environment in old age, it is also important to remind us that old age is not necessarily a synonym to disability and dependence. While theses such as the 'demographic time bomb' tend to paint a negative picture of population ageing (see, for example, Mullan, 2002), increased longevity is considered a positive and successful outcome of contemporary social advancement such as advanced medicine and technology as well as policy measures including public health, education and social security. Due to the increased longevity, many people spend an emerging life-stage of the 'third age' in maturity, independence and personal fulfilment (Laslett, 1996). However, the 'fourth age' of decline and dependency eventually come to many people, especially since longevity has been extended to well over eighties in a 'super-aged' society. The last stage may require older persons to move into nursing homes, supported accommodation, or bringing extensive care services and adaptation into their home (Baltes and Smith, 2003). This stage in later life in particular illustrates the importance of the link between housing and care, including where older persons live to receive long-term care and how they fund such services (see Izuhara, 2009).

Another distinctive demographic characteristic of Japan, which is shared among many East Asia societies such as South Korea and China but contrasted from other developed Western societies, is its pace of social transformations. In many European societies, the process of societal ageing started much earlier, sometime in the late nineteenth or early twentieth century, and took much longer, such as 85 years for Sweden and even 115 years for France to double their rate of older people aged 65 and over in the total population from 7 per cent (to enter the UN defined 'ageing society') to

14 per cent ('aged society') (US Census Bureau, 2016). In comparison, the same process has taken place more recently and much faster in East Asia. It took Japan only 25 years (1970–1995) to double the ageing rate from 7 to 14 per cent, and it is predicted to take South Korea only 18 years and China 23 years, both of which only entered the 'ageing society' in 2000 and 2001, respectively. The time to further increase the percentage of older people from 14 to enter the 'super-aged society' of 21 per cent will be even faster in Japan at 12 years, and is predicted to take 11 years in China and only 9 years in South Korea (US Census Bureau, 2016).

The issue here is how the infrastructure and resources including housing stock, health and social care services or supported accommodations with care provision would cope with such tremendous pace of societal ageing. In this context, many developed welfare states have shifted their approach from developing institutions and residential care facilities to 'community care' encouraging older people to 'age in place' and providing long-term care services in their own dwellings, reflecting the preference of older people and their families as much as a cost containment exercise. This is also the policy direction of Japan and other East Asian societies such as China, Taiwan and South Korea since home-based care and care in the community are widely promoted in the current policy discourse which is evident in the long-term care policy and practice. An important fact is that the vast majority of older people live in an ordinary dwelling, not institutions or purpose-built housing specially designed for older people. Moreover, the home-based care approach always contains expectations to draw upon extended family resources. Familisation, which is an over-arching trend in post-growth housing policy and practice in Japan, is inevitably found in the area of housing and older people as well.

As discussed in the previous chapter, promoting a revival of co-residency is increasingly considered by policy makers as one of the strategies to address care issues in the super-aged society with ultra-low fertility (Hirayama, 2016). Rapidly changing household structures are part of the post-growth demographic change. Over the last three decades, a shift from the traditional form of three-generation family living arrangements to nuclear family households has been taking place, reflecting the affluence brought to the older generation with established pensions and personal wealth. However, co-residency still persists and the twist of contemporary co-residency in post-growth society is the rising number of ageing parents living with their unmarried adult children (see Chapter 5). In the post-growth policy context, co-residency or living near-by are increasingly promoted in order to strengthen the intergenerational support mechanisms. It is partly a strategic response to the fertility decline as co-resident couples on average have higher fertility rates (see Chapter 5). This form of co-residency has a particular policy implication in relation to employment (especially for working mothers), fertility and care provision. A periodic income tax concession to facilitate co-residency was proposed and introduced by the Cabinet Office in 2015 while many local authorities provide cash subsidies and vouchers for family generations to live together or near-by (see Chapter 5 for the detail).

In this context, it is interesting to unpack who is depending on whom within the extended family households. Different types of support including financial resources, time, practical and personal support are likely to flow in different directions within families (see Finch, 1989). Financial resources tend to flow from the wealthier generation to the poorer one to alleviate inequality in families. In co-residency, which generation owns their home may be an important factor determining the flow of support. The ownership of their residential property may also create power relationships between the generations in the household. In case of public or private rental accommodations, who has a legal tenancy contract and whether the tenancy right could be transferrable to their co-resident family member(s) could be another critical question. There are issues around housing asset transfers and future maintenance risks among dependent adult children, especially those with insecure, casual or no employment. It is closely linked to emerging social issues among young adults, or dependent adult children in precarious employment status in this context, and their access to and maintenance of housing in post-growth society (see Chapter 4).

The last point in this section is that the current older generation is 'house-rich' in Japanese society. Given the post-war economic cycle and home ownership-centred housing policies, the vast majority of households with older members own their own home and the demographic location of (housing) wealth tends to be on the older generation instead of the middle or younger generations within families as well as the society as a whole (Forrest and Izuhara, 2009). This provides a rationale behind the popular academic and policy debates on the (housing) asset-based welfare approach. Home ownership for older people is increasingly considered as financial resources for use in their own old age. Since current older people hold a significant proportion of the nation's wealth in Japan, it has been an integral part of Japan's fiscal policy to encourage older people to transfer their wealth to their adult children and directly to grandchildren through tax concessions in order to stimulate the stagnated national economy. In this context, families as opposed to the state are expected to provide social protection and housing and educational funds to their members, but the asset-based welfare debate, the expectation and mechanisms of liquidising housing assets for their own care needs is not necessarily central to the fiscal policy. We will return to examine the limitations of the housing asset-based welfare approach in the Japanese context later in this chapter.

Housing and social divisions among older people

Linking to the wider social system and recent policy reforms, this section explores how the conventional post-war housing approach and how the focus around assisting mainstream families to achieve home ownership has contributed to produce differentiated outcomes among older households at the arrival of post-growth society. Increasing social inequalities in home ownership society, particularly through intergenerational asset transfers, have been well documented in recent years (Spilerman, 2000; Piketty, 2014). Japan is a case in point where policy promoting intergenerational asset transfers instead of wider redistribution through taxations or other measures may alleviate inequalities between generations at the macro social level, but it contributes to the persistence of wealth inequalities between haves and have-nots at the micro level of families and households.

First, we look at the significant wealth gap which exists across different tenure groups. This is not surprising in society with a great emphasis on home ownership. Households can only achieve high-quality housing, in both size and quality, in the owner-occupied sector as public investments in other sectors have been minimal (see Chapter 1). Although inheritance and lifetime gifts have become important resources for family wealth accumulation, the current generation of homeowners were more likely to have acquired their residential property through their own income earned in the labour market in the economic growth period. Secure employment and stable income were the prerequisites of securing a mortgage towards home ownership. Such processes clearly explained how the employment status and conditions translated to housing tenure and the gap became more accentuated when people entered old age.

One of the major characteristics of households with older members in Japan is the high rate of home ownership. According to the micro data calculated from the 2005 Population Census, on average, 83.2 per cent of households with older member/s aged 65 and over lived in owner occupation (see Table 6.1) (Hirayama, 2015). In particular, home ownership is common tenure for married couples, which is in line with the earlier argument regarding different sections of society such as women and younger people (see Chapters 4 and 5). The stability of family and family formation has been particularly important among this generation, which divides their fortune in old age: 87 per cent of households with more than two members (including older couples and an older parent with other family member/s) lived in their own home. Marital status is also an important determinant among elderly-only households as widows were more likely to live in owner-occupied home (74.6%) compared to their never married (48.4%) and divorced (38.5%) counterparts, respectively. This explained how home ownership has been closely entwined with family formation in Japan as house purchase had usually come after marriage in the conventional post-war life-course (see Chapter 5). When home-owning couples become separated or divorced, it is also evident that at least one of the partners, if not both, leaves the home ownership sector (see Kawata and Hirayama, 2010).

In contrast to the security of home ownership shared among the majority of older Japanese people, the insecurity and vulnerability in housing situations have been observed in a small minority of older tenants. This is where one of the divides is particularly prevalent, and poverty among older tenants presents a major issue in post-growth society. The percentage of tenants among households containing older members was 16.6 per cent in 2005 (see Table 6.1). Among those, 9.3 per cent lived in private rented accommodation while 6.4 per cent in publicly rented accommodation. Among single-elderly households, the rate in private rental was even higher at 20.6 per cent, partly because single people are often excluded from the priority need groups of public rentals. In particular, unmarried older people (34.4 per cent) and divorcees (38.7 per cent) lived in a privately rented accommodation on their own.

Many factors underpinned the reasons behind the insecurity of private rented living in old age. In general, compared to owner occupation, dwellings available in private rentals are smaller, older and in a poorer state of repair. Security of tenure remains a major issue for older (single) tenants in the private rented sector as it is not usually guaranteed to private tenants. Moreover, older tenants are often unwelcome by private landlords due to risks of unpaid/delayed rent payment or even death in the accommodation. Rental accommodations offer limited flexibility in housing adaptation to meet the changing need in old age. Poverty among older tenants is severe in any society but the lack of public assistance in the form of direct provision of public rental and cash-based housing benefits in the Japanese welfare state makes life more difficult in old age, especially when the access to the formal and informal labour market is significantly restricted in the post-growth society.

'Housing costs induced poverty' has been well documented in other home-ownership societies such as the UK (see Tunstall et al., 2013). In the

Table 6.1 Tenure patterns of older households (2005)

	Single-person households					*Household with two or more members*	*Total*
	Sub total	*Never married*	*Married*	*Widowed*	*Divorced*		
	(%)	*(%)*	*(%)*	*(%)*	*(%)*	*(%)*	*(%)*
Owned houses	64.9	48.4	68.9	74.6	38.5	88.6	83.2
Public rented houses	12.0	12.9	7.7	11.0	19.3	4.7	6.4
Private rented houses	20.6	34.4	18.9	12.6	38.7	5.9	9.3
Company houses	1.9	2.8	2.9	1.5	2.6	0.6	0.9
Others	0.6	1.5	1.5	0.4	1.0	0.2	0.3
Total	100.0	100.0	100.0	100.0	100.0	100.0	100.0

Source: Hirayama (2015); author's calculations from micro-data on 2005 Population Census.

UK, for example, Tunstall and colleagues (2013) argue that millions of people fall below the poverty line after they pay their housing costs such as rents. In Japan, older homeowners are often better off than their younger home-owning counterparts. Older homeowners tend to be outright owners without a mortgage before retirement in Japan. However, home ownership also accompanies the continuous cost of maintenance and property tax (normally 1.4 per cent of estimated property values annually with some discretions). On the other hand, older tenants have to continue to bear the monthly housing cost in the form of rents and management fees, which often put high pressure on their already meagre income. In society where the system provides an advantage to homeowners, the disadvantages brought to tenants are thus substantial. For example, the elderly-only households in the private rented sector tend to have a heavy burden of housing costs in their often low incomes. According to the micro data of the 2004 National Survey of Family Income and Expenditure, compared to only 25.8 per cent of home-owning households, the vast majority (68.8%) of private tenants had annual income less than 3 million yen (24,000 euro [1 euro = 125 yen, May 2017]). The large majority (78.9%) of owner occupiers reported their monthly housing cost being less than 30,000 yen (240 euro), while much lower proportion (23.1%) of private tenants paid such small sum (see Figure 6.1). While 65.7 per cent of older homeowners spent less than 5 per cent of their income on housing, 64.3 per cent of private tenants spent more than a quarter of their income on housing cost. This is a considerable difference which divides haves and have-nots in housing costs in later life.

Thus, while many older public and private tenants are already in poverty before the housing costs are taken into account, the housing costs are also the reason to put them into poverty. Furthermore, the rising level of social insurance contributions such as the Long-Term Care Insurance (for those aged 40 and over including older people themselves, increased on national average from approx. 3,000 yen (24 euros) per month in 2000 when it was first introduced to 5,500 yen (44 euros) in 2015) among low-income tenants increasingly puts pressure on their household incomes and make them tighten other expenses. In order to reduce the burden, the latest reform on the Long-Term Care Insurance in April 2015 further reduced insurance contributions from 50 per cent of the standard rate to 30 per cent among low-income individuals including those recipients of the public assistance. However, it is still a major drain on their small income, especially if they do not use the scheme. Since there is no cash-based housing allowance available and the direct provision of social housing has been always marginal in Japan (see Chapter 1 for the more detailed discussion), the link between poverty and housing has not been sufficiently addressed in the policy term.

Social divisions within older homeowners

At a glance, the high rate of home ownership among older people paints a picture of 'secure old age' in housing terms with a high level of housing

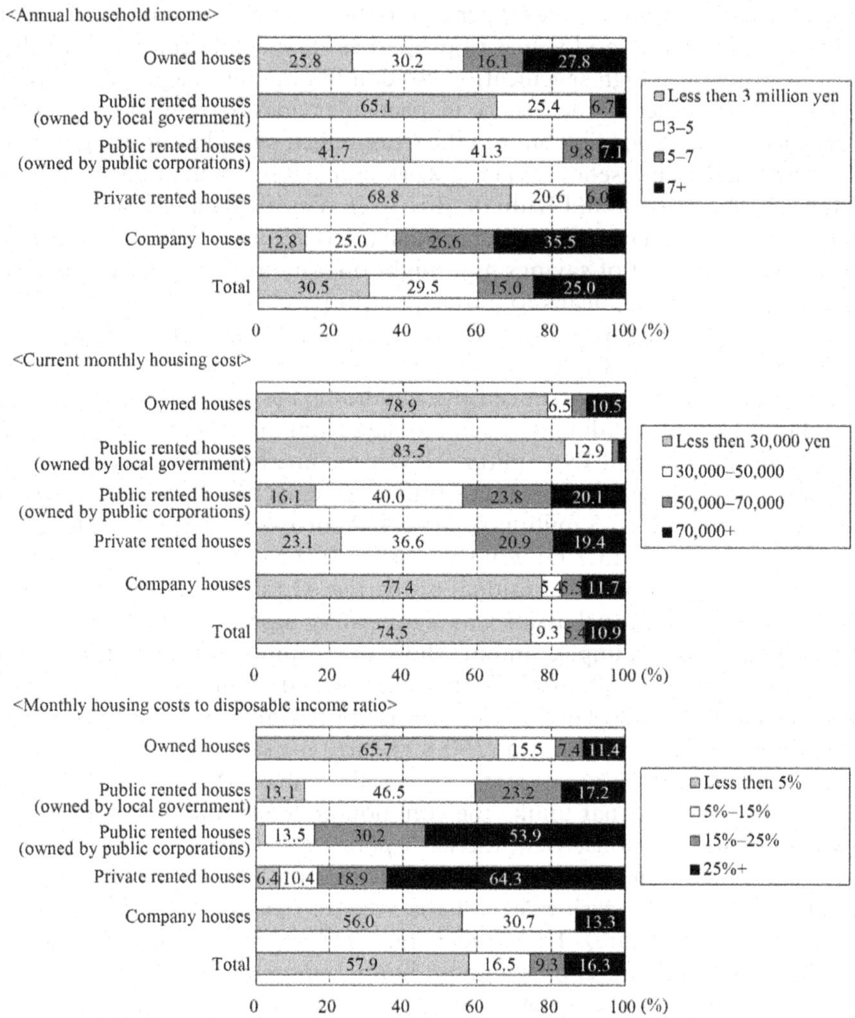

Figure 6.1 Annual household income and monthly housing costs of older households by tenure (2004)

Note: Data are for households with members aged 65 and over.

Source: Hirayama (2015); author's calculations from micro-data on 2004 National Survey of Family Income and Expenditure.

wealth in Japanese society. This picture is, however, not necessarily the reality as social stratifications in the home ownership sector itself have been widening in terms of household incomes and asset levels. Such housing inequalities among homeowners also exist in many societies, especially in countries like the People's Republic of China, where it has gone through the parallel shifts of privatisation and marketisation of housing in more recent decades. Among over 80 per cent of homeowners in urban China, for example, the quality and values of properties vary significantly as some live in a ultra-modern high specification condominium unit in a gated complex, while others, older homeowners in particular, may live in old one-room former work-unit housing built in the Communist period as housing used to be distributed to households via the work unit system (Wu, 2005; Wang and Murie, 1996; Forrest and Izuhara, 2012). In divided Japanese society, people tend to either have none or have them all. High-income households tend to have a high level of savings and might own multiple properties. Instead of using up financial means to purchase a property (so that you either have substantial savings OR additional properties), those who own tend to possess a great deal of both financial and real estate assets. Furthermore, multiple property owners can rent out their additional properties to earn further regular income. According to the micro data from the 2004 National Survey of Family Income and Expenditure, lower-income households with annual income less than 2 million yen (16,000 euro: €1=¥125 May 2017) had an average savings of 10.3 million yen (82,400 euro) and the real estate assets (land and dwelling) 23.7 million yen (189,600 euro). Only 10.6 per cent of those households owned additional properties. On the other hand, the level of financial and material assets was significantly higher among high-income households. For example, among those with annual income more than 10 million yen (80,000 euro), 35 per cent owned additional properties on top of their residence. The asset level was approximately three times higher on average at 32.6 million yen (260,800 euro) for savings and 68.5 million yen (548,000 euro) for real estate assets (Hirayama, 2015).

The data suggest that unlike the common understanding of older homeowners being 'the house rich, the cash poor' due to their reduced income after retirement, the dominant situation is that the house-rich older people tend to be also the cash-rich and the welfare-rich (with better access to private health and care). The same income and expenditure survey revealed that among those households with additional properties, 39.2 per cent earn incomes from renting out their real estates. The higher the asset level is, the higher their annual incomes are. The majority (79.2%) of the households with the annual income less than 3 million yen (24,000 euro) did not have any rental income source, while a third of the households with the annual income more than 7 million yen (56,000 euro) had rent income more than 2 million yen (16,000 euro) per annum (see Hirayama, 2015). In the low fertility society with the stable rate of home ownership, people are more likely to inherit housing assets from their parents. The redistribution of housing in the market is a largely neglected area of social policy in Japan. It is thus necessary to consider the role of the market transfers to alleviate the widening divisions created by intergenerational transfers of assets within families. The situation does not require one compensating for the lack of the other, which challenges a popular notion of asset-based welfare.

The myth of the housing asset-based welfare

In the home-owning society, the meaning of home goes beyond practical use and symbolic social values of housing such as a form of shelter or social status derived from the 'rite of passage' to adulthood. Housing can be also considered as a platform of wealth accumulation for individuals and families. It is especially the case in a housing boom period when housing asset values are expected to rise consistently and thus property purchase is viewed as an attractive investment (Forrest et al., 1999). In such buoyant housing market, housing assets, if effectively accumulated and liquidised, could indeed support the welfare need of family members throughout the life-course. One could release the housing equity early to fund children's education or towards the end of their life-course by downsising their property to supplement old age income or fund their own health or social care need (see, for example, Doling and Ronald, 2010; Lowe et al., 2011; Rowlingson, 2006). The idea of asset-based welfare originates in the US, and it is viewed as social inequalities in ownership of financial assets to be problematic and such inequalities could be alleviated by helping low-income individuals to accumulate assets through policy measures such as individual development account schemes (see, for example, Regan and Paxton, 2001; Moser, 2007). The idea of asset-based welfare has also been promoted in the housing context by ways of increasing owner occupation in societies including the UK through policy initiatives such as the Right to Buy (RTB) and Low Cost Home Ownership (LCHO) (Munro, 2007). Widening access to home ownership may be welcomed by many, but a question remains that the state withdrawal in the social housing sector leaves this section of society even more vulnerable. Moreover, this 'hard to access' group is a growing group in the post-growth society (see Chapter 4 on housing and young people).

Different stakeholders have different interests in equity release. In the stagnated economy of Japan, on one hand, the government is keen to encourage families and households to release their equity more and earlier in order to stimulate its economy. On the other hand, older people themselves would be interested in releasing some of their equity tied to their property to supplement their income or to meet their changing needs in old age if necessary. Various options can be deployed for individuals and households to release part or all of their equity tied to housing through equity release products, renting out extra rooms or additional properties which they own, downsizing their properties or moving into purpose-built rented accommodation for older people. The options can include both inter- and intra-tenure residential moves as well as staying put in their own home.

In this context, at the macro social level, widening access to home ownership and asset-building more generally, and integration of less-privileged households into mainstream society have been integral parts of the promotion of the asset-based welfare approach (Watson, 2009). In the economic growth period, home ownership was a 'social project' which promoted widening access and provided households with security, stability and social status. Such social project has, however, become a much more investment-focused 'economic project' under the neoliberal policy reforms (Forrest and Hirayama, 2014). In the post-growth context, security and stability associated with home ownership have now been replaced with risks, asset value volatility and differentiated access by households with different socio-economic characteristics. Therefore, home ownership may no longer be able to provide a secure welfare base to older households. For the post-growth debates, indeed, we need to consider two concurrent trends such as increasing levels of welfare need derived from the super-aged society and also actual and potential declines in housing asset values in the post-growth economy. There are significant implications of the trends on the potential and effective use of housing assets in welfare for older people in post-growth Japan.

First, the idea of the use of housing assets in welfare can be problematic since the nature of such assets compared to financial assets is not easy to liquidise in some social systems (Doling and Ford, 2007; Izuhara, 2007). The idea is much more embedded in societies such as the UK where the practice of equity release is progressive among homeowners (Toussaint and Elsinga, 2009; Quilgars and Jones, 2007). In those societies, the socio-political ideology of ownership has turned to become decumulation as well as accumulation of housing wealth (Fox O'mahony and Overton, 2015). In this scenario, homeowners are increasingly expected to use their assets including residential property assets to meet their welfare need. In this context, the changing meaning of home ownership among those who use the equity release products has been observed. While equity release products allow older home owners to retain some of the emotional and psychological attachments to their home, for example, some compromises may be made in other associated meanings of home ownership including security, success, control and freedom (Fox O'mahony and Overton, 2015).

In many East Asian societies such as Hong Kong and Singapore, housing assets have always been embedded in the wider context of welfare provision (see Groves et al., 2007; Lee, 2009). The combination of the population ageing and the economic downturn in post-growth society provides an interesting platform for provoking debate about potential options and strategies for the state, the market and the family in using accumulated housing assets in ageing society. There are common and differentiated policy approaches witnessed in the East Asian region given the differences in the housing market, economic cycles and the broader welfare structures (see Chua, 2003; Chou et al., 2006; Ronald and Doling, 2012). What makes a difference is that Japanese older people have distinctive saving patterns since the value of financial assets which households own steadily increases as people age. After the two decades of post-bubble deflation, the Japanese case is thus located somehow differently in the housing asset-based welfare debates (Hirayama, 2010; Izuhara, 2016). The experiences of Japan may be contrasted to a certain extent with those of other East Asian societies such as China since some societies have been still experiencing strong price appreciation (or property boom) in more recent years although a similar cycle of downturn is well predicted for some time. Moreover, different policy developments, institutions and markets combine to facilitate or hinder the practice of the use of housing wealth on welfare. Valuable lessons can be learnt from the Japanese case as many East Asian societies tend to follow Japan's path.

Equity release

Home ownership is now increasingly considered as a 'consumption good' and an 'individual financial safety net' in some national contexts (see Lowe et al., 2011). In order to encourage people to invest themselves in securing their long-term welfare, individuals are expected to become a 'financialised agent' by embracing the investment and saving culture (Watson, 2009). In Japan, there is a clear cultural practice of financial accumulation as people tend to save even after retirement instead of spending their accumulated assets in the post-retirement period. A major issue is, however, that the nature of housing assets compared to other financial assets such as savings is not easy to liquidise to fund welfare services or lifestyle need (Doling and Ford, 2007). There is also a number of institutional and market barriers to realise the potential of asset-based welfare approach in the Japanese context. The success also requires cultural shifts such as people's attitudinal change towards personal property assets.

In capitalist societies, accumulation of individual assets is often supported by institutional mechanisms such as home ownership, pension schemes and private insurance schemes. Thus, the reversing effect of equity release early in people's life-course also needs the structural support of institutions and markets to be materialised. For propertied families under the traditional family practice of many East Asian societies, real estate was often considered as 'family assets', which were expected to pass on from one generation to another following the male line. Such strong family practice has been always considered as the major drawback to promote the equity release products in Japan. There exist a number of equity release products offered by local authorities and private financial institutions. However, even with the pioneer of reverse mortgage schemes offered by one of the local authorities (Musashino City) in Tokyo, the take-up rates had been minimal (only 119 cases over thirty years), which questioned the sustainability of the schemes leading to their closure (*Nihon Keizai Shinbun*, 20 August 2013). One cultural reason which is often highlighted is that the scheme requires a guarantor when older homeowners want to sign up, and the guarantor is often their adult child. This institutional practice tends to perpetuate their understanding of shared responsibility over family generations and home ownership as family assets. However, the ideology and practice of the 'generational contract' involving obligations and responsibilities within families has been transforming albeit at different speed and extent across East Asian societies (see Izuhara, 2013). Older parents become much more independent financially, and also in their attitude towards family support and the meaning of assets in Japanese society compared to its regional counterparts. Comparing Japan and China regarding people's attitudes towards inheritance, for example, the primary bequest motives in both societies are largely 'selfish' based on the life-cycle model of saving for their own need as opposed to the 'altruistic' or 'dynasty' models of saving to support future generations (Horioka, 2014). It is evident that the cultural reason of intergenerational transfers is not the most pressing reason behind the stagnated liquidisation of individual assets since the nature of inheritance is often more accidental rather than planned. In Japan, older parents tend to leave unused residential property and financial assets to their off-springs instead of their active estate planning.

If the cultural practice is not the predominant reason, what is then undermining the practice of asset-based welfare, evident in the low take-up rates of reverse mortgage schemes in Japan? It is indeed the influence of the market together with the post-growth socio-economic conditions. As Doling and Ronald (2010) argue, in order to unlock the full potential of asset-based welfare, for example, the mortgage market needs to be developed and confident. The combination of the stagnated economy, the unstable financial market and volatile property values provides a ground to hinder the process and development of the asset-based welfare approach. Market mechanisms are the ones which closely intertwine to produce considerable challenges to potential equity release. First, volatility in housing prices are a major barrier to equity release as the maintenance of house prices is an important determinant. For typical equity release schemes in Japan, a series of restrictions are applied to the scheme, such as purpose-specific monthly payment limits and low borrowing limits against the properties (Okuda, 1999). The lack of confidence in the market is understandable in the post-growth society. When reverse mortgage schemes were originally introduced as a response to the arrival of the aged society in the late 1980s, the sharp decline in property values after the burst of the property bubble was not a part of the prediction.

The dual pricing system of land and housing in Japan presents another challenge in housing equity release. Land usually holds its value higher and longer, while building (housing) is considered to be more consumable commodities with a limited life span. Some private financial institutions which offer reverse mortgage schemes use tighter eligibility criteria allowing homeowners to release land-based equity only. Under the pioneering reserve mortgage scheme offered by the local government in Musashino, for example, condominium owners were only able to release a maximum 50 per cent of the market value of their housing equity as funds. According to the recent Housing and Land Survey, however, over 40 per cent of available dwellings were condominium units in 2013 (Ministry of Internal Affairs and Communications, 2014). The significant fall in the values of condominium units compared to single-family homes is evident (see Chapter 2). This dual pricing system thus makes the housing equity of condominium owners more vulnerable; and the condominium owners, who are increasingly become dominant tenure in the Japanese housing context, tend to be excluded from the equity release market (see the details in Chapter 2).

This leads to a question of to what extent the state has a role in maintaining the nation's housing market in relation to housing supply and demand which essentially have an influence in property values. The asset-based welfare approach would only work in a stable housing market. Examining the East Asian experiences, Singapore is a case in point where the state has a strong commitment for controlling and monitoring the nation's housing supply and demand. In the small city state, affordability issues together with the asset levels can be also addressed holistically. Unlike the construction-driven housing supply in Japan (see Chapters 1 to 2), the state strategically maintains and potentially enhances property values by balancing competing demands for new build and its commitment to upgrading old housing estates. In other words, the state is responsible for maintaining property values for existing owners and also making affordable access for new households without offering it as a welfare entitlement (Chua, 2014). In the Singaporean model, housing assets and social security are closely linked (Lee, 2009) and the asset-based approach is offered as an alternative to the welfare state (see, for example, Sherraden, 1997). A 'closed loop' financial transaction system (Chua, 2014) makes citizens save monthly into the Central Provident Fund (CPF) (tax-exempt, mandatory social security savings for retirement); using pre-retirement withdrawal from the Fund, people can purchase an apartment from the Housing and Development Board, which holds the mortgage, and the Provident Fund directly makes mortgage repayment to the Board. In the process, no commercial financial institution is involved. The feasibility of such system may only rest on the society dominated by public housing provision. By the late 1980s, approximately 90 per cent of the population had lived in public housing, more than 85 per cent of which owned a 99-year lease on their housing (Chua, 2014). In this context, the market is not the sector to dictate housing provision and values, but the 'visible hand' of the state has a direct and strong control in the housing supply and pricing (Phang, 2007). In addition, the asset-based welfare approach is evident in this state-orchestrated system since there is now a lease buy-back scheme which allows low-income leaseholders to raise funds by selling all but 30 years of the remaining lease to the Housing and Development Board while staying put in their property (Chua, 2014). This state-orchestrated system contrasts with the private construction-driven approach in Japan. As discussed in Chapter 2, a construction-focused approach undermines the maintenance of the existing housing stock and thus value of the properties, which jeopardises the potential of housing asset-based welfare. As the composition of housing supply has shifted towards condominiums and an increased number of vacant properties, however, the post-growth society requires the re-examination of the current approach.

The underdeveloped second-hand market is another strong determinant (see the detailed discussion in Chapter 2). One of the causes and consequences of the current older generation still holding the largest share of the nation's wealth and the low residential mobility once people acquired a single-family home in Japan is the under-developed second-hand housing market. The current system does not encourage people to move according to the need of their life-course, although inter- and intra-tenure residential moves such as trading down their property are usually effective to release part of their equity tied to housing.

Some policies have anti-asset elements by setting the asset limit to access welfare services such as long-term care services, or through punitive taxation system. However, the Long-Term Care Insurance scheme in Japan is a contribution-based social insurance system and the recipients of services are not means-tested. It thus remains as institutional incentive for individuals and families to accumulate and retain their housing and financial wealth while accessing public welfare services if the need arises. This approach is contrasted from the English approach, for example. Whether personal care for older people should be free or not has resulted in differentiated policy outcomes between England and Scotland in the late 1990s. While personal care is free in Scotland, those currently with over £23,250 of eligible capital including housing assets are expected to meet the full cost of social care in England. If necessary, therefore, it requires older homeowners to sell their home to raise the funds to move into residential care or to pay for extensive care services at home towards the end of their life. Although delayed changes to the means test will come into effect in April 2020 raising both upper and lower limits to £118,000 and £17,000, respectively (Age UK, 2015). The rationale behind the means-test was that public money should not be invested in individual asset accumulation. The similar principle exists in Japan since the recipients of the Public Livelihood Assistance are not allowed to use the funds for mortgage repayments. However, such disincentive does not apply to the social insurance schemes with universal eligibility. The Long-Term Care Insurance, which has been widely provided to those in need through the contributory social insurance scheme since 2000, is not means-tested. The link between care and housing assets is explicitly divorced in this scenario (Izuhara, 2009), allowing people to age in place and to access public long-term care while keeping their income and assets intact. Widening access and reducing the burden of informal family carers were the policy priority, resulting in widening the wealth gap while benefiting asset-rich older people who had substantive care needs.

Conclusions

This chapter highlighted the diversity and stratification which exist among households with older members in terms of housing tenure, conditions and wealth level. The post-growth characteristics and recent policy directions contribute to such widening inequalities. The link between housing and poverty is in particular evident in the private rented sector as a result of home-ownership-centred housing policy in the post-war period. The lack of policy measures to support older tenants in the private rented sector as well as the lack of subsidies available to support private or non-profit landlords remain an issue in society. Housing poverty also exists and is severe among low-income homeowners, which requires a greater recognition that tenure is not a simple indicator of housing wealth among older households. In post-growth Japan, current fiscal policy promotes asset transfers within families instead of wider redistribution through taxation or other measures. It may alleviate inequalities between generations at the macro social level, but it contributes to the persistence of wealth inequalities across families.

There is an intergenerational element in housing access and housing policy. Given the high proportion of home ownership among the current older generation on the one hand, and young adults struggling to access housing on the other hand, housing assets of older people are increasingly viewed as the key resources for the younger generations (as much as their own welfare base) in the post-growth social context. The housing privilege and housing questions will shift when the future generations start moving on in the life-course. However, if a housing safety-net continues to be developed and embedded predominantly around family resources, it will become another incubator for growing social inequality.

The lack of success in the housing asset-based welfare approach is evident in the Japanese housing and financial markets. It has already been well articulated that there are a number of barriers in promoting the asset-based welfare approach in the Japanese cultural and market context. Housing policy as well as economic policy have always focused on new construction of housing. Such approach has undermined the values of existing properties and thus hinders the sustainability and development of the second-hand housing market. A policy shift may be thus required to encourage more residential mobility of households to meet their changing need in the life-course. In order to stimulate such residential mobility, a shift in housing policy and provision is required from continuous construction of new housing developments to the state and the market investing more on maintaining and upgrading the existing housing stock as social stock. Major housing-building corporations have already started promoting home renovation as a new business opportunity and market development. Overall, the housing questions which we are facing now are likely to be specific to the current generation of older people, many of whom purchased their own home using the incomes earned in the labour market. With increasing potential of inheritance in mature home ownership society with low fertility, the future generation will face different housing issues, including the maintenance of the tenure.

References

Age UK (2015) Deprivation of assets in the means test for care home provision, *Factsheet 40*, London: Age UK.

Baltes, P. B. and Smith, J. (2003) New frontiers in the future of aging: From successful aging of the young old to the dilemmas of the fourth age, *Gerontology*, 49(2), 123–135.

Chou, K. L., Chow, N. W. S. and Chi, I. (2006) Willingness to consider applying for reverse mortgage in Hong Kong Chinese middle-aged homeowners, *Habitat International*, 30(3), 716–727.

Chua, B. H. (2003) Maintaining housing values under the condition of universal homeownership, *Housing Studies*, 18(3), 765–780.

Chua, B. H. (2014) Navigating between limits: The future of public housing in Singapore, *Housing Studies*, 29(4), 520–533.

Doling, J. and Ford, J. (2007) A union of home owners, editorial, *European Journal of Housing and Planning*, 7(2), 113–127.

Doling, J. and Ronald, R. (2010) Home ownership and asset-based welfare, *Journal of Housing and the Built Environment*, 25(2), 165–173.

Elsinga, M., De Decker, P., Teller, T. and Toussaint, J. (eds.) (2007) *Beyond Asset and Insecurity: On (In) Security of Home Ownership in Europe*, Amsterdam: IOS Press.

Evans, S. (2009) *Community and Ageing: Maintaining Quality of Life in Housing With Care Settings*, Bristol: The Policy Press.

Finch, J. (1989) *Family Obligations and Social Change*, Cambridge: Polity Press.

Forrest, R. and Hirayama, Y. (2014) The financialisation of the social project: Embedded liberalism, neoliberalism and home ownership, *Urban Studies*, 52(2), 233–244.

Forrest, R. and Izuhara, M. (2009) Exploring the demographic location of housing wealth in East Asia, *Journal of Asian Public Policy*, 2(2), 209–221.

Forrest, R. and Izuhara, M. (2012) The shaping of housing histories in Shanghai, *Housing Studies*, 27(1), 27–44.

Forrest, R., Kennett, P. and Leather, P. (1999) *Home Ownership in Crisis? The British Experience of Negative Equity*, Aldershot: Ashgate.

Fox O'mahony, L. and Overton, L. (2015) Asset-based welfare, equity release and the meaning of the owned home, *Housing Studies*, 30(3), 392–412.

Groves, R., Murie, A. and Watson, C. (eds.) (2007) *Housing and the New Welfare State: Perspectives From East Asia and Europe*, Aldershot: Ashgate.

Heywood, F., Oldman, C. and Means, R. (2002) *Housing and Home in Later Life*, Buckingham: Open University Press.

Hirayama, Y. (2010) The role of home ownership in Japan's aged society, *Journal of Housing and the Built Environment*, 25(2), 175–191.

Hirayama, Y. (2015) Choukoreishakai no jutaku jouken to sono kaisouka [Stratifying housing conditions in super-aged Japan], *Toshi Keikaku [City Planning Review]*, 64(6), 40–45.

Hirayama, Y. (2016) Sansedai doukyo sokushin no jutaku seisaku wo dou yomuka [How to assess housing policy promoting three-generation living], *Sekai* April (880), 107–118.

Horioka, C. Y. (2014) Are Americans and Indians more altruistic than the Japanese and Chinese?: Evidence from a new international survey of bequest plans, *Review of Economics of the Households*, 12(3), 411–437.

Izuhara, M. (2007) Turning stock into cash flow: Strategies using housing assets in an ageing society, in Y. Hirayama and R. Ronald (eds.) *Housing and Social Transition in Japan*, London: Routledge, 94–113.
Izuhara, M. (2009) *Housing, Care and Inheritance*, London: Routledge.
Izuhara, M. (2013) Housing wealth and family reciprocity in East Asia, in M. Izuhara (ed.) *Ageing and Intergenerational Relations: Family Reciprocity From a Global Perspective*, Bristol: Policy Press, 77–94.
Izuhara, M. (2016) Reconsidering the housing asset-based welfare approach: Reflection from East Asian experiences, *Social Policy & Society*, 15(2), 177–188.
Kawata, N. and Hirayama, Y. (2010) Housing conditions of single people in Japan: A cross-national perspective, *Journal of Architecture and Planning*, March, 75(649), 681–689.
Laslett, P. (1996) *A Fresh Map of Life: The Emergence of the Third Age* (2nd edition), Basingstoke: Macmillan.
Lee, J. (2009) Developmentalism, social welfare and state capacity in East Asia: Integrating housing and social security in Singapore, *Journal of Asian Public Policy*, 2(2), 157–170.
Lowe, S. G., Searle, B. A. and Smith, S. J. (2011) From housing wealth to mortgage debt: The emergence of Britain's asset-based welfare state, *Social Policy & Society*, 11(1), 105–116.
Ministry of Internal Affairs and Communications, Japan (2014) *Housing and Land Survey*, Tokyo: Statistics Bureau.
Moser, C. O. N. (ed.) (2007) *Reducing Global Poverty: The Case for Asset Accumulation*, Washington, DC: Brookings Institution Press.
Mullan, P. (2002) *The Imaginary Time Bomb: Why an Ageing Population Is Not a Social Problem*, London: I.B. Tauris.
Munro, M. (2007) Evaluating policy towards increasing owner occupation, *Housing Studies*, 22(2), 243–260.
Okuda, K. (1999) *Nihon ni okeru reverse mortgage no genjo* [Reverse mortgage schemes in Japan], *Yusei Kenkyusho Geppo*, 9, 109–114.
Phang, S. Y. (2007) The Singapore model of housing and the welfare state, in R. Grove, A. Murie and C. Watson (eds.) *Housing and the New Welfare State: Examples From East Asia and Europe*, Aldershot: Ashgate, 15–44.
Piketty, T. (2014) *Capital in the Twenty-First Century*, London: Belknap Press of Harvard University Press.
Quilgars, D. and Jones, A. (2007) United Kingdom: As safe as houses? In M. Elsinga, P. De Decker, T. Teller and J. Toussaint (eds.) *Beyond Asset and Insecurity: On (In)Security of Home Ownership in Europe*, Amsterdam: IOS Press, 259–286.
Regan, S. and Paxton, W. (2001) *Asset-Based Welfare: International Experiences*, London: IPPR.
Ronald, R. and Doling, J. (2012) Testing home ownership as the cornerstone of welfare: Lessons from East Asia for the West, *Housing Studies*, 27(7), 940–961.
Rowles, G. D. and Chaudbury, H. (eds.) (2005) *Home and Identity in Later Life*, New York: Springer.
Rowlingson, K. (2006) 'Living poor to die rich?' or 'spending the kids inheritance?' Attitudes to assets and inheritance in later life, *Journal of Social Policy*, 35, 175–192.
Sherraden, M. (1997) Provident funds and social protection: The case of Singapore, in M. Sherraden and J. Midgley (eds.) *Alternatives to Social Security: An International Inquiry*, Westport: Greenwood, 33–60.

Spilerman, S. (2000) Wealth and stratification processes, *Annual Review of Sociology*, 26(1), 497–524.

Toussaint, J. and Elsinga, M. (2009) Exploring "Housing Asset-Based Welfare" Can the UK be held up as an example for Europe? *Housing Studies*, 24(5), 669–692.

Tunstall, R., Bevan, M., Bradshaw, J., Croucher, K., Duffy, S., Hunter, C., Jones, A., Rugg, J., Wallace, A. and Wilcox, S. (2013) *The Links Between Housing and Poverty*, York: Joseph Rowntree Foundation.

US Census Bureau (2016) *An Aging World 2015: International Population Reports*, Washington, DC: US Government Printing Office.

Wang, Y. P. and Murie, A. (1996) The process of commercialisation of urban housing in China, *Urban Studies*, 33(6), 971–989.

Watson, M. (2009) Planning for a future of asset-based welfare? New labour, financialized economic agency and the housing market, *Planning, Practice & Research*, 24(1), 41–56.

Wu, F. (2005) Rediscovering the 'gate' under market transition: From work-unit compounds to commodity housing enclaves, *Housing Studies*, 20(2), 235–254.

Conclusions

Widening inequalities are the major consequences of the socio-economic shift to post-growth society. Throughout the volume, we identified that housing inequalities existed in many spheres of the society and the emergence of post-growth characteristics accentuated such social divisions among households in terms of housing access, conditions and wealth. To conclude this volume, we first remind ourselves where the housing divisions are and examine structural factors which facilitated the widening housing divisions. When the society has matured and entered the post-growth phase of socio-economic developments, the existing housing systems which have accompanied the growth model are no longer viable or sustainable. The consideration of new approaches in order to re-orientate the housing systems to fit for post-growth society will conclude this volume. Japan is indeed the cutting edge of transformations to post-growth society. The experiences of Japan thus provide some useful lessons for other East Asian societies and beyond, especially those of which showing converging socio-economic and policy trends.

Widening housing inequalities

The first division that exists is across generations. There are clear cohort effects on the distributions of material wealth including housing assets in the society. Considering the particular economic cycles including the booms and busts experienced in the post-war period together with the development of the labour market and social security, the current older generation holds substantial housing and financial wealth compared to the subsequent generations in Japan. The wealthy olds are often contrasted with the struggling youths in the post-growth economic context. Job security and housing policy providing stepping stones to home ownership are no longer guaranteed to the younger generation today. We have witnessed parallel trends of an expansion of independent elderly-only households due to affluence brought to older people through incomes, savings and pensions, and increased dependency on family resources among young adults. Both are the products of the transitions to post-growth society.

Second, tenure divides household fortune. In a society where housing policy focuses on promoting home ownership, public and private sector rentals are both marginal and residual in quality and quantity. It is apparent that tenure status dictates housing conditions and also represents the wealth of households. The contrast becomes even starker when people move on their life-course. Examining the current older generation, the large majority are owner-occupiers and some of them own multiple properties. The housing access and conditions of older tenants are extremely harsh due to their limited income and the lack of policy measures. In the post-war growth period, egalitarianism was a key social value and thus 'every household' had an opportunity to acquire their own home with the buoyant labour market and rising real incomes. However, opportunities to access home ownership have become more skewed and a privilege for a small few, with stable family and employment. Wealthy families could earn extra incomes through renting out their (inherited) properties, while the number of social housing has been reduced and still no cash-based housing allowance is available for tenants on low incomes in post-growth Japan.

Third, housing inequalities also exist between household types. Families are better off than single households in housing term since the three pillars of housing policy (the provision of low-income public housing, public corporation housing and public housing loans) in the growth period have always targeted 'new families' and thus benefited conventional married households. When we investigate the relationships between work, family and housing, those who have stable incomes are more likely to marry, and marriage often leads to home ownership. This also represents a gendered aspect of housing inequality in post-growth Japan. In general, marriage and home ownership have a strong correlation and women still tend to reside in housing which is earned and owned by their husband (or father in case of unmarried women). Such gendered inequalities had existed in the growth period but the expansion of non-conventional households due to divorce and never-married made such inequalities more visible.

Furthermore, the volume examined stark contrast in housing values, investments and thus future prospects of growth between Tokyo as a global city and disappearing regions, small towns and rural areas. House price deflation and volatility are distinctive characteristics of post-growth society. It is, however, only Tokyo which appears not to suffer from deflation in property values. Selective and targeted investments are current strategies for public resource allocation in post-growth Japan. To compete globally, Tokyo is still being further developed and booming with concentrated public and private investments which are predicted to continue up to and beyond the 2020 Olympic Games. Other regions and rural areas including those hit by the major disasters in the recent past, on the other hand, struggle to sustain their population and economic activities as well as property values. Depopulation means an increasing number of empty houses. Vacant properties have become a major concern in the regional context, especially when such regions are no longer the subject of public investment.

A new paradigm of growth in the housing sector

Post-growth society is often problematized by the disappearing or dearth of resources including natural resources, human resources, especially cheap labour supply, as well as ageing and shrinking of the populations. In other words, post-growth widely represents economic and demographic stagnation in society. This is indeed a global trend but a highly accentuated phenomenon in Japan. In the Japanese scenario, it is characterised by key features such as prolonged post-bubble recession, the world most aged society and yet the persistence of strict immigration policy to name but a few. The rise of neighbouring economies in the region such as South Korea and Taiwan followed by China in more recent years makes the features of post-growth Japan even more critical. It is in this context of post-growth society in which high GDP growth will no longer be expected and the welfare state no longer guarantees high labour and welfare costs, that the housing sector requires a new paradigm of growth. A shift in the conventional systems of housing policy and practice will be required as part of economic development to a more sustainable and innovative approach to promote well-being of the nation.

The term 'growth' needs to be re-defined in the current socio-economic context. Growth was an important conception in the housing context throughout the post-war period. Housing policy has focused on the mass construction of new housing units both to own and to rent. In the early post-war period, it was an effective strategy especially in urban areas to meet the housing shortage derived from the combination of war damage, urbanisation and an expansion of new households. Since then, the public funds have been constantly injected into the activities of the construction industry under the series of the Housing Construction Plans. Housing investment has been indeed a vehicle of the post-war economic growth. It was, however, in the late 1960s when the total number of housing units had already exceeded the total number of households. The over-supply of housing units in statistical term was already evident in every prefecture including metropolitan areas by the early 1970s (although the size and quality of such dwellings were uneven). What sorts of housing systems are required in the society where no further population growth is expected? A rising level of vacant properties has become a major policy issue especially in small towns and rural areas; and youth dependency and stagnated new household formation as well as extremely low fertility are serious social concerns.

In post-growth society, mere economic development along with more emphasis on the quality of life and well-being can be introduced. Well-being is considered to be an effective prescription to tackle widening inequality and polarisation as OECD also promotes well-being as a social development approach in the post-growth period. In the housing context, it could mean a shift away from expansion and new construction of housing units and housing finance but a more sustainable approach of maintenance and the use of the existing housing stock. How can the housing markets be developed and made functional, for example, without population increase and without further mass constructions of new housing units? A shift can be made to the re-organisation of the existing resources, the activation of under-developed markets and the stimulation of new household formations, especially among those who currently remain at their parental home.

A more effective use of the housing stock

A high volume of housing production was a marked feature of post-war housing systems not only in Japan but also in other East Asian societies such as South Korea and China. Within the framework of the developmental state, mass construction of housing was used as an engine for economic growth. In post-growth Japan, however, the ageing and shrinking of the population as well as stagnation in economy suggest the maintenance of such mass production is no longer feasible. It is predicted that other East Asian societies will follow suit reducing the quantity of housing construction. In post-growth society, the core of housing policy will thus shift from new construction to the effective use of the existing housing stock.

The consequence of such construction-led housing system is the underdeveloped nature of the second-hand housing market. There has been a persistent belief that what serves to stimulate the economy is not the improvement of existing dwellings but the construction of new dwellings. Despite the high rates of vacant houses, the Japanese government has repeatedly stimulated housing construction as a prescription to economic downturns. In addition, the construction and real estate industries have put pressure on the government to support mass housing construction. Nevertheless, economic and demographic changes brought an inevitable decline in the number of housing starts (newly constructed units). Since public and private investment in the existing housing stock remains stagnated, the decline in housing construction has directly led to the shrinking housing economy. The number of housing starts per capita is larger in Japan than in European countries but housing investments as percentage of GDP is larger in Europe than Japan. This means that within the context of mature economies, stock-oriented housing systems in European societies are more effective in maintaining a considerable level of housing investment compared to the construction-oriented Japanese system. Moreover, the underdeveloped second-hand property market tends to discourage homeowners from investing in improving their property due to the limited resale opportunities.

Post-growth economic stagnation creates some advantages for the second-hand housing market. A rising number of younger couples with or without children have started purchasing more affordable second-hand condominium units. Life-style change is another reason behind the new trend. In the high growth period, many baby-boomer households aspired to own a spacious single-family home filled with new furniture and electric appliances partly as a backrush of the lack of material resources experienced in the period immediately after the war. The younger households in post-growth Japan, however, often prefer simpler life-styles, which is evident in their choice of compact dwellings with fewer piece of furniture and appliances. Capital gains were a strong incentive for the baby-boomer households to purchase their house in the growth period. In contrast, current younger home owners can hardly expect capital gains unless they can afford a property in desirable locations of large cities. Thus, use values instead of exchange values have become an important factor for young people in their housing choice. In this context, purchasing an inexpensive second-hand property and renovating it to their taste are attractive options for the post-growth cohorts. This is an emerging trend in contemporary society which challenges the conventional home ownership ideology focused on social status and asset accumulation.

Indeed, an increasing number of vacant houses generate a new policy challenge. In central urban areas where demand for housing is chronically high, the development in the second-hand housing market is expected to facilitate the distribution of 'useable' vacant dwellings. However, the main issue is how to deal with vacant houses with poor state of repair in not only rural areas but also in urban core. In response to such phenomenon, the Vacant Houses Special Measures Act was put in practice in 2015, and local governments were provided various measures to deal with dilapidated vacant properties. The local government officers recently acquired power to warn or order the owners of dilapidated vacant houses to dismantle such properties. They can even enforce the administrative execution of demolition by proxy. How local governments will cope with unpopular and deteriorated vacant houses comes into focus in post-growth society.

Another related but separate issue is the future of the first generation of condominium complexes. Mid- and high-rise condominium complexes built in the 1970s started facing many problems including weakening of the structures (e.g., against earthquakes), rising vacancy rates and cumulative unpaid management fees by residents. Nevertheless, given the multiple individual ownership of such complexes and the lack of funds, building consensus among the residents for redevelopment is far from easy. There has been only a small minority of successful cases for the redevelopment of existing condominium complexes despite a rapidly increasing number of such ageing condominiums requiring substantial renovation or reconstruction. Lowering the proportion of agreements required from the individual unit owners for reconstruction has been used as a means to achieve the redevelopment but such measures often benefit the private developers, not ageing owners with limited financial means who cannot re-purchase their property. How the government and ageing individual owners deal with such issues is distinctively a matter of post-growth society. The Japanese experiences will provide valuable references to neighbouring countries, especially whose dominant housing type is high-rise condominiums.

Enhancing re-distribution in the housing system

Widening inequalities challenge housing systems in post-growth society. Housing policy in post-war Japan was not particularly redistributive in terms of allocating public resources directly to lower-income households. Housing policy promoted the growth of home ownership among the middle-income households, while residualising the provision of low-income public housing. However, the expansion of the owner-occupied housing sector encouraged an increasing number of households to access home ownership, leading to the maintenance of a relatively egalitarian society centred on the property-owning mass. Nevertheless, with entry to the post-growth era, neoliberal policy combined with economic slow-down has resulted in increased inequalities in housing opportunities. Widened economic gaps among the people are now one of the most critical social concerns in Japan, raising questions as to whether and how a redistributive housing system can be developed in the post-growth age.

In mature economies that have accumulated a large amount of housing and financial assets, as growth slows, the deployment of family wealth, rather than incomes earned in the labour market, becomes more significant as a driver of social stratification. Rollbacks of state provisions in welfare foster reliance on family resources, which in turn further exacerbates social inequalities according to family wealth. Widening gaps are thus visible between those who inherit residential properties from parents and those who do not; and between those who can receive financial assistance from parents in purchasing housing and those who cannot. In response to economic stagnation, the Japanese government reduced gift taxes on inter-vivo asset transfers in relation to house purchase. Such measures further widened inequalities among younger cohorts. Moreover, in super-aged Japanese society, the government currently promotes the form of extended families by facilitating co- and near-residency in order to encourage families to provide care to children as well as older members. These policies of facilitating the distribution of family resources within families help widen socio-economic cleavages between propertied families that further accumulate housing assets over generations, modest families that experience the dissipation of their property assets accumulated in the past, and perpetual tenant families that are increasingly finding themselves excluded from mainstream society centred on property ownership.

In the era of pervasive neoliberalism, a reduction in state housing subsidies has increasingly been normalised along with the rise of the 'austerity state'. However, it is assumed that post-growth socio-economic changes progressively impose limits on the sustainability of neoliberal policy. In the sluggish economic climate, a decline in the redistributive functions of housing and social policy combined with emphasis on family resources leads to a relentless and continuous expansion of inequalities and, thus, inevitably undermines social integration and state legitimacy. In Japan, there is a notable increase in those faced by difficulties in securing adequate and affordable housing when age, tenure, marital and employment status interact to produce multiple disadvantages: for example, unmarried young adults in precarious employment living at parental home; one-person households on low incomes who remain in the private rented sector with few prospects of accessing home ownership; single-mother households who are trapped in housing poverty; low-income homeowners with an excessively heavy burden of mortgage repayments; and single elderly households with meagre pensions living in substandard private rented housing. A key question is thus how and to what extent new housing issues emerged in the post-growth era will stimulate changes in housing and social policy to address diverse needs of contemporary households.

Housing, diversity and cohesion

What role the housing system plays in maintaining social cohesion is a significant question in post-growth society. Japan has been a relatively homogeneous society characterised in the conventional family model and the standardised life-course, which underpinned social cohesion during the period of high economic growth. The home-ownership-centred housing system provided many conventional households with opportunities to climb up the property ladder. The majority experienced a transition from tenancy to owner-occupation as they progress in their life stages in parallel with the entry to the labour market, family formation and (housing) asset accumulation. Housing policy together with the labour market and social security systems was constructed around the 'male breadwinner family' model, which reinforced social homogeneity. Mass construction of *danchi* (multi-family housing estates) with a large number of uniform units and the development of suburban neighbourhoods filled with numerous standardised single-family homes produced post-war landscapes of uniformity. Although inequalities existed between tenants and homeowners, tenants were considered as future homeowners supported by the rise of real incomes. In this growth context, inequalities were thus viewed as temporary, and those tenants had a prospect to move up the socio-economic and housing escalator, which helped maintain social stability. The process of households moving through the standardised path to home ownership indeed shaped the contours of Japan's post-war social development.

As argued, however, post-growth society has diversified the patterns of people's life-course with an increase in the number of unmarried adults, one-person households, those on casual employment, urban professionals, dual-earner households, single-parent and elderly-only households. Such diversified life-courses reflect on diversified housing types. In urban areas, a number of *one-room mansions* (medium-rise complex consisting of one-room studio flats) and compact apartments accommodate one-person and small-size households, respectively, while a small but increasing number of

SOHO (Small Office Home Office) is provided to workers in the information and creative sectors who have more flexible working arrangements and who work both at the office and in their home. Lone-female households place particular importance on accessibility and security in their accommodation. In large cities, some apartments with high-spec amenities and securities and attractive design are developed exclusively for women. Some young people on low incomes have begun to choose living in a shared house with small private rooms and communal spaces. Male-breadwinner households in the growth period often moved to purchase suburban single-family homes, whereas contemporary dual-earner households in the post-growth era prefer to acquire a condominium located in city centres. Meanwhile, some old *danchi* developments have been renovated so that fashionably re-designed units start attracting young tenants. Moreover, in response to increased care need in super-aged society, various types of rented accommodations with care services have been developed and provided to mainly single-elderly households. Such rented housing with care services is located differently from both ordinary accommodations and institutions.

Therefore, an important question in the post-growth era is what role the housing system plays in constructing social cohesion with increasing diversity. Such challenges are likely to be shared with other East Asian societies that are experiencing staggered but rapid social change. Currently, the diversification in people's life-courses and life-styles is part of the structure of social stratification. A socio-economic hierarchy is spatially organised in contemporary society: units on the lower floors of super-high-rise condominium blocks in the central and waterfront areas of Tokyo are sold to middle-income households, while the super-rich purchase an extremely expensive and luxury penthouse. Extremely small rooms converted from offices and warehouses accommodate the poor at the bottom of urban society, whereas spacious single-family homes of traditional Japanese architectural styles in high-class neighbourhoods are lived by families of pedigree over generations. Developing more redistributive social systems is an urgent policy agenda in order to alleviate housing inequalities in particular and social inequalities as a whole. In this context, it is important to examine how emerging diversity in households can be nurtured in housing policy and practice. In post-growth society, social cohesion needs to be achieved without re-enforcing standardisation and homogeneity. This is certainly a policy challenge facing the nation leading the significant social transformations in the region.

Index

Note: Page numbers in *italics* denote references to Figures.